Vegan

ve·gan

(most commonly pronounced "VEE-gun")

A person who does not eat animal products,
including meat, fish, seafood, eggs
and dairy products; All-plant.

Vegan

The New Ethics of Eating

by Erik Marcus

McBooks Press

Ithaca, New York

Cover and page design by Rider Design

Cover photo © Index Stock Photography

Library of Congress Cataloging-in-Publication Data

Marcus, Erik, 1966–
    Vegan : the new ethics of eating / Erik Marcus.
        p.   cm.
    Includes bibliographical references and index.
    ISBN 0-935526-34-X (hardcover). -- ISBN 0-935526-35-8 (pbk.)
    1. Vegetarianism. 2. Vegetarianism--Moral and ethical aspects.
    I. Title.
RM236.M37   1997
613.2'62--dc21   97-10398
                                                 CIP

Additional copies of this book and other McBooks Press titles may be ordered from any bookstore or directly from McBooks Press, 120 West State Street, Ithaca, NY 14850; toll-free order line 1-888-266-5711. Add $3 shipping and handling for mail orders. New York State residents must add 8% sales tax to total.

Ask us about bulk purchase discounts for your business or organization.

Visit the McBooks website at http://www.mcbooks.com

This book is distributed to the book trade by
Login Trade, a Division of LPC Group
1436 West Randolph Street
Chicago, IL 60607
1-800-243-0138; fax 1-800-334-3892

Printed in the United States of America

9876543

AUTHOR'S NOTE

Some conversations quoted in this book were, for the sake of clarity and cohesiveness, adapted from a composite of personal interviews, letters, e-mails, telephone conversations, and other communications which occurred over a period of time. Occasionally, these quotations were rephrased to remove abstruse technical wording. The persons who were quoted were given the opportunity to review the resultant quotes and approve them as representative of their expert opinions.

To Henry Spira, a tireless defender of animals

Acknowledgments

Thank you to:

My parents, Sonja and David Marcus, for help and encouragement of every kind.

Wendy Skinner, *Vegan*'s editor, for her dedication to producing a quality book.

Alex Skutt, Sandy List, and Patricia Zafiriadis of McBooks Press for their absolute commitment to this project.

Henry Spira and James Weishaupt for additional support during the writing of this book.

To the following people for answering my many questions so patiently and thoroughly:

Gene Bauston
Lorri Bauston
T. Colin Campbell, *Ph.D.*
Stephen Dealler, *M.B., Ch.B., D.C.M., D.T.M.H., F.R.S.T.M.H., M.R.C., M.D.*
Dina Fitzsimons, *M.S., R.D.*
Suzanne Havala, *M.S., R.D., F.A.D.A.*
Lynn Jacobs
Mark Messina, *Ph.D.*
Virginia Messina, *R.D., M.P.H.*
Dean Ornish, *M.D.*
Carl Phillips, *Ph.D.*
David Pimentel, *Ph.D.*
Bernard Rollin, *Ph.D.*
Terry Shintani, *M.D., M.P.H., J.D.*
David J. Wolfson, *J.D.*

In addition, I would like to thank:

Michael Rider for the book's cover and page design.

Dan Winkler for editing early drafts.

My past associate Michael Greger, for researching much of the mad cow and heart disease chapters, contributing some text to the mad cow chapter, and reviewing most of the manuscript.

Elizabeth J. Conrey, for her gracious help in researching and writing material that eventually became the milk chapter.

Debra Wasserman, of the Vegetarian Resource Group, for critiquing several chapters.

Alec Shuldiner, Neil Switz, Laura Greger, and many others for reading and commenting on several chapters.

Leor Jacobi at Vegan Action, for aiding my earliest research efforts, and for putting me in touch with many of the people who helped to make this book a reality.

Werner and Eva Hebenstreit for sharing many hours with me recounting their experiences on the Ornish Program.

The Physicians Commitee for Responsible Medicine for permission to reprint their New Four Food Groups text.

Anthony Arciola, Bill Beane, Al Young, and Rudolf Flesch for teaching me how to write.

Tim Polk, Margaret Marr, Jean Ednie, Scott Twombly, Rick Kaplan, Tony White, and also Drew Mitty, Phil Lynott, and Ainslie Perrault.

And finally, Alka.

Contents

Foreword

ALMOST 70 PERCENT OF ALL AMERICANS, according to former Surgeon General C. Everett Koop, are dying from ailments associated with their diets. About half of us will die of one thing: heart disease. Another third of all Americans will have cancer, and one-quarter will die of it. Study after study proves the inseparable link between diet and health. We can no longer afford to stick our heads in the sand and ignore these facts, if we expect to lead long and healthy lives.

However, the American people can change the odds dramatically if they adopt two very simple practices: refrain from eating animal products and spend the grocery budget on organically produced fruits and vegetables. A study at Loma Linda University has shown that a group of vegetarian men lived about seven years longer than their meat-eating counterparts. Studies in Germany and Finland also have shown that people who eat no animal products—vegans—may live an additional 15 years over the animal-eating population.

I made this lifestyle change several years ago, undeniably improving my life and possibly extending it as well. If a person like me can understand the necessity for such a change, anyone can. I am a fourth-generation farmer, rancher, and feedlot operator. I raised beef cattle, I poured pesticides and herbicides onto my grain crops, and I ate meat with the best of them.

I now travel around the world telling people that the proper amount of animal products to include in their diets is zero. I have made the transition from animal producer to a practicing vegan and president of the International Vegetarian Union all in one lifetime!

My life started on a small organic dairy farm in rural Montana during World War II. Child care back then amounted to being set to work in the garden, and this was the beginning of my love of the soil and of growing crops. The only thing I ever wanted to be was a farmer. I went to college where I learned about "better living through chemistry." I graduated with a degree in agriculture and returned home determined to turn the small organic farm into a large agribusiness.

Within a few years, I was operating a farm with thousands of acres of crops, thousands of heads of cattle, and many employees. It was almost a dream come true. The only problem was that the farm environment was changing drastically. The birds were dying, the trees were dying, and the soil was changing. I was using thousands of dollars' worth of chemicals each year, and they were making significant and damaging changes in my farm.

I saw the changes, but I thought they were just the price of being on the cutting edge. Then in 1979, I was paralyzed from the waist down from a tumor on my spinal cord. I had less than one chance in a million of ever walking again.

Fear has a way of making us reassess and see a lifetime of mistakes with a newfound clarity. Lying in the hospital at night, waiting for morning and surgery, many of the things I had previously ignored started to play on my mind. I realized I was killing my family's farm. I was killing the soil, the birds, and the trees with chemicals. I had to admit that I was killing the things I loved most.

I was blessed with a great gift the day I walked out of the hospital. From December, 1979 until today, my life has been very different. I read *Silent Spring* by Rachel Carson, and I could see all around me on my own farm what she was talking about, what chemicals were doing to our world. Retreating from the new way was much more difficult than I imagined, and in 1983, I had to give up and sell most of my farm to repay debts. However, I never gave up on my commitment to change the way we produce our food.

The number of people living on this planet today is twice what it was the day I was born. If I live the average American lifetime of 75.5 years, I may see that number double again. To think that the world population would quadruple in my lifetime is mind-boggling. We are running out of resources to support the human race. We are behaving like parasites, blindly consuming and ravaging our host with little thought for ourselves, our future, and the future of the entire planet. Never in man's history on the earth have we had less clean water, less topsoil, and fewer trees.

The United States is considered to be the breadbasket of the world, but our food production methods show little concern for the planet or the future. For every calorie of grain we produce with our chemical-mechanical system of agriculture, we expend 16 calories of energy. For every calorie of meat we produce, we expend 70 calories of energy. You don't have to be a rocket scientist to see that we are headed toward disaster if we continue to pursue the present course of using large amounts of energy to support a meat-based, non-organic national diet.

Reading Erik Marcus's *Vegan* is a critical first step for anyone wanting to extend both the quality and length of their life, and the planet's life. The future of the planet depends on the decisions we make every day. Every consumer who spends a dollar on organic produce and not on meat is voting for the future. This is the kind of action that is heard in Washington; it's the kind of action that comes from education and awareness.

Making the public aware of the dangerous and critical state of our food supply is my ultimate goal. The education contained in this book fits comfortably with the commitment I made many years ago while lying paralyzed in a hospital bed.

A vegan lifestyle is not only a healthy one; it is a kind and intelligent one. Add a large dose of love for yourself and all the things around you and you have a prescription that can't be topped.

— *Howard Lyman*

Director, Eating with Conscience Campaign
Humane Society of the United States
January 1997

Introduction

AN AWAKENING IS AT HAND. From hot dogs at a ballpark to the Thanksgiving turkey, America's national diet has long centered around meat. But now, substantial numbers of people are becoming vegetarians. In the past decade, millions of people who have eaten meat all their lives have decided never to take another bite of beef, pork, turkey, chicken, fish, wild or domestic game, or any other animal. Many people are also becoming vegans—eliminating from their diets not just flesh foods but milk, eggs, and all other animal products.

Why the growing interest in vegetarian diets? Individual reasons range from wanting to stay healthy to being concerned about the future of the earth and its population. Whatever the personal motivation, more and more people are realizing that being vegetarian makes sense—today more than ever. In the 1990s, we've discovered that vegetarian diets, and especially vegan diets, deliver far greater rewards than previously thought. This book examines some of these new discoveries and shows why a change in what you eat can be so simple and yet so significant.

The first chapters present some of the remarkable health advantages provided by vegan diets. Strong evidence shows that a low-fat vegan diet can practically eliminate the possibility of having a heart attack. Not only that, such a diet dramatically reduces cancer risk and can add years to your life. A vegan diet can also help you to reach and maintain your ideal weight, as well as providing a foundation for lasting health and greater energy. In addition, with many experts warning that mad cow disease could surface in the United States, there's no need to be exposed to possible infection: a vegan diet eliminates the risk of eating contaminated beef.

The second section of the book examines the modern meat and animal products industries. In many ways, these stories offer even more compelling reasons to switch to an all-plant diet. It is hard to deny that animals deserve some measure of compassion, and the technology for raising and slaughtering farm animals has grown increasingly inhumane over the past two decades. Modern "factory farming" methods mean that many of today's food animals never see sunlight or soil. They live under conditions of intense crowding in a world of cages, conveyor belts, and artificial light. I have been particularly careful not to exaggerate any of the facts presented in this book, especially those relating to animal production. The plain truth is enough to appeal to most people's sense of ethics. The stories and photos in this section are intended to help you make the mental link between the miserable lives and deaths of animals raised for your consumption, and what you eat for dinner.

A further concern about meat production is its effect on world food supplies. As the human population grows, our world is becoming less able to afford the inefficiencies of cycling massive amounts of food resources through livestock. By moving to plant-based diets, we can do our part to push back the worldwide food shortages that scientists warn are probable in the coming decades.

Our food choices also affect the environment. To touch on this issue, this book follows the story of a man who was determined to expose the consequences to the environment of cattle ranching in the Western U.S. Destruction of fragile rangeland, water pollution, and the decimation of wildlife are among the "side effects" of raising beef cattle.

This book is also about people—doctors, scientists, activists, people who were sick and got well, people who care about humanity, people who want to make the world a better place. You'll meet them in the chapters that follow.

The book ends with a brief explanation of how I came to be a vegan and why it has been so important to me.

Eating meat is a strong tradition in this culture, and the meat, dairy, and egg industries have a large interest in seeing that tradition continue. In their efforts to maintain the status quo, they can call on huge financial resources, armadas of experts, and some of the slickest advertising campaigns ever created. Yet despite their many strengths, these industries are being called into question. Why? Because on so many levels, the arguments against the eating of animal products are overwhelmingly convincing. In this book, I have tried to consistently avoid exaggeration or misstatements. Hyperbole is unnecessary when the facts come down so strongly in favor of being a vegan. And that is why I can state here my belief, which I think is amply justified by the evidence presented in the following pages:

A vegan diet Is most in harmony with our bodies' needs, our innate sense of compassion, and our ability to survive on earth. Moving to a plant-based diet is comparatively easy and it opens the door to a gentler, healthier, and happier way of being.

To your health

"Nothing will benefit
human health and
increase chances for
survival on Earth
as much as the
evolution to a
vegetarian diet."

— *Albert Einstein*

CHAPTER

Heart disease—America's number one killer—has met its match. A landmark program established by Dr. Dean Ornish has shown that changes in diet and lifestyle can stop and, in some cases, reverse the damage done by heart disease. The diet that Ornish recommends is largely vegan.

The beat goes on

Think of all the people you know—from world leaders to a beloved relative—whose lives have been diminished by heart disease, or who have died of a heart attack or stroke. Think of the complex surgeries they undergo, the shelves of drugs they consume, the bills we all share in paying, the lost time and talents, the ruined lives, the grieving. Think about the irony of our acceptance of this set of tragedies as commonplace and "normal," when "normal" really should mean long life and many years of good health.

We have been prey to a disease of our own making. In our pursuit of the good life, we've piled our plates high with meats and creamy sauces. We've believed in the virtue of drinking big glasses of milk, even as grown-ups. In fast-food restaurants, we choose our meat, cheese, egg, and high-fat foods from appealing, full-color pictures.

"It's no surprise that half of all Americans develop heart disease," says researcher and clinician Dr. Dean Ornish, "because the typical U.S. diet puts everyone at risk."

The diet of prosperity has turned out to be a killer. A high-fat, animal-based diet is the single most significant cause of death from heart disease.[1]

The good news is that, for many people, America's leading cause of death is no longer inevitable. Living healthy lives in general—not smoking, reducing stress, exercising—can help, but the most effective way to stop the progress of heart disease is to switch to an all-plant or nearly all-plant diet.

Let's look at the story of a man who, after suffering two heart attacks and a severe degree of disability, enrolled in Dr. Ornish's Opening Your Heart program. His health rapidly regained, this man—now 82—hikes mountain trails as a pastime.

THE DEALMAKER

Midway on a transcontinental flight, an older man kept checking his watch. Nobody noticed. The passengers around him were caught up in the banalities of the flight—watching a forgettable movie, reading, and choosing between steak or chicken when the flight attendants wheeled the meal cart down the aisle. Pale, his forehead clammy with perspiration, and with his watch reminding him that the flight wouldn't touch down for another four hours, Werner Hebenstreit wondered if he would reach the San Francisco airport alive.

Worried that a second heart attack was striking, Werner felt confused by this invisible enemy.

Five years earlier, his first heart attack had nearly killed him. In the aftermath of this frightening experience, Werner, always a man to follow instructions to the letter, did exactly what the cardiologists told him to do. He stopped eating red meat and cut back on eggs. He swallowed a fistful of pills every day, enduring their numerous side effects. He tried to exercise moderately. Despite all this, his condition worsened. When out walking, he would sometimes be unable to finish crossing the street before the light changed. As honking cars sped by, Werner would stand exhausted in the middle of the intersection while his oxygen-starved heart struggled to keep beating. Neither medical advice nor his own determination was enough to stave off Werner's heart disease. Sick and weak, the 71-year-old Werner had boarded this flight in a wheelchair.

For most of his life, Werner had felt himself to be very healthy. He had excelled in boyhood sports, and as an adult, he was strong and vigorous. A courageous man whose life was forever changed by events in Nazi Germany, Werner had overcome a series of ordeals unthinkable to most Americans. Now, worried that **a second heart attack** was striking, Werner felt confused by this invisible enemy. He looked around the airplane and felt cheated, and very alone.

In fact, Werner need not have felt singled out—he merely topped the list of those on board whom heart disease would eventually kill. Sooner or later, nearly half his 400 fellow passengers would share his fate.

After decades of eating meat, dairy products, and eggs, Werner had unwittingly clogged his arteries to such an extent that the blood flow to his heart was seriously impeded. The buildup of cholesterol, fat, and cellular debris had so narrowed these major pipelines, that Werner's heart wasn't getting enough blood. Short episodes of this deprivation of blood, and hence oxygen, could bring on chest pains, or angina. If a blood clot were to get caught in one of the narrow places in Werner's arteries, cutting off the flow, it could result in the actual death of heart tissue; in other words, a heart attack.

Werner's fears were confirmed. He had his second heart attack on the airplane. He was met by an ambulance when the flight landed, and the other passengers saw him whisked

FACING THE ULTIMATE ENEMY

In 1935, the Nazis began rounding up Jews in Werner Hebenstreit's native Germany. Werner was barely 20 years old when, on a moonless night, he kayaked down the Danube river into the safety of Austria. From there, it took him until the end of 1937 to reach India by hitchhiking east from country to country. He made his living playing a concertina in third rate nightclubs. He decided to make India his home, though without a university education or even a trade or craft, opportunity was scarce. Nevertheless, he raised enough money to get his parents and sister out of Germany shortly before the outbreak of war in Europe. Once war was declared, the British sent Werner to an internment camp for two years, in the erroneous belief that he was a German spy.

Werner survived the internment and managed to keep his family alive. In 1946, they emigrated to San Francisco. Werner had a photographic memory and a business aptitude that he had honed during years of desperate wartime conditions. Shortly ▶

The Hebenstreits at the San Francisco airport on their way to Germany. Werner had been following Dr. Ornish's program for five years when this photo was taken.

Courtesy of Werner Hebenstreit

◄ after arriving in San Francisco, he obtained a broker's license and began insuring German immigrants. Werner made the most of his skills of salesmanship and deal-making. In the 1950s he wrote thousands of insurance contracts. By the 1960s he was negotiating for a partnership in one of San Francisco's most prestigious brokerage firms.

Life was rewarding and full for Werner until his first heart attack in 1981. He slowed down and followed his doctors' orders, but became progressively more debilitated until his second attack in January, 1986. "After that, I felt nearly dead," says Werner. Four months later, tired and discouraged, Werner joined the first group of patients to enter Dr. Dean Ornish's program for reversing heart disease.

away across the tarmac, not knowing if he would live or die.

In Werner's career as an insurance broker, he had mastered the art of negotiation. And once he made a deal, he would move heaven and earth to hold up his end of the bargain. Werner survived the in-flight heart attack, but he knew now that it was time to make the deal of his life. A cardiogram had revealed the worst possible news: one coronary artery was completely closed up, and two others showed severe blockages.

"What can I do to get better?" he asked his cardiologist. "What kind of deal can I make to stay alive?" is what he was thinking.

The doctor wrote several new prescriptions for more powerful medication and sent Werner home. He was now armed with propanolol and nifedipine, whose effects helped to combat the angina pain, Isordil to reduce the load on his heart, and Persantine to prevent blood clots. The medications, while potentially saving his life, made him feel worse. Headaches, dizziness, nausea, depression, and fatigue were among the side effects.

Werner's life settled into a routine of sitting in a chair in his living room, swallowing fourteen pills throughout the day, and feeling constant pain, weakness, and fear. Any physical exertion, even shaving or combing his hair, shot fierce pains through his chest. As the weeks went by, Werner shrank further into his brown easy chair, awaiting the end. His only uncertainty was whether the heart attack that would finish him would strike in months or in hours. He was angry and bitter, and his tongue grew so sharp that only his wife Eva would spend time with him.

Then one day the Hebenstreits got an unexpected phone call. Eva answered it, listened for awhile, and then said to her husband, "A Dr.

Dean Ornish wants to speak to you about a heart study." Another doctor wanting to make deals. Werner didn't hesitate: "Tell him I'm sick and tired of doctors."

But Dr. Ornish kept Eva on the line, telling her about his program. "Your husband fits exactly the profile we think we can help the most," he explained. Werner gestured angrily for Eva to hang up, but instead she carried the phone across the room to the brown easy chair. "At least listen to what he has to say." Werner scowled, then took the receiver and said icily, "Okay, Doctor, whatever you have to sell—I'm not buying."

Ornish laughed. "That's good, because I'm not trying to sell anything. Mr. Hebenstreit, I'm putting together a study of Bay Area residents who have had recent heart attacks and angiograms. We've developed a program that we think offers an effective treatment and a real possibility for improvement. I was hoping to get together with you to see if this is a program you would like to pursue."

"No offense, Dr. Ornish, but I don't see any reason to. I've already done everything my doctors advise. I'm so sick from the drugs I'm taking, I'm just not interested in experimental treatments."

"I understand, Mr. Hebenstreit. But a main

LOVE AND MEDICINE

Courtesy of Dean Ornish

A medical doctor and researcher whose patients include celebrities and public figures, Dean Ornish is something of a celebrity in his own right. (A *People* magazine photograph published in June 1995 captured him clutching a guitar and leaping like a rock star across his living room floor.) Ornish was the first clinician to present findings that showed that changes in diet and lifestyle can reverse even severe heart disease without surgery or drugs. The results of his groundbreaking study appeared in the *Journal of the American Medical Association* (*JAMA*) in 1983 and in the British journal, *The Lancet*, in 1990. That same year, Ornish shared his revolutionary findings with the general public in a book titled *Dr. Dean Ornish's Program for Reversing Heart Disease*. The book quickly hopped onto *The New York Times* bestseller list, and each of Ornish's other books has enjoyed similar success. *Eat More, Weigh Less*, published in 1994, was reviewed in publications ranging from *JAMA* to *Glamour*.

Ornish grew up in Dallas, Texas. His father was a dentist and his mother a historian. A National Merit Scholar, Ornish entered Rice University only to drop out in his sophomore year. Feelings of depression led him to discover the healing qualities of meditation and a vegetarian diet. A year later, he resumed his studies, this time at the University of Texas. In 1975 he ▶

◀ graduated first in his class. He enrolled in Baylor College of Medicine, where he became interested in cardiology and first began to research the potentially beneficial effects of diet and meditation in treating heart patients. Ornish received his M.D. in 1980, became a clinical fellow at Harvard Medical School, and fulfilled his internship and residency in internal medicine at Massachusetts General Hospital in Boston.

In 1984, Ornish founded the nonprofit Preventive Medicine Research Institute in Sausalito, California, where he and his colleagues focus on alternatives to surgery and drugs for the care and prevention of heart disease. A firm believer in such stress-relievers as meditation, yoga, moderate exercise, and group sessions to relieve feelings of isolation, Ornish combines many techniques in his Opening Your Heart program. In his book on reversing heart disease, he explains:

"Physically, this program can help you begin to open your heart's arteries and to feel stronger and more energetic, freer of pain. Emotionally, it can help you open your heart to others and to experience greater happiness, intimacy, and love in your relationships. Spiritually, it can help you open your heart to a higher force (however you experience it) and to rediscover your inner sources of peace and joy."

point of this study is to replace drugs with dietary changes, moderate exercise, stress management, and group support. In my past studies, most of my patients soon became able to stop taking much of their medication."

"That sounds very nice, Doctor, but I'm tired. And I really don't want to pay for another program that probably won't work. Good day."

But before Werner could hang up, Ornish responded, "Don't worry about cost—this study is funded. It won't cost you a dime to participate. Now if you and your wife can come to my office, I'd love to explain the program to you. What have you got to lose?"

After a long pause Werner sighed. "All right, Dr. Ornish," he said. "We will meet with you."

With that phone conversation, Werner had started on the road back to health and a full and active life. He didn't know it yet, but he was about to share in the success of a study that would redefine cardiac treatment. Werner was about to become one of the first Americans to experience a reversal of advanced heart disease.

THE EXPECTED WAY TO DIE

Heart disease is the leading killer of men and women in the United States.[2] Almost one of every two Americans will die from heart disease.[3] The numbers associated with it are staggering: 40 million diagnosed with heart disease, and 1.5 million a year having heart attacks.[4] Cardiovascular disease kills over 700,000 U.S. citizens each year; one-fourth of the victims are under age 65.[5] Much effort has gone into developing surgeries and drugs to help victims survive, but in the end, heart attacks are seen as a natural and expected way to die.

But heart disease is much less common in countries where people consistently eat low-fat diets containing minimal amounts of animal products. Low-fat, plant-based diets keep blood cholesterol levels low.

According to Antonio Gotto, past president of the American Heart Association, societies whose average blood cholesterol is very low have virtually no coronary heart disease or atherosclerosis—hardening of the arteries which leads to cardiovascular disease.[6] The risk of **heart disease in China** is only about 5 percent of the risk Western populations face.[7] In Japan, life expectancies exceed those in the U.S. at every age, but when Japanese people move to this country and start to eat as we do, their mortality rates become indistinguishable from ours.[8]

In fact, over 200 studies involving migrants—people who move from one country to settle in another—have shown that atherosclerosis is largely a disease of dietary lifestyle.[9] New arrivals in this country who adopt the American diet, or supplement their largely plant-based meals with American fast-food or meat-centered dishes, often give up their freedom from heart disease.

Over the past several years, the evidence implicating elevated serum, or "blood," cholesterol as a major risk and causal factor in cardiovascular disease has grown conclusive. A 1984 National Institutes of Health panel of experts agreed that an "elevated blood cholesterol level is a major cause of coronary heart disease,"[10] and in 1990, the American Heart Association issued a report stating: "The evidence linking elevated serum cholesterol to coronary heart disease is overwhelming."[11] By 1995, medical textbooks covered the issue with phrases like, "Evidence incriminating cholesterol in coronary heart disease is extensive and unequivocal."[12]

High blood cholesterol is one of three major risk factors for cardiovascular disease, along with smoking and high blood pressure.[13]

> The risk of heart disease in China is only about 5 percent of the risk Western populations face.

Lack of exercise, obesity, stress, diabetes, or a family history of heart disease are also contributing factors. Esteemed cardiology expert, William Roberts, however, has concluded that the most significant risk factor for heart disease is the lifetime presence of a blood cholesterol level above 150.[14] (Cholesterol is measured in milligrams per deciliter of blood. People at high risk for heart disease may have cholesterol levels of over 300.[15] The average cholesterol level of vegans in the U.S. is 128.)[16] Roberts pointed out that even in the presence of other common risk factors, arteries just will not harden when cholesterol levels are low.[17]

The connection between low cholesterol levels and reduced risk of death by heart disease is upheld by the often-cited Framingham Heart Study. Framingham, Massachusetts is a town near Boston where scientists have been monitoring about 5,000 people since 1948. They have considered every conceivable cause of heart disease, including cholesterol levels. The data produced by the Framingham study have been extremely useful in identifying such risk factors as smoking, obesity, and diabetes, but perhaps the most important finding is this: In the nearly four decades of the study, other than a few individuals with overall severe health problems, no person whose blood cholesterol was less than 150 ever had a heart attack.[18]

GETTING CHOLESTEROL UNDER CONTROL

More than anything else, blood cholesterol determines your likelihood of having a heart attack.[19] Fortunately, cholesterol levels can be lowered, and even a small reduction can produce substantial health benefits. For every 1 percent that your blood cholesterol drops, your risk of having a heart attack falls by 2 to 3 percent.[20]

Researchers have long known that high blood cholesterol levels—and consequently the risk of heart disease—tend to run in families. And while it's true that the genes you've inherited do have an influence, diet can counter most genetic risk. Indeed, people with a genetic propensity to heart disease are among those who should be most concerned with diet.

Almost everyone can reduce high blood cholesterol simply by making appropriate food choices. The best way to do this is to minimize your daily intake of dietary cholesterol, saturated fat, and total fat. Vegans, in general, have low blood cholesterol levels because they tend to eat less total fat, much less saturated fat, and *no* dietary cholesterol—since plants don't contain cholesterol.[21]

Cholesterol is a waxy yellow substance that all animal cells require in order to function. Produced by the liver, cholesterol circulates through the blood and into the body's cells. Cholesterol is essential for all animal life, and it is found in large quantities in meat of any kind, eggs, and whole dairy products.[22]

Like other animals, human beings also require cholesterol to survive. This might lead one to believe that it's a good idea to consume food that contains cholesterol. It isn't. Because the human liver makes all the cholesterol the body needs, any cholesterol obtained through diet provides no benefit.[23] Indeed, the excess cholesterol that we eat can wreak havoc with our health.

Harvard nutrition expert Walter Willet advises: "The optimal intake of cholesterol is probably zero, meaning the avoidance of animal products; people will need to balance their desire to minimize the risk of coronary heart disease against their taste for meat and dairy foods."[24]

Choosing a longer and healthier life over steak and ice cream seems like an easy decision to make. It's even easier to figure out which foods contain cholesterol and which don't. Plants have no need for cholesterol to survive, nor do they have the ability to manufacture it. If a food comes from a plant, then it has no cholesterol. This means that the surest way to completely eliminate cholesterol consumption is to follow a vegan diet. What's more, vegan diets minimize saturated fat, which is an even greater health hazard than dietary cholesterol.

Saturated fat intake determines what your cholesterol levels will be. If you eat foods containing high percentages of saturated fat, your cholesterol levels will go up. Too much saturated fat can also

> Almost everyone
> can reduce
> high blood
> cholesterol
> simply
> by making
> appropriate
> food choices.

upset the optimal balance between the two kinds of cholesterol carried in the blood stream.

By now, most people have heard about "good" cholesterol and "bad" cholesterol. The designation has to do with the way in which cholesterol is ferried around the blood stream. Cholesterol attaches to protein for transport. The combination is called a lipoprotein. The so-called good cholesterol is a component of high-density lipoproteins, or HDLs. HDLs transport cholesterol away from the arteries and allow it to be broken down. HDLs can even clean up the arteries by picking up and carrying away fatty deposits. A relatively high HDL level is considered good protection against heart disease.

LDL, or low-density lipoprotein, contains the "bad" cholesterol. LDLs carry cholesterol to the arteries, where it is deposited. High levels of LDL lead to the build-up of plaques inside the arteries, constricting the passageways and leading to heart disease or heart attacks. The main source of elevated LDLs is saturated fat. Saturated fat causes the liver to produce mainly low-density cholesterol. The best way to increase your ratio of "good" to "bad" cholesterol is to stay away from saturated fats.

LOW-FAT EATING

In epidemiological studies, the consumption of saturated fat is more strongly correlated with mortality than stress or even cigarette smoking.[25] Belgium epidemiologist H. Kesteloot, who presided over two international nutrition and health symposiums, writes "A decrease in the dietary intake of saturated fat . . . should get the highest priority as a means to improve public health."[26]

What is the greatest source of saturated fat? Dairy products supply about one-third of the saturated fat in the typical American diet. Red meat supplies another third, and poultry and fish contribute the next highest amounts. The vegan diet tends to contain very little saturated fat, and the proportion of saturated fat to total fat tends to be low as well. The only concentrated sources of saturated fat in the plant kingdom are tropical oils and artificially hydrogenated oils like margarine.

Thirty-seven percent of the calories in the average American diet come from fat. The most conservative experts—such as the U.S. government—say that total fat consumption should be no more than 30 percent of calories. Others suggest that the most healthful diet contains no more than 20 percent of calories from fat. But it's usually quite difficult to follow a truly low-fat diet when you're eating meat and other animal products.

An effective step in **reducing saturated fat** in your diet is to replace animal foods with vegetable foods. Because almost all grains, fruits, and vegetables are fat-free, just by eliminating animal foods from your diet, you can reduce your total fat intake. About the only way to have a high-fat vegan diet is to eat large amounts of the few vegan foods that are high in fat—nuts, seeds, and avocados, for instance—or to cook with large amounts of vegetable oils. If you follow a balanced vegan diet, you will automatically be eating less fat than with almost any non-vegetarian diet.

Beware, however, of assuming that vegetarians will automatically enjoy similar reductions in fat. A vegetarian diet that includes eggs and whole dairy products can contain as much fat as a meat-based diet.

YOUTH OFFERS NO BARRIERS

Although heart attacks typically strike people who are middle-aged or older, the factors that lead to heart disease can begin much earlier in life. In fact, signs of the disease have been revealed in outwardly healthy young people under 20 years of age.

During the Korean and Vietnamese wars, U.S. doctors discovered that many young men were already developing coronary disease. In these wartime studies, surgeons removed the hearts of soldiers killed in battle. Most of the dead soldiers were barely into their twenties and many were still in their teens; the average age of death was 22 years. Not only were these soldiers too young to be considered candidates for heart disease,

An effective step in reducing saturated fat in your diet is to replace animal foods with vegetable foods.

they were also apparently in prime physical health. Most had recently undergone the rigors of basic training, a program demanding extraordinary physical exertion to foster unparalled fitness.

Yet even with their youth and their high physical fitness levels, many of these soldiers already had clear indications of heart disease. When doctors studied their hearts, they discovered that many had atherosclerotic plaques on the coronary artery walls. The typical dairy, egg, and meat-centered diet that was then considered the best thing for active people had already started many of these young men down the road toward a potentially fatal heart attack.

In the Korean War heart studies, over 75 percent of war casualties showed signs of atherosclerosis.[27] Among Vietnam War casualties studied, 45 percent showed indications of atherosclerosis, with around 5 percent showing "gross evidence of severe coronary atherosclerosis."[28]

The Vietnam War casualty study was the last of its kind done by American doctors. However, recent autopsies of healthy children killed in accidents have revealed cholesterol buildup, and there is strong reason to suspect that many Americans continue to develop the first stages of heart disease at a young age. A 1996 study examined risk factors among 82 teenagers at a Midwestern high school. The study evaluated the teenagers' rate of obesity, blood pressure, blood cholesterol levels, and substance abuse. More than one-third of the group had at least one risk factor for developing heart disease.[29]

PUBLIC POLICY SHROUDS THE TRUTH ABOUT DIET

Because vegans eat no cholesterol and typically consume less saturated and total fat, their cholesterol levels are generally much lower than that of the general population. In the United States, the average cholesterol level in vegetarians (who eat dairy products and/or eggs) is 14 percent lower than in non-vegetarians. Vegans do even better, having cholesterol levels that are 35 percent lower than average!

Given the clear health benefits, why doesn't the U.S. government promote vegetarian or vegan diets? Part of the answer can be found in a paper prepared by the Food and Drug Administration. The paper uses negatively charged words, indicating that a move to a low-fat vegetarian diet is "severe" and "extreme" and that the average American will only "accept" and consider "palatable" the standard meat-based diet. For example:

"The diet need contain no cholesterol for health, and any dietary cholesterol will raise LDL [or "bad"] cholesterol to some extent. Considerations or recommendations thus are based on practicality.

"It would be desirable if cholesterol intake could be reduced by another 200 mg/d; but in practical terms, this probably is impossible for a majority of adult Americans. Such a change would require a severe reduction in consumption of animal products, a change that may not be acceptable to some persons."[30]

Ornish takes umbrage at this sort of language, calling it "patronizing." The public is fully capable of making wise decisions based on sound information, he contends. **Government officials now know what the most healthful diet is, and yet will not recommend it.** Professor T. Colin Campbell, a Cornell University nutrition expert profiled elsewhere in this book, also thinks such advice betrays the public: "We, as scientists, can no longer take the attitude that the public cannot benefit from information they are not ready for. I personally have great faith in the public."

A LIFE RECLAIMED

The morning after Dr. Ornish telephoned, Werner and Eva took their car for the twenty-minute drive across the Golden Gate Bridge to his medical office in Sausalito. Ornish greeted them with a smile and a warm handshake. Werner immediately noticed that Ornish appeared in much better health than any of the other cardiologists he had visited. He also lacked the distant attitude Werner had observed in his other cardiologists, conveying instead a manner of approachability and warmth. For the first time in weeks, Werner felt a bit at ease.

Government officials now know what the most healthful diet is, and yet will not recommend it.

"So why are we here today?" Ornish began, "Why do so many Americans develop heart trouble? You are certainly not alone, Mr. Hebenstreit, in struggling with this illness."

Ornish continued, "Let's start with cholesterol. Your body knows exactly how much cholesterol it needs. Even if you eat no cholesterol at all and limit your fat intake to no more than ten percent of calories, your body automatically manufactures enough cholesterol to ensure good health. **Plant foods**—from fruit to rice to vegetables to beans—tend to be quite low in saturated fat and are always 100 percent free of cholesterol. But Americans eat all kinds of meat and dairy products, which short-circuit how our bodies manage cholesterol.

"Let's look at how the average person eats during a typical day on the American diet. Many people start their day with a breakfast containing generous quantities of bacon or eggs or dairy products. At lunch it's more fatty animal products, and your body hasn't even finished handling the fat and cholesterol from breakfast! By six o'clock the bloodstream is overloaded with cholesterol and the body is trying to get rid of it when the dinner bell rings. Then, for most people, it's the biggest meal of the day, with more meat and more fat than even the first two meals. Some people eat a sirloin, while other people convince themselves they are eating healthy by cooking a chicken. What does your body do with all this fat? Much of it gets carried into the bloodstream, where it accumulates on artery walls.

"Imagine the long-term effect of this lifestyle, day in and day out, for decades on end. To stop the process a heart patient should eat entirely vegetarian food with no added fats. That gives the body a chance to start healing."

Werner responded, "But I've always avoided beef, and rarely have bacon. I used to eat 14 eggs a week and now eat only four. Why should I have developed heart disease?"

"Because even on your improved diet, the odds are still against you. Chicken has as much cholesterol, ounce-for-ounce, as beef. And

"Plant foods
are always
100 percent
free of
cholesterol."

whether your fat comes from meat, poultry, eggs, or milk, a high ratio of the fat will be saturated, which further drives up your blood cholesterol levels.

"This link between animal products and heart disease is now very well documented. It's no surprise that half of all Americans develop heart disease, because the typical U.S. diet puts almost everyone at risk. Every meal that is rich in fatty animal products has an immediate impact on heart risks. The blood literally becomes thick with cholesterol and other lipids, which are deposited on the body's arteries."

Werner asked, "So what's your solution?"

"The dietary component of our program is to attack the problem at its source. It's easy to construct a diet based on plant foods that markedly lowers cholesterol in just about everyone. The basis of the diet is simple—it's vegetarian, and made up of whole grains, fruits, vegetables, and beans. We also allow limited quantities of egg whites and non-fat milk and yogurt. There are other factors which play an important part in the development of heart disease. Therefore, we also focus on lifestyle changes, in particular, stress management and group support sessions to recognize one's feelings of isolation and hostility."

Werner grew suddenly suspicious. In his kitchen, "low in fat" had always meant "low in taste." He asked, "What's the food like?"

"In designing the program, we knew we had to make the food delicious or people wouldn't stay on the diet. Plus, if you've got a sweet tooth, our dessert recipes are unbelievable."

Werner looked at Eva, and she nodded back in approval. He took a breath and said, "I'm willing to give this a shot. How long a commitment do I have to make?"

"The study runs for one year. At the end of the year, it's all up to you if the program is worthwhile to continue."

"Okay, Dr. Ornish," said Werner, extending his hand, "I will commit to one year of meeting every requirement you set. You've got yourself a deal."

Driving back, Werner and Eva made plans for adjusting to the program. Upon arriving home, they gave the chicken, eggs, and milk in their refrigerator to a neighbor. They then looked over some recipes from the program, and Eva drove to the store to purchase the necessary ingredients. That night, they dined on egg-free pasta, non-fat marinara sauce with vegetables and mushrooms sautéed in non-fat salad dressing.

Improvement came more quickly than Werner had dared hope. Within days, the angina pains greatly diminished. He even had the energy to get out of his easy chair and walk around the house. He began looking forward to his twice-weekly trips to Sausalito, meeting other Ornish program members, and learning the relaxation and gentle exercise techniques that would help to restore his health.

Not everything was solved overnight. He felt that the heart medication still soured his mood, and he still had a hair-trigger temper. But four months after beginning the program, a follow-up test provided the first solid basis for hope in years. Dr. Ornish telephoned with the results.

"Congratulations, Werner. Your cholesterol level has dropped by over 100 points. This drop, coupled with the results of your other tests, means that it's now safe for you to discontinue your propranolol, nifedipine, and Isordil medications, and to cut your Persantine in half."

Freedom from most of the pills, plus exercise, stress reduction classes, and group support sessions all contributed to Werner's improving health. When Werner went on a short hike for the first time in six months, he knew his recovery was underway.

The improvements kept coming. Within months, all his angina pains had vanished. He and Eva began taking lengthy hikes through Muir Woods, all over Mount Tamalpais, and in other scenic areas near San Francisco. On his one-year anniversary in the Ornish program, Werner's cholesterol level had dropped from 320 after his second heart attack to 145. By then, at Ornish's recommendation, he stopped taking any medications except one baby aspirin every other day.

As the years went by, Werner's angiograms showed a remarkable reversal of his blockages. A 54 percent blockage at the beginning of the program went down to 40 percent after one year and to 13 percent after four years. Even his totally blocked artery began to open up again and after four years showed a 71 percent blockage. In his first six years in the program, Werner underwent five coronary Positron Emission Tomography (PET) scans. PET scans use an advanced computer technology to show the condition of coronary arteries in great detail. At the time, the only center for PET scans was in Houston, and Werner was flown there every year. Without exception the PET scans showed continuing improvement in the blood flow to Werner's heart.

When I caught up with Werner in San Francisco, he had just returned from one of his regular hikes along Mount Tamalpais' Matt Davis Trail where he often chooses the extended loop which stretches on for miles. Now 82, he has left all worries of heart disease behind him.

Eleven years after his second heart attack, Werner has not only survived but has become fit and vigorous. For the past nine years, his cholesterol level has remained around 145. Like several other participants in Ornish's program, Werner now travels and lectures about the Opening Your Heart program. He recently spoke to what he terms "prime candidates" for heart disease, a firm of stockbrokers in Boston.

Werner's friends call his recovery miraculous. Yet his story is not uncommon among patients in the Ornish program. Most people who closely follow the program have similar stories of recovery to tell, complete with improved fitness and a reduction or stoppage of medication.

A 1995 study published in the *Journal of the American Medical Association* compared Ornish's patients against a control group following standard anti-angina care. The study used PET scans to measure blood flow and clogging in the heart's arteries. The PET scans were taken at the beginning of the study, and again five years later at the

> Werner's friends call his recovery miraculous.

study's conclusion. Each measurement followed the same pattern: Ornish's group improved while the condition of patients following standard treatment deteriorated.[31]

Ornish says, "Many doctors still say it's perfectly reasonable to treat heart disease through high-risk bypasses and angioplasties. In the same breath, they'll call a vegetarian diet, regular exercise, and stress management too radical. Personally, I don't understand how doctors can recommend their heart patients face major surgery without first considering our non-surgical approach. I think the majority of heart patients would gladly choose diet and lifestyle changes over heart surgery. And the most recent studies, utilizing the latest in testing technologies, are now squarely on our side."

William C. Roberts, M.D., editor in chief of the *American Journal of Cardiology,* agrees: "Dr. Ornish is on the right road and we need to get on it also."

A PLEASURABLE WAY TO GET WELL

Each year, Ornish's organization, the Preventive Medicine Research Institute, hosts four one-week retreats at the Claremont Hotel in Berkeley, California. Up to a hundred new and long-time patients arrive. Like Werner, many were once so sick with heart disease they could no longer walk. The meals are one of the retreat's highlights—a chance for participants to sample some of the finest vegetarian cooking available in the country. Dozens of former and new heart patients crowd around the table, laughing and talking as they enjoy pastas, soups, and all kinds of **special dishes**.

A 1994 article in *Forbes* magazine, while acknowledging the success of Ornish patients who stick to his program, criticized the diet he recommends as "severe" and "radical." Such language, whether part of government advisories, conventional doctors' advice, or popular media reports, misrepresents the myriad possibilities for vegan or vegetarian meals that are colorful, flavorful, and satisfying. Although it may be radical to suggest that delicious food can help heal an ailing heart, calling Ornish's diet "severe" misses a main point: The recipes Ornish and his helpers have collected are extraordinarily pleasing.

Almost a third of Ornish's bestselling book, *Dr. Dean Ornish's Program for Reversing Heart Disease* is devoted to recipes and cooking tips. "Some of the country's leading chefs developed our recipes," explains Ornish. "They produced slimmed-down versions of old favorites as well as dozens of creative new dishes. We've got main dishes like linguine with roasted red pepper and herbed tomato sauce, refried bean burritos, Indian curries, Southwestern vegetable stew, and dozens more. There's not a boring dish among them."

For people who may be reluctant to leave their cuts of meat behind all at once, Ornish's book suggests a gradual transition. Substitutes and replacements for cheese, eggs, fish, red meat, and poultry can be gradually introduced. Ornish's recommendations stop short of an entirely vegan diet, retaining the occasional egg white, for instance, and suggesting fat-free yogurt as a substitute for salad dressing, but the direction is clearly mapped out: As far as possible, replace the high-fat, high-cholesterol meat, eggs, and dairy with low-fat, low-cholesterol vegetables, grains, and legumes. The change is made easier by using the recipes, which have been chosen for their palate-pleasing flavors and textures. And, although it is not overtly expressed, the fun of cooking and eating these tempting dishes could easily qualify as a stress reducer.

Ornish and his colleagues understand quite well that the notion of vegetarian and vegan food as bland, brownish, or strange-tasting needs to be dispelled quickly. "This is not a diet of deprivation," Ornish's book states. "It is, on the contrary, a diet vibrant with color and rich with the flavors and textures of many different foods—fresh vegetables, tangy herbs and pungent spices, chewy, wholesome grains, savory beans, elegant pastas, and sweet, enticing fruit dishes. There are enough deli-

> Dozens of patients crowd around the table, laughing and talking as they enjoy pastas, soups, and all kinds of special dishes.

cious and beautiful dishes here for you to cook something different every day for months. And you will quickly appreciate how light and satisfied these meals leave you feeling."

A VEGAN BY ANY OTHER NAME

Robert Siegel is a chef who loves to cook and loves to eat. He was also once at very high risk for heart disease. "Every male member of my family had quadruple bypass surgery," says Siegel. He started taking heart medicines at the age of 42, and was told by his doctors he would have to stay on the pills for the rest of his life. For the next eight years, Siegel swallowed the medicines twice a day. But on his 50th birthday, he decided he had had enough. "I was overweight, and I felt sick all the time," he says.

"This isn't about '-isms.' It's about what you have for dinner."

In an effort to bring his cholesterol level down the natural way, Siegel gave up eating meat and became a lacto-ovo vegetarian. He felt a little better, but his cholesterol level barely budged and he weighed as much as ever. Why? He was still consuming eggs, dairy fats, and was still cooking with liberal quantities of oil.

Then Siegel discovered the work of doctors like Dean Ornish and John McDougall (author of *The McDougall Program*, a plan for changing to an all-vegan diet) and took his personal health experiment one step further.

"I did it. I switched to a low-fat vegan diet," Siegel recalls. "Guess what? I started to feel really good. My cholesterol level tumbled. I had much more energy, and before long, I was able to stop taking the medications."

As a gourmet chef for 25 years, Siegel knew he wasn't going to be satisfied with an uninteresting diet. He began to adapt his old recipes and invent new ones until he had a great repertoire to draw on. The vegan diet, Siegel explains, does not imply loss or sacrifice, just different choices—and so many choices! Siegel smiles as only a true hedonist can when he describes the great variety of pastas, beans, grains, vegetables, fruits, herbs and spices at his disposal.

Siegel teaches classes in healthy cooking and recently published a book titled *Fat Free and Delicious: 176 Tasty Fat Free and Ultra Low Fat Recipes*. All of the recipes are vegan, although Siegel avoids the term, substituting—warily—vegetarian. "Veganism, vegetarianism—it all sounds so serious. **This isn't about '-isms,'"** says Siegel. "It's about what you have for dinner. It's about having fun and feeling good. I just call it healthy eating."

Siegel is still a big man, although obviously trim and energetic, and he has a big laugh. Enjoyment of life and life's pleasures rate high with him.

"Some people like to tell me that the way I eat is radical," he comments. "Well, I think it's radical when they take you into the hospital on a gurney and they decide you need a $40,000 operation. I think it's radical when they saw your ribs open and then they take pieces of artery from your legs and they sew them onto your heart.

"*That's* radical. Eating beans and delicious vegetables and grains is *not* radical."

2

Mounting scientific evidence shows that a low-fat diet of fruits, vegetables, grains, and legumes can ward off many kinds of cancer. Experts are now saying that Americans may cut their cancer risk *in half* by adopting vegetarian, and especially vegan, diets.

Cutting your cancer risk

My grandmother had much in common with Werner Hebenstreit (profiled in the previous chapter). Like Werner, she was a Jew in Europe when the Nazis seized power. She lived with her husband and two daughters in Norway, but after Nazi soldiers carried my grandfather away to a concentration camp, Grandma Rexie and the two girls fled. They eventually settled in New York City where my grandmother worked for the Norwegian government while raising my mother and my aunt.

My mother and Grandma Rexie were always very close, but in 1961, a year after my mother graduated college and got married, my grandmother returned to Norway and moved back into her original house. Although separated by thousands of miles, my mother and grandmother remained in close contact. I know this because, when I was growing up, I used to bring in the mail after school. Among the letters, I'd often find an Aerogramme from Norway. The Aerogrammes were printed on flimsy blue paper that often became creased and battered on the transatlantic flight. My mother always opened these fragile messages first.

My mother received at least one Aerogramme each week. Then halfway through my senior year of high school, Grandma's letters abruptly stopped coming. One evening, after two weeks without an Aerogramme, my mother answered a long-distance phone call. When she got off the phone, she went to her room and wept.

Grandma Rexie was rapidly losing weight and had gone to a hospital for tests. The results took weeks to arrive, but at last she was diagnosed with pancreatic cancer. Mother called a cousin who worked as a doctor in Norway. She learned that pancreatic cancer is almost invariably fatal, and that most victims live no more than a year after being diagnosed. Mother booked a flight to Norway, knowing that this would almost certainly be her final visit. When she arrived, Grandma Rexie's health was quickly deteriorating. She telephoned us with the news: "She lost a lot of weight. She's so weak and fragile I don't know how long she'll last."

When my mother visited the hospital, there were times when my grandmother was alert and could carry on conversations. But as the days passed, she became less communicative. She would often lie silently with half-closed eyes. **Their connection grew as wispy** as Aerogramme paper.

Grandma Rexie died, and my mother returned home from Norway. She went back to her job and resumed her usual schedule. But my grandmother's death had changed her. She was sad in a way that I had never seen before, and she feared that she, too, could end up dying of cancer. One night my mother told me: "Cancer runs in both my mother's and father's side of the family. When I die it will probably be from that."

In 1985, when my mother said this, her fears were justified. Aside from avoiding cigarettes, there appeared to be no way to significantly reduce cancer risk. Some research reports were already showing promising links between diet and cancer, but the connection was not yet widely accepted in the medical community. In the years since my grandmother died, however, there has been remarkable progress in what science understands about cancer.

Today, cancer is less fearsome and mysterious than ever before,

Their

connection

grew as

wispy as

Aerogramme

paper.

and these are exciting times for people who want to reduce their risk. The best news is that people from high-risk families need no longer feel helpless. In fact, they are more able than anyone else to improve their odds. Diet can help everyone, *especially* people in the highest risk groups.

T. Colin Campbell, a professor of nutrition and biomedical science at Cornell University, says: "Thanks to our current knowledge of nutrition, **we now have the opportunity** to live the longest, most disease-free lives in history."

THE CHINA PROJECT

Dr. Campbell directs the China Health Project, which is arguably the most important dietary study ever conducted. *The New York Times*, which called the China Project the "'Grand Prix' of Epidemiology," also noted that it is "the most comprehensive study ever undertaken of the relationship between diet and the risk of developing disease." Dr. Mark Hegsted, professor emeritus of nutrition at Harvard agreed: "This is a very, very important study—unique and well done."

China may be the perfect place to study how food affects health. The country's reliance upon local agriculture means that diet—and disease rates—vary greatly between villages. Some villages are nearly vegan, while other villages eat large amounts of animal products. By comparing disease rates in different villages, researchers can determine which diets are healthiest. Rural Chinese are also ideal for study because they tend to spend their whole lives in one geographic spot and to maintain the same diet and lifestyle throughout their lifetimes.

Besides having at its disposal this stable information source, the China Project's scope sets it apart from other studies. The China Project is a population study, and population studies in general have not been considered the most valid way to reach conclusions. That's because most studies of this type take in just a few pieces of informa-

We now have the opportunity to live the longest, most disease-free lives in history.

tion per person, making it easy to cast doubt on the results. For example, previous population studies have shown that vegetarians have lower cancer rates than non-vegetarians. It has been pointed out, however, that perhaps the people who eat the most vegetables also exercise more or smoke less, and that these are reasons for the lower disease rates. It's also possible that other lifestyle patterns, that were not recorded and analyzed, hold the answer.

The first sign that the China Project would be a population study of unprecedented scope and validity came when Dr. Chen Junshi, a preventive medicine researcher from Beijing, spent a sabbatic year working in Campbell's lab at Cornell. Junshi told Campbell that the Chinese Academy of Medical Sciences had compiled cause-of-death data on 800 million Chinese citizens. The two scientists realized that this treasure-trove of information could be the foundation for determining the link between diet and disease. They secured funding from the National Cancer Institute, and Dr. Junshi organized the huge survey.

The Chinese government wanted to make the China Project as authoritative as possible, and they threw their full support behind the study, supplying dozens of doctors and researchers to help gather the data. Scientists from England, France, the U.S., and other countries joined their Chinese counterparts, and in 1983 and again in 1989, they roamed China's countryside, often spending days at a time hiking in and out of remote rural villages. They went to 65 different counties, stretching from the southern coastal regions to the Gobi desert. They brought in computers, and introduced China to its first fax machine. They gathered information on everything from exercise habits to cigarette smoking to contaminants in the drinking water supply. They observed eating habits, home environments, and interviewed, tested, and examined each participant and their families over a period of days. In the 1989 survey, over 1,000 pieces of information were recorded for each of the 10,200 people studied!

As a result, the China Project has the most robust set of population data on diet and health ever assembled. Richard Peto, one of the world's top statisticians, has coordinated the China Project's statistical analysis. Professor Campbell summarizes the early results: "The China Health Project's primary finding is that the Chinese who eat the least fat and animal products have substantially lower rates of cancer, heart attack, and several other chronic degenerative diseases."

Campbell stands by his findings, and his subsequent recommendations for eliminating animal products from one's diet, because the China study has looked at diet and lifestyle in a very comprehensive way. "Most contemporary research focuses narrowly on relationships between single nutrients, single foods, single diseases, and—if possible—single molecules!" Campbell observes. The China Project is different, he contends, because it focuses on the relationship of *whole diet* and lifestyle patterns to *whole health*.

One of the initial findings of the China Project was that similar diseases tend to group according to geographic and economic areas. The less affluent, rural populations in China succumb more often to diseases that in many Western countries are no longer so great a threat. Among these diseases are pneumonia, parasite-caused ailments, and tuberculosis. On the other hand, the poorer, more rural residents often have dramatically lower rates of what are sometimes called the "diseases of affluence." These include diabetes, heart disease, and colon, breast, and lung cancer.

The higher incidence of common cancers and other "affluent" diseases, the researchers found, tend to occur in richer, more urban areas of China where incomes and lifestyles allow for more meat, oil, and animal protein consumption. Furthermore, the higher rates of cancer and other diseases are directly linked to higher levels of total blood cholesterol and urea nitrogen. High cholesterol levels can be attributed to eating fats, animal proteins, and meat. High levels of urea nitrogen, a product left in the blood after protein is metabolized, result from excess protein intake. People who rely on meat, eggs, and milk for a large part of their food are in danger of consuming too much protein, Campbell warns.

"We found that a high level of blood cholesterol was consistently associated with many cancers—including leukemia, liver, colon,

"We found that a high level of blood cholesterol was consistently associated with many cancers."

rectum, lung, and brain," reports Campbell. The China Project data show that as both cholesterol and urea levels rise, so do the instances of cancer, heart disease, and diabetes. The project results also suggest that even small amounts of animal products in the diet produce significant increases in disease. However, the more plant foods a diet contains, the lower the disease rates.

"Quite simply, the more you substitute plant foods for animal foods, the healthier you are likely to be," says Campbell. "I now consider veganism to be the ideal diet. A vegan diet—particularly one that is low in fat—will substantially reduce disease risks. Plus, we've seen no disadvantages from veganism. In every respect, vegans appear to enjoy equal or better health in comparison to both vegetarians and non-vegetarians."

REDUCING YOUR RISK

Campbell's work comes at a time of intense scientific interest in food choices. In the United States, diet is now believed to be a leading factor in 35 percent of cancer deaths. Cigarettes and tobacco use cause 30 percent of America's cancer deaths.[1] If you don't smoke, food choices become even more relevant. Walter C. Willett, of Harvard University's Departments of Nutrition and Epidemiology, says that ". . . in the non-smokers, diet is likely to account for a substantially larger percentage of cancers, probably more than 50 percent."[2]

What kind of diet does Professor Willett recommend? "Although much remains to be learned, most epidemiological data suggest that optimal

THE CAUSES OF CANCER DEATHS[3]

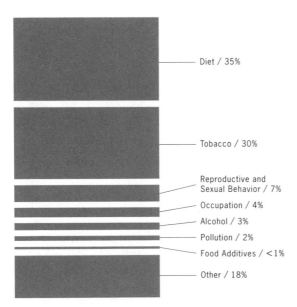

Diet / 35%

Tobacco / 30%

Reproductive and Sexual Behavior / 7%

Occupation / 4%

Alcohol / 3%

Pollution / 2%

Food Additives / <1%

Other / 18%

health can be achieved from a diet that emphasizes a generous intake of vegetables and fruit." Willett's comments about the protective properties of vegetables and fruits are well borne out in the nutrition literature. He cites over two hundred studies suggesting reduced cancer rates in people who eat more vegetables and fruits.[4] Willett writes that his own Nurses' Health Study, which is one of the largest and most highly regarded of these studies, found that: ". . . a 20–30% reduction in [breast cancer] risk was seen among women consuming more than one serving of vegetables per day."[5]

But *why* do fruits and vegetables prevent cancer? Researchers have had surprising difficulty deciding which plant-based compounds offer protection. In the 1980s, one of the best candidates for study was beta carotene. Beta carotene is produced only by plants. Not surprisingly, therefore, people who eat plenty of fruits and vegetables usually have high blood levels of beta carotene. In 1981, a very influential article that appeared in *Nature* reported that people with high beta carotene levels had lower rates of cancer. The article suggested that beta carotene might be an anti-cancer agent and called on researchers to investigate. In response, six extensive studies involving beta carotene supplements were launched during the 1980s.

The studies went poorly. Not only did the supplements

◄ beginning, attended not only by students but by other Cornell faculty and interested members of the public. Campbell has also been the senior science advisor to the American Institute of Cancer Research and has authored more than 300 scientific publications.

Campbell, now 62, has become the leading scientific proponent of an all-plant diet. His work, however, has met with resistance from some in the scientific community. Much of the problem is that many who have worked their whole lives in the nutritional sciences are reluctant to change their viewpoints, Campbell says. Another problem is that vegetarianism has in the past tended to support a somewhat dogmatic belief system, adhering zealously to the "rights" and "wrongs" of diet. Both parties need to lighten up, Campbell suggests, for the truth to be found. More objective, open-minded science needs to be applied to vegetarian and vegan diets, and followers of such diets need to support their choice with facts, not blind faith or exaggerated claims.

When Campbell, a former animal-protein researcher, saw his studies indicate that animal foods are unhealthy, he took a giant step in redirecting his career—but this is what good scientists do, he says. "I was just paying attention to what the scientific evidence was showing me."

fail to reduce cancer risk, they actually *increased* rates of lung cancer. Reporting on these dismal results, the *New Scientist* wrote: "The search for the life-saving ingredient of fruit and vegetables was knocked back to square one this week, after the leading candidate—the plant pigment beta carotene—was ruled out."[6]

Two of the six largest beta carotene studies were called off early because of the possible risk to volunteers. Charles Hennekens, who authored one of the studies, wrote: "These results now clearly tell us that for the general public beta carotene is not a magic bullet—that taking a supplement of beta carotene is not equivalent to eating a diet that is rich in fruit and vegetables."[7]

But Harvard's William von Eggers Doering says it's still too early to rule out beta carotene. The problem, says Dr. von Eggers Doering, is that supplement-makers synthesize just one type of beta carotene commercially, whereas there are numerous other varieties found naturally in fruits and vegetables. Until the full range of plant-based beta carotenes are tested, it will be too soon to give up on beta carotene.

Researchers have run similar health studies on vitamins C and E, which like beta carotene, are found primarily in plant-based foods.[8] They have encountered similarly unimpressive results when administering supplements to volunteers. Once again, though, they may be testing the wrong molecules. Vitamin E supplements contain just one member of the tocopherol family, of which there are at least eight members found naturally in plants. As with beta carotene, any of these other members might be offering vegetable eaters protection.

While *supplements* appear ineffective, the evidence that *fruits and vegetables* guard against cancer has never been stronger. One 1996 review of the failure of vitamin C, E, and beta carotene supplements, published by the *Journal of the American Dietetic Association*, notes: "Dietitians need to recognize the possibility that those micronutrients, particularly vitamin C and the carotenoids, may simply be markers for another biologically active component . . . that is truly the active agent. Thus, a focus on diet, such as eating more fruits and vegetables, is currently the recommended, scientifically based strategy for disease prevention."[9]

The failure of these supplement trials should tell us one thing: we may not know exactly *what* the anti-cancer substances are, but we now definitely know *where* they are. As Professor Campbell says: "Every bite of **vegetables or fruits** supplies the body with numerous powerful anti-cancer substances. Scientists may have a tough time isolating these agents, and they may not work individually as supplements, but it's now indisputable that fruits and vegetables exert tremendous anti-cancer activity."

"Every bite of vegetables or fruits supplies the body with numerous powerful anti-cancer substances."

COLON AND BREAST CANCER

Colon and breast cancer are the two most deadly cancers in the United States. Let's look at them for an indication of how far diet can go toward cancer prevention.

Of all cancers, colon cancer is the most directly related to food choices.[10] Seventh-day Adventists in the U.S. have *40 percent less colorectal cancer* than the general population.[11] Since about half of Seventh-day Adventists do not eat meat, researchers believe that diet may be the primary reason for their lower colon cancer rates.[12]

In the *Dietitian's Guide to Vegetarian Diets*, Mark and Virginia

Messina have identified numerous reasons why vegetarians have less colon cancer risk. They note that cell proliferation in the colon is reduced in vegetarians,[13] so tumors have fewer opportunities to develop, and that vegetarians have a lower concentration of potentially carcinogenic bile acids. Vegans have even lower levels of these acids.[14] Colon pH is lower in vegetarians, which may reduce enzymes that turn bile acids into carcinogenic secondary bile acids.[15]

The key to all of this may be that vegetarians and vegans eat more fiber, which moves waste material through the bowel in a speedy manner.[16] This may limit the time that carcinogens carried by the feces contact the lining of the colon.[17] Fruit, vegetables, and grains are all rich in fiber, whereas meat has no dietary fiber. Although some health-conscious people take daily doses of fiber supplements, recent evidence indicates that the variety of plant fiber that is ingested may be just as important as the fiber itself. Therefore, it is wise to eat a variety of fiber-containing foods.

Breast cancer is a very real threat in this country, but studies suggest that the risk can be reduced through diet. U.S. breast cancer deaths are three times Mexico's rates, four times Japan's rate, and five times China's rate.[18] These rates correspond closely to the amount of animal products in each country's diet.

A 1995 investigation was the first of three independently conducted studies that have shown vegan foods to protect against breast cancer. It examined 115 types of foods and beverages. The conclusion: "Vegetable consumption and fruit consumption were independently associated with statistically significant reductions of breast cancer risk . . . [and] no significant associations were evident for the other food groups examined."[19]

In 1996, another breast cancer study looked into the role of nutrition in breast cancer. It sampled 64 food categories, and found that four were associated with breast cancer: meat, red meat, saturated fat, and total fat. Red meat had the strongest association.[20]

Another 1996 study found that the more vegetables women ate, the less likely they were to get breast cancer.[21] The study could not, however, pinpoint which vegetable nutrients were responsible. The study's authors encountered the same problem we saw earlier with the beta carotene researchers. That is, although it's easy to see that vegetables reduce cancer risk, it's very hard to isolate which substances in vegetables are responsible. The authors suggest that individual nutrients from plant foods may not reduce risk by themselves, but that fruits and vegetables eaten in their entirety can reduce risk. They also believe that other yet-to-be-identified nutrients present in the vegetarian foods may offer greater protection than the ones that were studied.[22]

ANIMAL FOODS AS A CANCER TRIGGER

Although identifying the anti-cancer agents in plants has been more difficult than expected, researchers have had great success with the other part of the equation—figuring out the substances in animal products that increase cancer risk. During the 1980s and 1990s, biochemists have discovered that **animal products** contain numerous compounds that can trigger cancer tumors or hasten their development. Researchers are now especially concerned about free radicals, a class of molecules often found in cooked meat. First discovered in the early 1980s, they have aroused ever greater scientific interest as their behavior has become clear.

> Animal products contain numerous compounds that can trigger cancer.

Free radicals are the back-alley muggers of biology, roving the body in search of oxygen atoms they can steal from healthy cells. They break through cells' protective membranes looking for weakly bonded oxygen atoms. There's nothing delicate about this theft—during encounters with free radicals, the attacked cells' DNA may become damaged. These damaged cells may later pose great dangers to the body. When such cells divide, their damaged DNA can produce cancer cells. Substances that can cause this genetic damage to cells are called mutagens or carcinogens.

Perhaps the most dangerous group of free radicals are the heterocyclic amines (HAs). One team of researchers warns that: "These compounds have much higher mutagenic activity than other typical mutagens-carcinogens. . . . It is desirable to limit intake of heterocyclic amines to a minimum."[23]

HAs are generated in meat when it is cooked. When researchers wanted to discover which foods will produce the most HAs, they experimented by frying ground-beef hamburgers, bacon, and tempeh (vegan, soybean-based) burgers. They found that during cooking, both the hamburgers and bacon generate significant amounts of HAs. By contrast, cooking the tempeh burgers produced absolutely no HAs.[24]

Heating any food to cooking temperatures causes some carcinogenic materials to form. So even though tempeh burgers won't form HAs, they can and do form other carcinogenic compounds upon cooking. However, the same amount of cooking will generate far more potent carcinogens on meats than on these soybean-based "burgers." When the researchers investigated the total carcinogenic content, they found that "when fried to a well-done state, the beef and bacon had 44 and 346 times the mutagenic activity of the tempeh patties."[25]

In the HA study we just reviewed, cooking times and temperatures were carefully monitored under laboratory conditions. A truer picture of risk emerges when we consider the average fast-food restaurant, where grilling times and temperatures are not rigorously controlled. One group of researchers investigated the HAs found in meats purchased from various fast-food outlets. They found that mutagenic powers can vary *by more than ten times* from one hamburger to the next.[26]

As with other free radicals, HAs form in ever greater numbers with increased cooking temperatures and cooking times. In response to growing food safety problems, many restaurants are now cooking their meat longer and at higher temperatures than ever. For example, after Jack-in-the-Box burgers caused a large E. Coli outbreak in 1993, the restaurant chain raised grilling temperatures in an effort to guarantee safe burgers. Although increased grilling may prevent E. Coli infection from spreading, it also aggravates long-term cancer risks by increasing the amount of HAs in the meat.

People who eat meat consistently have elevated rates of cancer. One major study published in the *British Medical Journal* involving 6,000 adults determined that meat eaters are twice as likely to die from cancer as vegetarians.[27] After adjusting for non-dietary lifestyle factors, the vegetarians' risk of dying of cancer was still 40 percent less than that of the meat eaters!

These findings corroborate studies from Britain,[28] Germany,[29] Japan,[30] and Sweden,[31] all showing that meat eaters suffer greater overall cancer deaths than do vegetarians.

Campbell's China Project shows that not just meat but all animal proteins have the potential to promote cancer, and Campbell cites other studies that show that **carcinogenesis can be "turned on"** by animal protein and "turned off" by plant protein.

"It appears that once the body has all the protein it needs—which it gets at only about 8–10 percent of the entire diet—then the excess protein begins to feed precancerous lesions and tumors," reports Campbell. The average American diet contains more than twice the amount of protein than is needed, and much of it comes from meat, eggs, or dairy products.

I asked Campbell how much meat, milk, or eggs can a person safely eat.

"I think risk begins with the first bite, and increases with every mouthful thereafter. Different people respond differently, but the safest diet you can eat is totally vegan," he said.

"So why," I asked, "do some life-long meat eaters avoid cancer?"

"You could ask the same question about smoking," he said, "Some people can smoke heavily for fifty years and not get cancer. It has to do with risk thresholds. Risk thresholds indicate how much of a given substance a person can withstand before they develop a disease. For people with low risk thresholds, I think even tiny amounts of animal products can dramatically increase risk. On the other side, there are people with

> Carcinogenesis can be "turned on" by animal protein and "turned off" by plant protein.

much resistance to the hazards in animal products. The problem, of course, is that it's difficult to know your risk threshold in advance. You can have some idea of your risk threshold based on your family history, but it will still vary greatly between individuals."

S P R E A D I N G   T H E   W O R D

Professor Campbell has had a difficult time publicizing his message. "My path during the past twenty years has been quite rocky," he says, "at times very rocky." Why has a scientist of Campbell's stature faced such stiff opposition? In part, it's because many of his fellow nutrition researchers received their education when meat and dairy products were considered essential foods. Many powerful posts are held by people who are unwilling to re-examine beliefs that they have held for decades. It's also a hard fact of life that **many nutrition authorities** receive grants and other funding from various livestock and dairy industry interests.

"We've got a great many people in the nutrition community who will never give veganism a fair hearing," says Campbell, "They have an intemperate belief that animal products belong in the diet, and cling stubbornly to this belief no matter what evidence emerges. You wouldn't believe how much criticism I get from scientists who haven't even bothered to read my articles."

Yet despite Campbell's difficulties, his message *is* gaining acceptance. There is a lag time between when a discovery is made about cancer prevention and when public recommendations are put in place. Most of the discoveries about nutrition and cancer that have been highlighted in this chapter were made between 1980 and 1995. Now, the latest recommendations on diet are only starting to be shaped by these discoveries. As researchers get a better handle on which nutrients in fruits and vegetables are responsible for lowering disease risk, the U.S. government will likely strengthen its advice to consume vegetables.

Meanwhile, the American Cancer Society's nutritional guidelines,

Many nutrition authorities receive grants and other funding from various livestock and dairy industry interests.

issued in late 1996, begin by noting that: "The introduction of healthful diet and exercise practices at any time from childhood to old age can promote health and reduce cancer risk."[32] From there, the guidelines get explicit about which foods to eat and which to avoid. The guidelines advise people to "limit consumption of meats, especially high-fat meats." And they go even further—sounding almost as if they were written by the Vegan Society—in stating: "Emphasize beans, grains, and vegetables in meals to help shift dietary patterns to include more foods from plant rather than animal sources."[33]

The message is unambiguous. The guidelines contain four main recommendations. The first is to eat more plant-based foods, and the second is to eat less fat and animal products. (The final two recommendations deal with exercise and alcohol.)

AMERICAN CANCER SOCIETY GUIDELINES ON DIET, NUTRITION, AND CANCER PREVENTION (1996)

1 Choose most of the foods you eat from plant sources.

Eat five or more servings of fruits and vegetables each day.

Eat other foods from plant sources, such as breads, cereals, grain products, rice, pasta, or beans several times each day.

2 Limit your intake of high-fat foods, particularly from animal sources.

Choose foods low in fat.

Limit consumption of meats, especially high-fat meats.

3 Be physically active. Achieve and maintain a healthy weight.

Be at least moderately active for 30 minutes or more on most days of the week.

Stay within your healthy weight range.

4 Limit consumption of alcoholic beverages, if you drink at all.

Still, nowhere do the guidelines specifically recommend a vegetarian or vegan diet. So I contacted the chair of the panel that drafted the guidelines, Marion Nestle, Ph.D., M.P.H. I asked Dr. Nestle to compare the cancer risk of vegetarians to that of the general population. Her response: "Vegetarians and vegans have one-third to one-half the cancer risk of omnivores."[34]

The Physicians Committee for Responsible Medicine (PCRM) promotes a vegan diet—although its popular literature tends to use the word "vegetarian," undoubtedly because vegetarian is a more acceptable term to the general public and because a lacto-ovo vegetarian diet is perceived as being easier to follow. In a booklet that the not-for-profit organization makes available to the public, PCRM states: "While there is considerable advantage to a lacto-ovo vegetarian pattern, vegan diets are the healthiest of all, reducing risk of a broad range of health concerns," and "The major killers of Americans—heart disease, cancer, and stroke—have a dramatically lower incidence among people consuming primarily plant-based diets."

The Physicians Committee for Responsible Medicine promotes a vegan diet.

PCRM has defined the ideal diet as one made up of adequate servings from four food groups: vegetables, whole grains, fruit, and legumes. Meat, eggs, and dairy products are completely omitted from PCRM's recommendations. See the appendix of this book for a more complete list of PCRM's food recommendations and information on how to access the group's library of information.

PCRM, headed by Dr. Neal Barnard, is made up of about 3,400 physicians and 60,000 non-medical members. The group's mission is to promote nutrition, preventive medicine, ethical research practices, and compassionate medical policy. In many ways, the group offers leadership and awareness that is lacking in other institutions.

No other major health organization has yet publicized veganism as the most effective way to reduce cancer risk. The advice is generally to "limit" animal products rather than to eliminate them. If animal products cause risk (and even the most traditionally oriented nutritionists must now admit that they do), why aren't people being advised that cutting them out entirely is the best approach? Isn't a vegan diet the surest way to "limit" animal products?

Perhaps a reluctance to promote veganism stems from a fear that people will be overwhelmed and do nothing at all. If people thought they had to be completely vegan to reduce risk, they might be frightened away from making smaller changes that would at least offer some protection. Of course, going vegan may be the best way to reduce your risk, but it doesn't have to be an all-or-nothing proposition. The closer you come—the more fruits and vegetables and the less fatty animal products you eat—the lower your cancer risk is likely to be.

Professor Campbell says, "There is now strong reason to conclude that a vegan diet is the most effective way to reduce cancer risk. If you aren't willing to go totally vegan, then it makes sense to at least center most of your diet around vegan foods. That way, most of the foods you eat will be reducing, rather than increasing, your risk of cancer."

CHAPTER 3

It seems too good to be true: Heap your plate with as much food as you want, eat till you're full, lose weight. The key to the formula is that the food you'll be enjoying must be all or nearly all vegan. The key to success is that these foods will satisfy your hunger drive without topping out your calories. The key to enjoyment comes with the discovery that vegan foods—a vast variety of fruits, vegetables, grains, pastas, bread, sauces, spices, desserts, and much more—can be prepared in limitless ways.

Eat well to weigh less

Ruth Payne was vacationing in Hawaii when she read an article about a weight reduction talk to be held at the local library. The speaker was to be Dr. Terry Shintani, a Hawaiian doctor who ran a special clinic devoted to helping overweight Hawaiians slim down and live healthier lives. Besides being an M.D., the article said, Shintani also held a doctorate in law, and a master's degree in public health from Harvard. He had won all sorts of awards for his work in preventive medicine and community health. Ruth was intrigued, and in spite of her past failures with diets, decided to go to the talk.

Ruth's doctor at home had recently told her that she was almost fifty pounds overweight and that the excess weight was aggravating her already high blood pressure. This information came as no surprise. Ruth had experienced weight problems for most of her life. Over the years, she had paid hundreds of dollars to participate in a variety of weight-loss programs. Some programs had failed her completely while others had worked—but only for a while. Staying on the diets was a constant struggle and any weight Ruth lost, she always gained back.

Even though she arrived a few minutes early for Dr. Shintani's talk, the library's conference room was already packed. All the seats were taken and Ruth had to squeeze in with the people who were standing along the back wall.

Shintani was introduced, and within a few minutes Ruth forgot the crowd and the uncomfortable spot she had claimed in the room. For one thing, she felt she liked this smiling, soft-spoken man who seemed to really care about what he was saying. More important, what he was saying made so much sense. Ruth felt hope brightening as she settled down to listen.

"So many of my patients come to me complaining that they are always hungry," began Shintani. "Does anybody here have this problem?"

Many people in the room nodded.

"Let's think about this. Our bodies have three physical drives: air, water, and food. So tell me, when was the last time you knew anyone who had a problem breathing too much air? How about drinking too much water? Does your neighbor phone you and chat for hours about how she just can't keep from breathing too much air or drinking too much water? Does she say, 'Help me, Betty, I'm drowning! I just pigged out on tap-water!'? It doesn't happen, does it?"

The audience laughed.

"So what about food?" asked Shintani, "How could we be designed with perfect drives for water and air, yet somehow with a major defect when it comes to food? Now, there *are* a few people with psychological or medical problems that cause them to eat too much. But for most of us, our hunger drive actually works as perfectly as our drive for air or water—when you're hungry, you should satisfy your hunger and eat! We gain weight, **not by eating too much,** but by filling up on the wrong kinds of foods.

"Tonight I'll show you how to select foods that will fill your stomach without causing weight gain. I know this sounds hard to believe, but stay with me and I'll show you how it works. There is nothing new-fangled

"We gain weight, not by eating too much, but by filling up on the wrong kinds of foods."

about this. I have no special pills, no protein powders, nothing high-tech at all. I'm just going to teach you a few simple things about food that will make it easy for you to drop those pounds."

HEALTH RISKS OF BEING OVERWEIGHT

Dr. Shintani reaches an eager audience with his approach to weight control. During the 1980s and 1990s, the U.S. population has gained weight every year. Between 1980 and 1991, the weight of the average U.S. adult increased by over seven pounds.[1] A similar trend has occurred in England, where the percentage of overweight men has nearly doubled in less than five years.[2] A 1994 article published in the *Journal of the American Medical Association* reports that one-third of all adults in the U.S. are overweight.[3]

Obesity can create serious health risks. Obese people have much higher than average rates of heart disease, hypertension, and stroke.[4] Large-scale studies have also linked obesity to gallbladder disease, arthritis, and gout.[5] One study of 750,000 people found that people who weigh 40 percent or more above optimum have 30 percent higher cancer rates.[6] Obese people are almost three times more likely to develop diabetes,[7] and overweight women who become pregnant may face greater risk of delivery complications.[8]

As obesity rates surged during the 1980s, many doctors were giving up hope that dieting offered any solution. Several doctors suggested that it was best to just accept that large numbers of people would always be overweight, and nothing could change this. The editor of Harvard Medical School's *Health Letter* confessed: "I can see no ethical basis for continuing research or treatment on weight loss."[9]

Why were doctors so gloomy? At any given time, one out of every five men and two of every five women are now on a diet.[10] Believing that bizarre diets are the only effective option to lose weight, many people take desperate measures. One in five dieters tries to take off the pounds by skipping meals.[11] Other people turn to diet pills and going to weight-loss centers.[12] But regardless of the method, most people who lose significant weight quickly gain it back.[13]

Registered Dietitian Dina Fitzsimons, says, "The reason most diets fail is that people accustomed to high-fat foods believe they must feel deprived in order to lose weight. Eventually people give up because no one can endure these feelings for long. It is very possible—in fact, favorable—to always satisfy hunger by eating fresh fruits and vegetables, whole grains, and legumes. In my practice, people learn that by choosing a low-fat, plant-based diet, they'll never go hungry, and the calorie intake will remain low enough for effective weight control."

NO GIMMICKS

In our weight-obsessed culture, promises of easy weight loss are common—and often involve fees for "secrets" or meal programs. But Shintani sounded different, Ruth thought. She correctly surmised that he wasn't using weight-loss promises to promote a get-rich-quick scheme.

"Here in Hawaii," Shintani told the group at the library, "the native Hawaiian people have almost the highest rate of obesity in the world. But just 100 years ago, well before Hawaii was annexed by the U.S., almost no Hawaiians had weight problems. As a medical student, I used to look at photographs and other records of nineteenth-century Hawaiians. I wondered why yesterday's Hawaiians stayed thin while so many today have problems with their weight.

"I started researching what and how traditional Hawaiians ate. They raised no cattle. While some natives ate a lot of fish, the people who enjoyed the best health filled their plates with fruits and vegetables. Three of the most common foods eaten in Hawaii 100 years ago were taro, sweet potatoes, and poi."

Taro is a root vegetable, and poi is a traditional Hawaiian food made from the taro root.

Shintani continued: "Hawaiians centered their diets on these three

"The reason many of us have weight problems is that we're eating a lot of animal-based foods."

main staples. I wondered why people stayed thin when they ate primarily taro, sweet potatoes, and poi. It was when I looked at caloric density of these foods that I discovered the Hawaiian weight-loss secret. You see, most people need three or four pounds of food each day to satisfy their hunger. But you would have to eat *nine* pounds of taro and poi, and over five pounds of sweet potatoes, to get a full day's calories.

"Does everyone see why it's practically impossible to gain weight by eating these foods? To maintain our weight, our food must deliver from 2,000 to 2,500 calories a day. Any calories above this range will probably cause weight gain. Most of us would explode before we consumed 2,500 calories worth of these foods.

"The reason many of us have **weight problems** is that we're eating a lot of animal-based foods. Did you know that Hawaii now leads the nation in per-capita consumption of Spam®? Animal foods are so rich in calories that you probably can't satisfy your hunger with them without gaining weight. When you fill up on animal foods, you'll reach your daily calorie limit long before you satisfy your hunger."

CHEESE OR PEACHES?

The average person needs 3 to 4 pounds of food each day to satisfy hunger. The average person also needs no more than 2,500 calories a day to maintain an ideal weight. Animal foods deliver the calories but not the bulk we need to feel satisfied, while plant foods allow us to eat as much as we like—without consuming extra calories.

CHEDDAR CHEESE
2,500 calories —————————————— 1.4 lbs

HAM
2,500 calories —————————————— 2.1 lbs

FRIED CHICKEN
2,500 calories —————————————— 2.2 lbs

BROWN RICE
2,500 calories —————————————— 4.6 lbs

APPLES
2,500 calories —————————————— 9.4 lbs

CARROTS
2,500 calories —————————————— 13.0 lbs

PEACHES
2,500 calories —————————————— 16.6 lbs

Ruth was beginning to wonder what taro root tastes like when another woman in the audience raised her hand. "I can find taro, sweet potatoes, and poi at the local markets, but are you suggesting that this is all I'm supposed to eat?" she said, "What about when I travel to the mainland? How am I supposed to stay on your diet?"

"Many common plant-based foods are just as suitable for weight loss as taro and other traditional Hawaiian foods. In fact, the traditional plant-based foods of most cultures are just as healthy as the Hawaiian foods we've looked at. The point of this diet is not to eat only taro or pineapples. Most plant-based foods have caloric densities every bit as low as our traditional Hawaiian foods. No matter where you live or travel, I encourage you to **eat the widest possible variety** of fruits, vegetables, whole grains, and beans."

"Are all plant foods this low in calories?" another person asked.

"No. There are a few exceptions," replied Dr. Shintani. "Nuts, seeds, avocados, coconuts, and vegetable oils are very fatty. You can gain weight on avocados just as easily as you can on milk or cheese. But aside from these items, just about any plant-based food will help you to keep your weight ideal."

The question-and-answer session that followed was filled with enthusiasm. Many people remarked that they remembered their grandparents and great-grandparents eating taro, sweet potatoes, and poi. They had always wondered why the older generation had stayed thin while the younger generation developed weight problems.

Ruth left the talk feeling good about what she had heard. Still, she waited another year before she began to follow Shintani's advice, a year of discomfort and confusion about her health and her weight. Later, when she learned more about Shintani's personal history, she realized he had once had much in common with her.

SHINTANI'S DISCOVERIES

Dr. Shintani, who is of Japanese descent, was born and raised in Hawaii. Like most people in his age group, he grew up eating lots of meat and processed foods. After entering college, his weight began creeping up. By the time he started law school he, like many Americans, was definitely overweight. He also felt sluggish and lacked the energy he needed to apply himself to his studies. Everything changed when a friend convinced him to stop eating an obvious source of calories, junk food, as

> "Eat the widest
> possible variety
> of fruits,
> vegetables,
> whole grains,
> and beans."

well as the less obvious high-calorie culprits: meat, dairy products, and eggs. In just a few months, Shintani lost 30 pounds, and he felt great. He graduated from law school trim and healthy, but he found he was far more interested in learning more about nutrition than he was in being a lawyer.

The next fall, he enrolled at the University of Hawaii's medical school. Although he excelled in his studies, he gradually realized that while he was learning a great deal about the pathology and treatment of disease, he received very little instruction on how to stay healthy in the first place. Nutrition was almost never mentioned in his classes. In four years of medical school, Shintani received just *three hours* of instruction on nutrition. Not three credit hours, he explains, three actual hours.

To pursue some of the areas that were not a part of his medical school training, he enrolled at Harvard to study public health and to specialize in preventive medicine. It was while he was at Harvard that he started to explore the causes of obesity. He developed a weight-loss program in which participants lost weight while eating more food.

Shintani returned to Hawaii in 1987 after his studies were complete, and he turned his attention to treating nutrition-related illnesses. Two years later he was making headlines with his revolutionary Hawaiian weight-loss plan. Hawaiians who had been plagued with obesity and its many attendant health problems were dropping pounds with ease. By 1993, a year after the library talk Ruth attended, Shintani had published his first major book on weight loss.

In The Eat More, Weigh Less™ Diet, Shintani expands on what he told Ruth's audience. The main idea behind his program is that some foods make you gain weight, and others help you to lose it. Dr. Shintani developed the Eat More Index (EMI) to show which foods are which.

Shintani's EMI scale contains over a hundred common foods, and each food item has a number next to it. The number tells how many pounds of each food it takes to provide a day's calories. Shintani discovered that most vegan foods are almost absurdly low in calories.

For example, the EMI for potatoes is 9.5, so if you ate only potatoes, you would have to eat almost ten pounds to get a full day's calories. Dozens of vegan foods have even higher EMIs. Oranges, green beans, and eggplant, for example, have EMIs of 15.6, 21.8, and 28.75. These numbers mean that any of these foods are practically impossible to gain weight on. You would have to eat almost 30 pounds of eggplant to get a full days' calories. And you can eat any combination of these high-EMI foods and still lose weight.

Once you've lost your excess poundage, vegan foods are good for maintaining body weight. The EMI for bread, chickpeas, and yams are 4.7, 5.5 and 5.3, respectively. The EMI values of most animal foods, by contrast, are a dieter's nightmare. Butter is .76, mayonnaise is .77, cheddar cheese is 1.37, bologna is 1.72, and fried chicken is 2.23. With these animal foods, it doesn't take much to have eaten more calories than your body needs, and when it happens you will probably still be hungry.

Shintani's EMI values are helpful in identifying the high-calorie foods to avoid, but an elaborate system of counting calories isn't necessary. Once your eating habits have changed, nature takes care of things, and your trusty hunger drive becomes your most reliable gauge. As long as you're adhering to a well-balanced vegan diet, your motto can be: eat when you're hungry; stop when you're full. The ease and the enjoyability of this diet are what make it the last one you ever have to adopt. The whole idea, explains Shintani, is to make a change for life.

A N E W Y E A R ' S R E S O L U T I O N

After hearing Dr. Shintani talk at the library, Ruth did not immediately change her diet. She was on vacation, and did not feel motivated to seek foods that were new to her. When she returned home to Texas, Ruth thought about Shintani's advice but still did not follow it. She continued eating as much meat and milk as ever, and her weight problems persisted.

The next year, Ruth and her husband bought a house in Honolulu. When it came time to choose a personal physician, Ruth thought of Dr.

Shintani. She went back to the King Street Library and was able to obtain Shintani's office telephone number.

At her first appointment with Dr. Shintani, she asked him if he could help her with her weight problem. Shintani replied: "Now that you're getting settled in Hawaii, you might want to try some of the wonderful produce we grow here. I really think you'll have no problem dropping your excess weight if you just shift your diet to high-EMI foods. My book can explain."

Dr. Shintani also told Ruth that many of his patients are able to quit taking blood pressure medication after dropping the animal products and fatty foods from their diets. He gave Ruth a copy of his book, and advised her to follow its step-by-step approach to weight loss.

Using the book's advice and recipes, Ruth found it easy to drop weight without feeling hunger. But she still had years of ingrained habits to overcome.

"I was raised in the Midwest," Ruth says, "and I'd always find myself going back to fried chicken, pork chops, and steak. It wasn't ever out of hunger, but just because I was still in the habit of eating meat. Whenever I ate meat or dairy products, the weight would come right back on."

Ruth continued to include substantial amounts of animal

A "F O O D   H E R O"

Terry Shintani has not strayed far from his boyhood home in Hawaii, even though he studied at Harvard, and his work has been written about in national publications, including *Newsweek*. Shintani has been honored with several community service and health prevention awards, primarily for his work with the native Hawaiian population.

He runs a health center in Hawaii where many of his patients are obese and overweight native Hawaiians. Shintani helps these patients discover how to use their traditional diet to lose weight and control or prevent disease. Shintani also reaches out to a broader audience by teaching, lecturing, and writing in both professional and popular arenas; leading conferences; and making personal appearances on radio and TV, from CBS to CNN.

Since his days as a graduate student, Shintani has focused on diet as a key component in good health. His trademarked "eat more, weigh less" program has helped untold numbers of people discover a solid foundation for feeling good, looking good, and staying healthy.

A man who has been honored many times (starting in his first year of medical school when he was lauded by the American Medical Student Association) by governments, civic and professional associations, the honor that perhaps best defines Dr. Shintani's work came in 1995 when *Eating Well* magazine named him a "food hero." That same year, his work was described in an article in the *Encyclopedia Britannica*.

products in her diet, and by the time of her next visit to Dr. Shintani, she had lost only a few pounds. She was afraid she would be lectured for not following the program, but Shintani didn't pass judgment. Ruth remembers, "He was the first doctor I ever liked to go to. He isn't pushy and he isn't demanding. Just by his example, his advice became easy to follow."

Some weeks Ruth would follow Shintani's advice to the letter, and on other weeks she would revert to her old habits. But her "trial-runs" convinced her she could stick with it if she made the commitment. On the morning of January 1, 1995, she made a New Year's resolution to follow all of Dr. Shintani's diet recommendations.

She breakfasted on bread and fresh fruit. She began cooking fat-free soup using barley, rice, and beans. She also tried some Japanese recipes from Dr. Shintani's book. She started paying attention to which vegetables were in season when she did her grocery shopping, and was amazed at the endless variety of textures, colors, and flavors each season had to offer.

The pounds came off, and she became more energetic. She began taking long hikes, which made her feel better than she had in years. The exercise sped her weight loss. By the end of 1995, she had lost 40 pounds. Her weight has since dropped further—stabilizing at exactly 48 pounds below what it had been.

Ruth's experience with veganism is similar to the vast majority of Dr. Shintani's weight loss patients.

Shintani says, "When my patients lose weight, they often act as if I've discovered a magical diet, whereas all I've actually done is shown them how to eat sensibly. Being able to control your weight is a natural outcome of a low-fat vegan diet."

IT'S EASIER THAN YOU THINK

Most diets tell people they can eat the same or similar foods that they've always eaten. But isn't this what has created the problem in the first place? Shintani's program differs from other treatments. His approach requires a willingness to try new foods—an approach that most other

The pounds came off, and she became more energetic.

diet programs deliberately avoid. Many dieters think Shintani is asking for too much. Ruth, who had long put animal products at the center of her diet, resisted Shintani's advice for almost two years.

Dr. Shintani says that, **"The people who say** the changes are too difficult are almost always the people who haven't tried it." People who make the leap toward Shintani's recommendations almost invariably find doing so much easier than expected. Shintani acknowledges that "it takes some of my patients a few months to become comfortable with the diet." But over time, many of his patients end up preferring vegan foods to the foods they grew up on.

Most importantly, Shintani's program delivers what other diet programs only promise. It really *is* a program in which you can eat all you want and still lose weight. Ruth believes that the low-fat plant-based foods made an immediate and lasting difference in how she looks and how she feels. She says, "After I made the commitment, I quickly realized how sensible and delicious this diet can be. I've been able to lose all this weight and keep it off without ever feeling hungry. Once you're on this diet for a few weeks, sticking to it becomes second nature. I think it's really neat that somebody like me could make a change like that and be happy about it too."

> "The people who say the changes are too difficult are almost always the people who haven't tried it."

VEGAN, SLIM, AND RELAXED

Finding a way to control your weight can lead to an overall sense of well-being. The emotional stress and worry about being "fat" can melt away at the same time the physical stress of carrying the extra weight is relieved.

Jean Ednie is a 28-year-old state beach lifeguard in Santa Barbara, California. She told me, "I've had trouble with my weight since I was eleven. But I've finally found a way of eating that has effortlessly solved my weight problems."

For Jean, maintaining a healthy body weight is important for her job. Each season, the lifeguards must take a strenuous ocean-swimming examination. Anyone who cannot perform adequately is not hired for the season. During the winter off-season, Jean's weight would usually creep up, and she had difficulty getting in shape for the annual swim test:

"My life became a winter/summer roller coaster of trying to lose weight in the spring and summer, and then gaining it back in the fall and winter. My weight fluctuated by 15 pounds every year, but even worse, I was becoming more prone to injuries by overtraining to work off all the calories. I did not have a healthy attitude toward food, and I hated that I kept eating so much."

In 1995, Jean decided to try a vegan diet, primarily to spare the lives of animals. Although she didn't initially become a vegan for weight control reasons, she found her chronic weight problems quickly diminished. "During my first year on a vegan diet, I lost ten pounds, very gradually, and at the same time my weight ceased to be a source of stress for me."

Now that Jean has found a way to stay thin without excessive exercise, she says she is no longer compulsive about her workouts. She suffers fewer injuries, and can run twice as often as she did when she carried her extra weight. She has noticed an improvement in her muscle tone. Her fellow lifeguards have noticed the difference, and several have approached her for information about how she has done it.

I asked her to sum up her experience after following a vegan diet for one year:

"When I began giving up meat and dairy, I immediately started enjoying food and the experience of eating again. I savored foods again, especially sprouts and salads. Raw vegetables gave me so much joy, it was almost funny. I lost the neurotic tendency to overeat, and I felt a deep intuitive knowledge that my body was being nurtured.

"I began to have more fun at work, and now, in my seventh lifeguarding season—my second season as a vegan—I weigh 135 pounds without having to torture myself in workouts every day. I enjoy my work more, and I've taken on more responsibilities. My outlook on

> "Sometimes I forget that something as simple as food could have such a profound influence on my state of mind."

life is more positive, and I laugh more with my co-workers. I am not as sensitive and embarrassed by feelings that I'm ugly or too fat. My shoulders are leaner, and my legs are stronger, and my posture is straighter.

"Sometimes I forget that something as simple as food could have such a profound influence on my state of mind, but it is so true. When I eat something loaded with sugar or cooked starchy food, I feel sad, like I've punished myself for something I didn't do. That's how I felt about food in high school and college, like I was feeding a bottomless hunger I had no control over. The lethargy and heaviness I felt after eating sugary or cooked foods, including meat, reinforced my belief that eating was a source of humiliation and a chore.

"Now I appreciate food, and I treat it with reverence. I believe that freeing myself of my cravings for meat and other animal products is one of the most loving gifts I can give myself, and my success has given me a deep sense of pride in myself, and a compassion for others."

Milk, cheese, and dairy products are a staple of the standard American diet—the same diet that is responsible for many of our highest disease rates. It's time to take a critical look at milk and consider whether it lives up to its reputation as "the perfect food."

The perfect food isn't

From the beginning of their schooling, nutrition students are fed a strong message. One standard first-year college nutrition textbook states unequivocally: "Milk is the most nutritious food in the diet at any age,"[1] and "Most authorities agree that milk is the single most important food in the diet."[2] With training like this, it's no surprise that many dietitians still promote milk as an essential food for children and adults, even though dairy products—like all other animal products—are associated with several degenerative diseases.

Registered Dietitian Suzanne Havala experienced first-hand how effective the dairy industry is in targeting dietitians. "Back in 1980, all we heard in undergraduate nutrition courses was that dairy products were all-important," recounts Havala. "You heard about it in class, you read the advertisements in nutrition journals, even nutrition textbooks told us that drinking milk was a good idea."

Havala accepted the importance of dairy products wholeheartedly, even though she scrutinized the meat industry's claims with a skepticism absent in most of her classmates. "I was caught up in the wholesome image of milk. I even wished for a job with the Dairy Council after graduation. Most nutritionists at that time thought a position with the Dairy Council was a dream job. In the eyes of an undergraduate, the Dairy Council jobs had great hours and cushy offices. The Dairy Council also gives employees beautiful, glossy nutrition education materials to hand to clients. My professors reinforced the concept that milk was a healthy food, so I thought that working for the Dairy Council would be an ideal job."

Havala remembers watching one of her nutrition professors load two tall glasses of milk on her cafeteria tray during lunch. "I asked if she was drinking all that milk because she was trying to get the recommended daily number of servings of milk and she said she was. And I remember being so impressed that she was so wonderfully health-conscious!"

It was not until after college that Havala began looking critically at dairy products. After college, she became aware that cow's milk often conflicts with the human body's needs. Milk causes day-to-day problems among many adults to a degree unseen in other foods. Milk-related digestive problems arise mostly from lactose, a type of sugar found only in dairy products. In order for the body to properly absorb the sugar in milk, the body requires lactase—the enzyme which breaks down lactose into its simple constituents, which can then be digested by the body. During childhood, many people stop producing enough lactase to properly digest milk. When these people drink milk, bacteria in the lower intestine ferments the undigested lactose, causing gas and cramps. Depending on the person, the symptoms vary from mild to severe.

More than 50 million Americans—upwards of one in every six people—have this problem resulting from drinking milk.[3] **Worldwide estimates** are higher, suggesting that two-thirds of the population has trouble digesting milk after childhood.[4]

Many people who suffer symptoms never suspect milk products are responsible. One victim writes:

"I had no notion that dairy products could be the root of the perpetual bloating, gas cramps and diarrhea that had plagued my life

Worldwide estimates suggest that two-thirds of the population has trouble digesting milk after childhood.

for years. Milk! Milk had 'something for every body.' Milk was nature's perfect food. Milk was the all-American drink. Milk was so important that government subsidies kept the price of a half-pint in my high school cafeteria down to only three cents, so that everybody could afford to have it every day. . . . With perverse irony, well meaning friends advised me to drink milk to 'soothe' my stomach. Each day, possibly each meal, I had milk, milk and more milk, some visible, much hidden, making it impossible for me to isolate any particular food as the source of my distress."[5]

Even with the frequent lack of diagnosis, milk allergies are actually the most common of all food allergies. Milk contains more than 25 proteins that can lead to allergies.[6] Frank A. Oski, when chief of pediatrics at Johns Hopkins School of Medicine, said that evidence suggests that around 50 percent of all U.S. children are allergic to cow's milk, with most of these allergies going undiagnosed.[7] Children of African-American or Asian descent are likely to be even more sensitive. But since milk is so deeply trusted by children and parents alike, a child can suffer chronic allergic reactions without the parent ever suspecting milk

Courtesy of Suzanne Havala

After completing her degree and becoming a registered dietitian, Suzanne Havala continued to study nutrition. Her doubts about the promotion of milk as the perfect food were heightened as she learned that it is actually quite easy to be well nourished without the consumption of meat or milk. She began to rethink the emphasis that her professors had attached to animal products, when so many less fatty and more nutritious foods exist in the plant kingdom. Havala gradually realized that the American way of eating was fundamentally flawed, and that most university nutrition departments were perpetuating a myth.

Havala found, however, that her ideas inspired great resistance from other dietitians. "For many years, most of my colleagues thought that vegetarian diets were risky and strange. They had no personal experience with them, and were frankly uncomfortable dealing with vegetarians. Given the concepts we learned as dietitians, communicating with vegetarians was almost like speaking a different language. I realized that dietitians were oriented to standards that were geared to Americans and the American way of eating. They were educated in an American system that assumes that people are always going to eat a meat-centered American diet. The belief was that, 'people eat this ▶

could be responsible. Another health problem associated with milk is infant colic, a digestive upset that affects one in five infants and may be caused by the dairy products nursing mothers consume.

WHAT'S IN MILK?

One thing milk has plenty of, unless it's completely skimmed off, is fat. The fat content in whole milk products is much higher than the dairy industry would like you to believe. The fat in whole milk accounts for 48 percent of its calories. The fat in so-called "2% milk" equals 34 percent of its calories. (By *weight*, the fat makes up 2 percent of the product.) Cheddar cheese gets 73 percent of its calories from fat, and butter, of course, is 100 percent fat. To put this into perspective, a baked potato contains 1 calorie of fat; a banana, 5 calories of fat.[8] Fat intake, and especially animal fat intake, is unequivocally a culprit in heart disease and has been identified as contributing to breast cancer.

The federal government specifies that vitamin D be added to milk, but the difficulty of mixing in just the right amount can result in levels that are too low or too high. In addition, varying amounts of antibiotics and growth hormones used on dairy herds are passed on to humans in milk.

Milk is a source of protein, but increasing evidence shows that milk protein may trigger the onset of insulin-dependent diabetes in children. Certain children develop antibodies to the protein, which in turn destroy insulin-producing cells in the pancreas. The Physicians Committee for Responsible Medicine reports a study of 142 diabetic children showed that every one had high levels of the milk protein antibody.[9]

Milk's biggest claim to fame is its calcium content. Indeed, a scenario has been built

◄ way, they'll always eat this way, and it's not right to tell them to eat differently.'

"I used to view veganism as a very extreme form of the vegetarian diet and not something to necessarily aspire to. Now I believe that a sensibly planned vegan diet is far healthier than anything Americans follow."

Havala has become an expert in the field of vegetarian and vegan nutrition and is on the advisory boards of *Vegetarian Times* magazine and The Vegetarian Resource Group.

around calcium-rich milk as a hero and osteoporosis as the villain. The story isn't so simple, however, and the push for milk consumption as a panacea for calcium loss may be a push in the wrong direction.

Dietitians are repeatedly exposed to the dairy industry's message that milk is the best source of calcium. One advertisement directed at registered dietitians says: "Encourage your female patients to drink milk regularly."[10] The ad goes on to say, "With 20 million women suffering from osteoporosis, it's important to raise awareness about milk's role in a healthy diet."[11]

Osteoporosis rates are very high in the United States, as the Milk Board ad suggests. Our hip fracture rates are among the highest in the world.[12] And yet we are also one of the highest dairy consumers in the world. Something doesn't compute, and scientists are beginning to discover why. **New evidence suggests** that high-protein diets can actually *cause* calcium loss. While milk contains calcium, as well as vitamin D that helps your body retain calcium, it also boosts your protein intake. Considering how many good sources of calcium exist in the plant world, it seems unnecessary to rely on milk. Good plant sources of calcium include kale, collards, mustard and turnip greens, broccoli, bok choy, black beans, chick peas, calcium-processed tofu, calcium-fortified soymilk, calcium-fortified orange juice, and blackstrap molasses. Spinach is an unreliable source of calcium because its oxalate content inhibits absorption.

Many factors yet to be understood influence bone health. It is wise for vegans to strive to meet the RDA for calcium both because of these uncertainties and because high calcium intakes have been shown to be beneficial not only for bone health but also for other health aspects. It is possible to meet the RDA for calcium on a vegan diet by eating a variety of calcium-rich plant foods. As with anyone on any diet, total bone health rather than just calcium intake should be emphasized. Your best assurance against osteoporosis (based on current data) is to encourage peak bone mass up to the early 20s through adequate calcium intake, sufficient vitamin D, and

New evidence suggests that high-protein diets can actually <u>cause</u> calcium loss.

exercise. After age 30, bone loss can be discouraged through exercise, proper calcium and vitamin D status, and avoidance of smoking, caffeine, soft drinks, and excesses of alcohol, protein, and sodium.

THINKING FOR YOURSELF

The notion that milk and dairy products are completely wholesome, healthful foods is a hard one to shake. The dairy industry has supported a series of brilliant advertising campaigns over the years, appealing to our vanity and senses of humor as well as our concern for good health. The most recent "Got Milk?" campaign plays on the milk-and-cookies theme with wit and flawless comedic timing. It's hard not to be swept along by the apparently harmless fun of it all.

Havala is unsympathetic to the ads and has suggested that milk promotion is potentially harmful and could even be construed as racist. Lactose intolerance, with its attendant bloating, abdominal pain, flatulence, and diarrhea, is much higher in black and Asian populations, while people of Northern European extraction fare much better. Milk intolerance among Southeast Asians is almost 100 percent; for blacks it is approximately 75 percent. Worldwide, Scandinavian populations have the least problem. Only about 3 to 8 percent are adversely affected by milk products. The degree of intolerance increases in southern and eastern directions until it reaches about 70 percent in southern Italy and Turkey. Most Africans—except for cattle-raising nomadic peoples—are unable to digest milk.[13] To promote milk to African-American and Asian populations without any caveat about probable intolerance or allergy is wrong, Havala feels. Nevertheless, the word is getting out. A 1993 article in the popular magazine, *Essence*, detailed the experience of a black woman who, over time, pinpointed milk as the source of her and her children's lethargy and chronic sinus congestion. "Growing up, most of us were told that dairy products—cheese, yogurt, ice cream and especially milk—were as American as apple pie," the article states. "But no one ever mentioned the downside . . . that the majority of Black folks can't digest them." [14]

Children start getting the National Dairy Council message almost as soon as they set foot in school. The Dairy Council has long provided educational materials to public school classrooms, starting in the earliest grades. However, several prominent pediatricians, including Charles Attwood and Benjamin Spock, have called attention to the problems with dairy products. The New Four Food Groups put forward by the Physicians Committee for Responsible Medicine leave out dairy products (and meat) altogether. This group of physicians, whose mission includes preventive medicine, endorses a dairy-free diet.

Americans will no doubt be exposed to a continuing series of charming and benign-seeming advertisements for milk. The wisest observers will consider the source and look for more objective information. Sorting out the information is a personal responsibility, just as choosing to eat dairy products is a personal choice. The important thing to remember is that you do have a choice.

C H A P T E R

5

Great Britain was shaken by an outbreak of a deadly brain disease in humans that most experts link to a similar disease in cattle. The deaths of several young Britons focused worldwide attention on British politicians who at first denied the problem. Add to this unresolved story the apparent discovery of an almost indestructible disease-causing agent, and it would appear that there definitely is a problem, and not only in Great Britain.

How now, mad cow

In 1957, Howard Lyman became one of the first 300-pound linemen in college football history. He was so big, so strong, and so fast that he could often block two defensive linemen in a single play. Coaches told him that he had the size and speed to be an NFL player. But Howard had other things in mind.

Howard's main interest was cattle ranching. Back in 1908, his great-grandfather purchased a 540-acre spread near Montana's Great Falls. The ranch had been handed down through three generations of Lymans. Every new generation of the Lyman family enlarged the ranch and made it more prosperous. Howard was the family's only surviving son and he wanted to be ready when his turn came to take over the ranch. He spent his college years studying agriculture at Montana State University. When he graduated from college, his father put the ranch in his hands.

Howard wasted no time in applying the new ranching techniques he had learned in college, and all his changes quickly paid off. Every year the ranch raised more cattle and turned greater profits. Howard succeeded for many reasons. He kept up with the most recent developments in ranching and crop-growing and made sure that his operation maintained every possible competitive advantage. He worked hard—often 18 hours a day—and he knew how to motivate the ranch hands who worked for him.

Howard was proud of his work. He ate beef with almost every meal and considered it an essential part of a healthy diet. But in 1983, he gave it all up—not just his ranch but also the whole lifestyle that centered around being a rancher. "Many common ranching practices began to trouble me," he says. "The longer I stayed in the cattle business, the more reasons I found to worry about the safety of our beef supply."

Lyman switched to a vegan diet eight years later, in 1991. Since then, he has openly come out against the cattle industry, as well as the use of chemicals in ranching and farming. Why has he done it? He says: "Running the ranch paid well, it was challenging, it was my family tradition. But my conscience told me that I needed to speak out about this industry—there's just too much that the cattle industry hides from the public."

FEEDING COWS TO COWS

I met Howard Lyman for the first time in 1994. Since he had run his family ranch for two decades, I eagerly sought his opinions about beef safety.

Lyman is an enormous man. He was drinking a soda, and the can was almost completely hidden inside his massive hand. He wore a checkered cowboy shirt and a pair of blue jeans. His graying hair was cut short and combed casually to one side. He looked keenly into my eyes and talked articulately and expertly about his fears of mad cow disease.

"I've been afraid for over a decade now," Howard began, "that one of the meat industry's shortcuts would end up hurting a lot of people. I always thought it would be the result of some of the drugs we inject into cattle—the growth promoting hormones, the antibiotics—but I never gave much concern to protein concentrates."

"What are protein concentrates?" I asked.

"For about 15 years now," he said, "ranchers have been feeding protein concentrates, or what's called meat and bone meal, to their cattle. The phrase, 'protein concentrates' sounds innocent enough, until you find out where this protein comes from. **Protein concentrates are really** the internal organs, blood, and condemned flesh from cattle and other livestock. Feed factories grind everything up at high temperatures. When it's all done, the protein concentrates have the look and feel of brown sugar. In a way, it's really quite remarkable. The rendering industry takes something that would have been wasted and turns it into a protein-rich cattle feed. Like almost every other feedlot owner, I bought literally tons of the stuff. It was much cheaper than grains or soybeans, and I was convinced it was totally safe."

I asked, "Weren't you afraid that you might spread an infection from dead animals to the live ones when feeding cattle meat to cattle?"

"The rendering process safely and effectively wipes out all viruses, bacteria, and parasitic agents. For decades, we thought that nothing could survive rendering. Absolutely nothing."

Then Lyman shook his head. There was a look of remorse in his eyes. "Until 1986, mad cow disease was totally unknown. By now hundreds of thousands of cattle have been stricken with this fatal brain disease. The infective agent does not get destroyed by rendering. And if even one infected cow gets rendered into protein concentrates, the feed can potentially infect a thousand cattle."

In March 1996, the Centers for Disease Control, the World Health Organization and the British government concluded that the illnesses and deaths of ten British young people were tied to mad cow disease,[1] an epidemic that spread throughout the cattle population al-

> "Protein concentrates are the internal organs, blood, and condemned flesh from cattle and other livestock."

most certainly because of this cannibalistic feeding practice. Several other deaths are suspected of having the same cause.

THE INDESTRUCTIBLE PRION

Until the 1980s most theorists believed that viruses were the smallest possible kind of infective organism. Viruses are made up of genetic material (either DNA or RNA) and some protein. But in the 1980s, David Bolton and Stan Prusiner, medical scientists at the University of California at San Francisco, found evidence that there might be an infective agent even smaller and tougher than viruses—one made entirely of protein. Many biologists initially scoffed at Bolton's and Prusiner's theory since, without DNA or RNA, it was thought there would be no way for an infective substance to reproduce. But Prusiner hypothesized that prions could reproduce without DNA or RNA.

Prions, according to Prusiner, are an abnormal brain protein with the power to convert regular brain proteins into more prions. Once the prion conversion is in progress, it will accelerate rapidly as each new prion goes on to create another.

Prions are chemically identical to normal brain proteins down to the very last atom. They are merely *shaped* differently. For reasons unclearly defined, a prion can cause another protein to take on its oddly folded shape. The deformed proteins clump together, eventually leaving holes in the brain tissue. Since prions chemically match the brain's own proteins, the human immune system is unable to target them as foreign invaders. Passed over by the immune system, they may build up in infected brains for decades.

John Collinge, a professor of neurobiology at Imperial College, London, is an independent researcher who has contributed many key pieces to the prion puzzle. Collinge says: "It's a very strange observation that you have these two quite different forms of the same protein with quite different properties. One of them is a killer. If this protein is present in your brain you're in serious trouble. The other one is a normal constituent of all our brains. . . ."[2]

Because of their unusual structure, prions can survive extremes that destroy all known viruses and bacteria. Cooking is powerless against prions, and so are conditions even more extreme than those used for rendering. In fact, prions can withstand such assaults as exposure to bleach, contact with strong acids, steam autoclaving, and even incineration.[3]

1986 — MAD COW FIRST APPEARS

For the first several decades that protein concentrates were used by ranchers, they appeared to pose little danger to the world's people or cattle herds. But the appearance of the mad cow prion in Britain changed everything. All it takes to kick off an epidemic is one infected cow sent to a rendering plant. And a cow can become infected by eating just one teaspoon of heavily infected protein concentrate.[4]

Mad cow disease was first recognized and named in late 1986. Its scientific name is bovine spongiform encephalopathy, or BSE, because under a microscope the infected brain has a sponge-like appearance. The first BSE cases were detected when several cows at a British dairy started twitching and acting nervous. Week by week, their condition deteriorated. Veterinarians tried numerous treatments but nothing worked on these staggering and disoriented cows. The veterinarians were baffled. They could recognize and treat mineral deficiencies and viral infections and dozens of other cow afflictions. But nobody had ever seen symptoms quite like these. An even greater surprise came when samples from the deceased cows' brains were examined under the microscope. The samples were riddled with tiny holes.

In the final months of 1986, dairies across Britain began reporting similar cases. Soon after, troubling reports of this new disease began appearing in Britain's newspapers. The disease raised a number of tough questions. How many cattle would catch this sickness? If mad cow spread widely, could it create a financial disaster for Britain's beef and dairy farmers? Worse, some scientists were fearing the disease could spread to people who ate infected meat. John Collinge recounts that "the burning question became: Can BSE transmit to humans, and are we going to see an epidemic of human disease following exposure to BSE?"[5]

TO EAT BEEF OR NOT TO EAT BEEF?

By 1988, mad cow disease was well known throughout Britain. Confirmed cases numbered in the hundreds, and more cattle were developing infections every week. Public fears of mad cow disease were damaging the beef industry. Everyone wanted to know if beef eaters were at risk.

It fell to Britain's Ministry of Agriculture, Fisheries, and Food (MAFF) to determine the danger. MAFF is in the suspect position of looking out for the interests of both the consumers and the producers of British food. In retrospect, it seems obvious that the interests of the British beef industry came first in MAFF's public policy regarding mad cow disease. Sir Richard Southwood chaired a committee notably lacking in relevant scientific credentials. In February 1989, the Southwood Committee's report was published. The report concluded that BSE was unlikely to infect people. The report also predicted that the number of cases among cattle would probably not exceed 25,000.[6] (An Oxford study published in 1996 estimates that over 900,000 cattle were eventually infected. MAFF received and chose to ignore a report in 1993 that warned of similar numbers.)

Armed with the Southwood Committee's findings, Britain's Meat and Livestock Commission launched a 6.5 million dollar advertising blitz to restore consumer confidence in beef. As part of the effort, the Minister of Agriculture took his four-year-old daughter to a press conference, where **father and daughter** ate burgers in front of the cameras in an effort to calm the public's fears.[7]

The membership of the Southwood Committee did not include any

Father and daughter ate burgers in front of the cameras in an effort to calm the public's fears.

of the BSE researchers who were working overtime to unravel the puzzle. Many in the scientific community believed that there was much more to be learned about this mysterious disease, and until the answers were found, the last thing the government should be doing was actively encouraging people in Britain to eat more beef.

One of the most impeccably credentialed of these dissenters was Richard Lacey, a microbiology specialist and professor of clinical microbiology at the University of Leeds. Lacey has published over 200 papers and has won a number of awards for his work. Since 1986, he has advised the British Government as a member of the Ministry of Agriculture's Veterinary Products Committee. The World Health Organization retains him as a consultant in microbiology.

Professor Lacey was an unlikely person to warn against beef eating. For much of his career, he has taken the beef industry's side in many disputes with consumer advocates, writing, for example, that antibiotic use in livestock poses no serious threat to human health.

But Lacey became more and more concerned about the Southwood Committee and its findings. He observes: "What was quite extraordinary about the composition of the committee was the omission of experts on spongiform encephalopathies, and the failure of the committee, once appointed, to co-opt them." Lacey also noted that while the Southwood report claimed that the risk from BSE was negligible, it also acknowledged that no scientific evidence existed to prove meat's safety.

Since human tests could not be done, researchers working on the BSE question used animals. The idea was to deliberately try to infect many different species with BSE. The greater the percentage of species that developed spongiform encephalopathies, the more likely it would be that BSE could also infect human beings.

Alarmingly, **scientists found that the BSE prion** could infect practically every species in which it was introduced. Researcher Adriono Aguzzi reported: "it can infect basically all species where this has been

> Scientists found that the BSE prion could infect practically every species in which it was introduced.

tried. It will go into mice, it will go into cats, it will go into monkeys. So we are witnessing a very special disease that has different features from the other spongiform encephalopathies we knew before, and therefore we have to deal with the problem that it might even infect humans."[8]

Armed with these conclusions, Lacey argued that mad cow warranted an aggressive eradication policy, coupled with safeguards to protect British beef eaters. Lacey suggested that when mad cow disease appeared in a herd, the entire herd should be slaughtered and the carcasses incinerated.

Lacey's contention was that the Southwood Committee may have been horribly wrong in its recommendations. If so, the resultant government policies could provoke a catastrophic health crisis. Lacey warned that "we could virtually lose a generation of people." At this writing, in the late 1990s, Lacey contends that the vast majority of Britons have now consumed beef infected with the BSE agent and that nobody can reliably predict the outcome.

THE INEVITABLE ARRIVES

The most important difference between Lacey's position and that of the British government was this: Lacey predicted that mad cow disease was likely to spread to any species that ate cattle. The government, by contrast, called the disease a "dead-end host" meaning that it would infect cattle but could not jump the species barrier to infect humans and other animals.

In the early 1990s, evidence began piling up on Lacey's side of the argument. A variety of animals began getting sick with brain disorders that almost certainly derived from eating infected beef. In 1990, a pet cat named Max died of a feline spongiform encephalopathy.[9] As with the disease in cows, no one had ever seen anything like it in cats before.[10] Pet food which included ground-up cattle parts was considered overwhelmingly the most likely cause of Max's death.[11] Infected food has since also been blamed in the deaths of 80 more cats in

Britain along with half a dozen zoo animals including a monkey, ante-
lopes, and ostriches which succumbed to never-before described
spongiform encephalopathies.[12]

The incubation period—the time from when an animal is infected
to the time it starts showing symptoms—varies in direct relationship to
the animal's natural life expectancy. Mice, who live just a few years, can
incubate the disease within a few months. For cats, who can live to around
15 years of age, the incubation period is a few years. In humans, who
can live to over age 70, the incubation period has been estimated to be
20 or 30 years. Researchers worried that the deaths among cats and
zoo animals might foreshadow a similar disease that would not show up
in humans until after the year 2005. Based on the theory that the incubation period could be shorter for a minority of people, Lacey said in 1989
that he thought the first cases of the human disease could appear as
early as 1994.

As Lacey predicted, **the first human cases** showed up in 1994.
Several teenagers and young adults came down with a severe and debili-
tating illness unlike any before seen in young people. The first case involved Vicky Rimmer, a 16-year-old schoolgirl in Wales who was found to
have a new form of Creutzfeldt-Jakob disease (CJD),[13] a human spongiform
encephalopathy.

Months later, 18-year-old Steve Churchill became ill. A relative later
recalled his illness on a special BBC report: "One of the first things we
noticed when Steve became ill was that he started hallucinating. It started
off that he'd be watching television and he'd get very enthralled in what
was going on. If there was fire on the television he'd feel as though he
was burning, or if it was like an undersea, underwater scene he'd feel as
though he was drowning, and then it got to a stage where he was just
seeing things that just weren't there. Or he'd try and pick up a cup of
coffee, but he'd miss, but he wouldn't realize, he'd still continue to look
as though he was drinking and hadn't realized that he hadn't actually
picked up the cup, and these became more and more frightening for
him. He was absolutely terrified of whatever he was seeing, but he wasn't
able to explain to us what had happened."[14]

The first
human cases
showed up
in 1994.

Steve grew progressively weaker and more emaciated. He died May 21, 1995.

Creutzfeldt-Jakob disease was not unknown. It is a naturally-occuring illness, but one that is very rare, striking only one in a million people per year. A progressive and invariably fatal dementia, it usually attacks people in their sixties or older. Until the 1990's outbreak, cases involving people under age 30 were almost nonexistent. In the new CJD cases, the victims' average age was 27 as opposed to the usual age of around 63. The new victims also showed abnormal brainwave patterns, suffered extreme psychiatric symptoms, and took twice as long to die as any previously-known CJD victims—13 months as opposed to 6 months.[15] The autopsies were the clincher, though. The victims' brains revealed a previously unknown disease pattern.[16] This led the British government and the World Health Organization to conclude that the BSE epidemic—and not the naturally-occuring CJD—was the most likely reason for the wave of human deaths.

Even the scientists who believed that meat from "mad" cows might kill people were stunned when the deaths actually started to occur. Adriono Aguzzi said, "Like everybody else we were pretty shocked. I mean everybody was thinking that there might be a theoretical risk of transmission of BSE to humans, but one thing is to say okay, there may be a theoretical risk, another thing is to see patients dying from it, so this came as a very sobering experience to us."[17]

In April, 1996, Britain's Secretary of State for Health announced the confirmation of ten British cases of a new variant of Creutzfeldt-Jakob disease, acknowledging that the most likely cause was eating BSE-infected beef. The oldest of the victims was 39. Five were in their twenties; three were teenagers.

Clues to the potential danger to other Britons lie in the story of the first deaths. Had these young CJD victims somehow eaten from the same source of heavily contaminated food? If that were the case, then one would expect a geographical clustering or some other link among the victims. However, the cases were scattered throughout

Even the scientists were stunned when the deaths actually started to occur.

Britain and so far no evidence has suggested a common source of infected beef. Another explanation is that these deaths are the first of a much larger group yet to come.

The incubation period of spongiform diseases in humans is thought to be at least ten years and probably 20 or 30 years for most people. Assuming the period is at least ten years, those who died in the mid-1990s of the new CJD variant were presumably infected around 1986, when there were only a few hundred diseased cows. In subsequent years, the numbers of infected cattle grew. Experts estimate that 250,000 BSE-infected cows were eaten in 1990.[18] Just as a trickle of mad cows in 1986 turned into a flood by 1990, the trickle of human deaths in 1995 may also surge. If the incubation period for most people is over 20 years, experts may be right to predict a delayed response to the BSE epidemic.

HOW MANY MIGHT DIE?

British BSE researcher Stephen Dealler has attempted to determine how many Britons may actually die from Creutzfeldt-Jakob disease. In 1996 and 1997, I exchanged several e-mail messages with Dr. Dealler. One of my first questions was, "How many people will die from the human form of mad cow disease?"

"At the moment we surely don't know," he wrote back. "John Collinge has tested mice genetically bred with the human gene for the prion, and these mice have not died rapidly when inoculated with BSE. So I doubt that we will see an enormous crash in the population. Nevertheless, since this type of disease affects a large proportion of animals from individual species (100 percent of mice, 100 percent of mink, 35 percent of goats, 25 percent of sheep, 4 percent of domestic dogs, and possibly 10 percent of domestic cats) when fed orally, I feel that we should not wait to find out. My own mathematics suggests that somewhere between 10,000 and 10 million British people will die over a period of 50 years."

I was staggered by this potential death toll. But why, I wondered, did Dealler's projections cover such a wide range? I asked him what his single best estimate would be.

"Given what we now know," he responded, "it's impossible to give a single number of deaths as a prediction. The size of this potential epidemic will depend upon the infectivity of beef and the human body's resistance to BSE prions. We have no way of knowing either of these things. So what I've done is calculate 21 scenarios giving the death tolls that will occur. Each scenario is based on a different level of beef infectivity and human resistance."

As our correspondence continued, I wrote: "Let's be optimistic for a moment. What's your prediction assuming that beef carries very low infectivity, and people are naturally quite resistant to the prion?"

"That would be the best of both possible worlds," wrote Dealler, "and we would witness very few deaths—probably somewhere in the dozens. We would be very lucky if things work out that way. Frankly I think things will turn out much worse."

"What do your other scenarios suggest?"

Dealler responded, "If beef is quite infective or if people aren't all that resistant to BSE, the potential death rate increases quite rapidly. As I mentioned, I've projected 21 scenarios for BSE, and each is in my opinion equally likely. Fifteen scenarios show at least 140,000 people at high risk for developing the disease. The six worst of these 15 scenarios predict that over 32 million people in Britain have already been exposed to a potentially fatal dose."

I responded, "Do you think there's a reasonable chance that you may have overestimated the numbers on some part of the equation?"

"No," wrote Dealler. "I want to stress here that I deliberately *underestimated* throughout the calculations. I did this to prevent Britain's agriculture ministry from denying the findings. I therefore believe that the numbers of people dying will actually be higher than the estimates I've published. We must now realize that a major risk has already been taken with Britain's population and **we should not be waiting** to see how many people will die. I am afraid that now is the time for the scientists to push the politicians aside and get on with finding methods of treatment, prevention and diagnosis."

"How would you summarize the risk in Britain?"

"We should not be waiting to see how many people will die."

"I believe that more than 90 percent of the people in Britain, myself included, could currently be incubating a potentially fatal infection brought about by eating beef during the late 1980s and early 1990s. However, there is a good chance that a much smaller percentage might develop disease, as crossing the species barrier often seems to cut this percentage from 100 percent down to much lower figures, possibly 5 percent. Even if our worst fears are confirmed, we probably shouldn't expect to see large numbers of people dying until about 2005. In the meantime, I think it's imperative that we begin a full-scale effort to discover effective drugs."

Dr. James Ironside, a member of Britain's National CJD Surveillance Unit is not optimistic about the possibility of developing such drugs. Even though a prion is an incredibly simple protein, finding drugs to counteract it may prove difficult, especially when working against a ticking clock. Says Ironside: "I think it's fairly unlikely that a cure for CJD would be developed in the foreseeable future, which means if we do see an enormous increase in numbers of patients in Britain there will be no prospect of specific treatment for them."[19]

"BUT COWS ARE HERBIVORES."

In April of 1996, Howard Lyman appeared with Dr. Gary Weber of the National Cattlemen's Association on the immensely popular Oprah Winfrey television talk show. Lyman had accepted Oprah's invitation to voice his concerns about the possibility of a BSE variant being spread among U.S. cattle. Her reactions to some of Lyman's revelations made the national news. (Oprah's spontaneous comments inspired the Cattlemen's Association to file suit against her and Lyman under the so-called "food disparagement" laws.)

Oprah began her questioning by asking Lyman, "You said this disease could make AIDS look like the common cold?"

Lyman looked at her calmly. "Absolutely," he said.

Oprah responded, "That's an extreme statement, you know?"

"Absolutely," said Lyman, "and what we're looking at right now is we're following exactly the same path that they followed in England. Ten years of dealing with it as public relations rather than doing something substantial about it. A hundred thousand cows per year in the United States are fine at night, dead in the morning. The majority of those cows are rounded up, ground up, fed back to other cows. If only one of them has mad cow disease, [this] has the potential to affect thousands. Remember today, [in] the United States, 14 percent of all cows by volume are ground up, turned into feed, and fed back to other animals."[20]

Oprah looked shocked and alarmed. "But cows are herbivores," she said, "they shouldn't be eating other cows."

"That's exactly right," said Lyman, "and what we should be doing is exactly what nature says, we should have them eating grass—not other cows. We've not only turned them into carnivores, we've turned them into cannibals."

Oprah broke in: "Now see, wait a minute, wait a minute," she said, "Let me just ask you this right now, Howard. How do you *know* the cows are ground up and fed back to the other cows?

"Oh, I've seen it," said Howard, remembering that he himself used to do it on his own ranch. "These are USDA statistics, they're not something we're making up."[21]

Oprah exclaimed, "It has just stopped me cold from eating another burger!"

Then Oprah turned to the Cattlemen's spokesperson, Dr. Weber. She gestured to him and asked, "Are we feeding cattle to the cattle?"

"There is a limited amount of that done in the United States . . ." responded Dr. Weber.

The audience cried out in disgust.

"Hang on just a second now," Weber continued, "the Food and Drug Administration. . . ."

Again, he was drowned out by the audience.

Oprah exclaimed,
"It has just
stopped me cold
from eating
another burger!"

Oprah broke in. "Because I have to just tell you that is alarming to me, that is alarming to me."

Dr. Weber: "Yeah, now keep in mind that before you view the ruminant animal, the cow, as simply vegetarian, remember that they drink milk."

TIME TO ACT

Feeding rendered animal remains to cattle, the most likely way for BSE to spread, is now banned in Britain and several other countries. Many American cattle ranchers, as of this writing, are still feeding rendered cattle protein to their animals at rates of thousands of tons a day,[22] despite the meat industry's call for a voluntary ban. Many industry observers are astounded that rendered feed is still permitted in this country. One such expert is Paul Brown, a medical director for the U.S. Public Health Service, who warns, **"We're playing with fire."**[23]

"I can't believe that American cattle producers are not taking greater precautions," says Howard Lyman. "It's like they're in denial over what happened In Britain."

When I asked Lyman what advice he had for the American consumers, he responded: "Remember what a huge mistake the British people made in trusting their government about beef. I pray that Americans don't make a similar mistake. The danger here may be just as real. The cattlemen are jumping up and down saying there's no BSE risk from American beef. I urge Americans to read the evidence first hand and to not blindly trust the cattlemen."

Indeed, the statements coming from America's cattlemen are eerily similar to those coming from Britain's Southwood Committee a decade ago. In 1996, the National Cattlemen's Association issued a report that contained the following soothing statements:

"BSE is an extremely rare, chronic degenerative disease affecting the central nervous system of cattle. BSE is not present in the U. S. but has been identified in the United Kingdom and a few other countries."[24]

"Consuming muscle meat or milk, even from contaminated animals, is not considered a health risk."[25]

"We're playing with fire."

"Efforts are underway to fully understand why the disease became such a problem in the U.K. This information will help ensure that we never acquire BSE in the U.S."[26]

The Cattlemen's reassurances appear to be based on two major claims: First, that BSE is not found in American cattle; and second, that even if BSE appeared in America, the cuts of beef the consumer buys cannot carry infective levels of prions. There are chinks in this armor of words, however, that should make us wary of complacency.

NO BSE IN THE U.S.?

As of this writing, there has not been a single confirmed case of BSE in the United States, but perhaps we should not rest easy just yet. Just as CJD can develop spontaneously in human beings, some researchers believe the same is true of BSE in cows. Some researchers think that a variation of Britain's BSE prion may already be here. James Gibbs, a National Institutes of Health expert who has been doing research in BSE-related fields for 20 years has said he thinks it's possible,[27] and Stanley Prusiner, the scientist who identified prions agrees that BSE must be present in the U.S. at low levels.[28] If one in a million cows has a naturally occuring BSE, as long as the practice of feeding cow tissue to other cows continues, an epidemic is possible. The United States raises tens of millions of cattle every year.

In 1985, nearly a year before BSE was reported in Britain, the late Richard Marsh, then chairman of the Department of Veterinary Science at the University of Wisconsin, Madison, was alerting dairy practitioners to the possibility that a "previously unrecognized scrapie-like disease in cattle" existed in the United States.

The story behind Dr. Marsh's warnings is somewhat involved. Since 1960 there have been four outbreaks of a mink spongiform encephalopathy on U.S. fur farms. (All spongiform encephalopathies progress the way BSE does in cows—they are marked by a riddling of the brain with holes and they inevitably lead to death.) Mink farmers believed that the mink had fallen ill from eating feed made from sheep which had died of a sheep prion disease called scrapie. There was a big problem with this theory—researchers were unable to orally infect mink with scrapie-infected sheep brains. A clue came in 1985 when prions wiped out a population of mink in Wisconsin who hadn't eaten any sheep at all. The meat portion of their diet consisted almost exclusively of dairy cattle called "downers," an industry term describing cows who collapse for unknown reasons and are too sick to stand up again. Based on his observations of mink, Dr. Marsh concluded that there was a form of BSE in the United States and that it manifests itself as more of a "downed" cow disease than a "mad" cow disease.

Downed cow syndrome is a major problem among dairy cattle, with tens of thousands of cows collapsing for largely undetermined reasons every year in the U.S.[29] If even a tiny percentage of these cows are falling victim to an undiscovered American version of BSE, this could have implications on a grand scale. If downed cows can be kept alive long enough to reach the slaughterhouse, the law allows them to be used directly for human consumption, and their bones (along with lips, head, knuckles, feet etc.) may be boiled to make gelatin, a main ingredient in products like marshmallows and jelled desserts.[30] If judged unfit for human consumption, the carcasses are often rendered into feed for other cattle.[31]

British cattle and meat have not been allowed into North America since 1989, and no U.S. downed cow has yet exhibited symptoms matching those of Britain's mad cows. We have already seen, however, that spongiform encephalopathies can emerge as variant forms, with different—although always fatal—disease patterns. **An American variant of** the British BSE prion could produce different symptoms and go unnoticed for several years. An American BSE prion (if it does in fact exist) could be like scrapie and not transmit to humans. Another possibility, though, is that an American variant BSE prion could indeed infect people, and potentially be at least as deadly as BSE in Britain.

As we have seen in Britain, conclusive answers to questions about mad cow disease can take decades to emerge. U.S. beef eaters

> An American
> variant of the
> British BSE
> prion could
> go unnoticed in
> its early
> stages.

could be exposed to a variant of Britain's BSE before we even know for certain that it is here.

Where did Britain's BSE prion come from in the first place? It is still thought by many that cows got it by eating scrapie-infected sheep. Another possible scenario is that it didn't come *from* anywhere, but instead generated spontaneously in a single cow. If Britain's BSE prion had appeared at some other time in history, the unlucky cow would have died and that would have been the end of the story. Cattle were not turned into cannibals until after 1950, and now the practice has been banned in Britain. But if this first infected cow were rendered into cattle feed, Britain's entire BSE epidemic could be attributable to a single infected animal.

THE POSSIBLE SPREAD OF INFECTION?

On the same Oprah Winfrey show described earlier, Gary Weber of the National Cattlemen's Association contended that no animal showing BSE symptoms could ever enter a U.S. slaughterhouse. However, most infected— and therefore infective—cattle in Britain were slaughtered before detectable symptoms appeared. There is no reason to assume that the situation would be different in the U.S. The only available tests for BSE (as of mid-1997) measure the presence of chemicals that are formed as the brain reaches its final stages of destruction. There is no test for the disease in its early stages.

In the United States, tissue from infected but healthy-looking cattle could easily enter the beef supply. More than half of U.S. dairy cows are killed before their fourth birthday, meaning that any cow carrying BSE would probably be sent to slaughter before the first symptoms appeared. Beef cattle are killed at less than two years of age, long before they would show symptoms of BSE.

In their 1996 report, the Cattlemen acknowledged the infectivity of brain and spinal cord tissue, while attempting to reassure consumers that beef muscle cannot carry the infection. One piece of evidence that beef muscle is safe is based on a study done on mice. A group of mice was injected with brains from infected cattle, while another group was injected with muscle tissue. Months later, the brain-injected mice were dying of spongiform diseases while the muscle-injected mice remained healthy.[32]

More testing may uphold these findings, although the species barrier question remains. We have no way of knowing if humans will react the same as mice. Meanwhile, the infectivity of brain and spinal cord tissue is still an important issue. It has been strongly suspected that much of the human risk in Britain came from ground beef contaminated with bits of brain or spinal cord tissue. This contamination was probably caused by mechanical meat separating devices used in slaughterhouses.

These **separation devices can transfer potentially infectious** tissue from the brain stem and spinal cord to the beef muscle people eat. The May 1996 issue of *Meat and Poultry* details the way meat products are obtained through the use of meat and bone separation machinery that pulls muscle tissue away from the spine. University of Nebraska researchers are quoted as writing, "When mechanical pressure is used to force meat away from vertebrae . . . certain components like spinal cord material show up. . . ."[33] Most beef obtained by mechanical separation devices becomes ground beef or hamburger meat.

Equally worrisome are findings about how stunning cattle before slaughter may increase the risk of BSE infection. In captive bolt stunning—a very common slaughterhouse practice—the animal is shot with a bolt through the forehead. (The creation of this severe head injury is considered more humane than cutting the animal's throat while it is fully conscious.) It has been well documented in medical literature, however, that people suffering head trauma may show brain tissue in other parts of their bodies. A group of Texas A&M researchers were curious as to whether captive bolt stunning of cattle would have the same effect. Their studies showed that the predominant stunning method used in the U.S. blows particles of brains into the animals' bloodstreams. A letter from the group, published in the British medical journal *Lancet* in August 1996,

Meat separation devices can transfer potentially infectious tissue from the brain stem and spinal cord to the beef muscle people eat.

ends with the observation that: "It is likely that prion proteins are found throughout the bodies of animals stunned for slaughter."[34]

Findings like these make the Cattlemen's statements less reassuring.

WHAT AMERICA CAN LEARN FROM BRITAIN

In January 1997, America's Food and Drug Administration finally proposed regulations to prohibit the feeding of cattle parts back to beef and dairy cattle. This proposal was passed into law in June 1997. If the resultant ban is seriously enforced, it could essentially eliminate the possibility of a British-style mad cow epidemic in America. Even though the occasional cow may come down with the disease spontaneously, stopping the practice of rendering cattle for feed will prevent the runaway spread of the infection.

However, the FDA legislation will still allow livestock producers to take several risks with America's meat supply. The cause of the mad cow epidemic was the feeding of cows to cows, a deep indication that the feeding of livestock to any other livestock is a mistake. Cattle were the first food animals to develop a disease-causing agent—presumably a prion—that is dangerous to people, but there is no way to be sure that a similar prion won't occur next in pigs or chickens. Pigs have already been shown to have developed spongiform diseases, and there is no reason to think that prions could not also infect poultry. [Editor's note: In February 1997, it was reported that Harash Narang, a prominent BSE researcher, had discovered what he believes are signs of spongiform disease in two chickens.] To suggest that pigs and chickens are somehow exempt from spongiform diseases would be recklessly optimistic— the same brand of dangerous optimism that once led authorities to insist that BSE could not infect people.

The FDA ruling exempts rendered pigs, horses, and chickens, as well as milk, blood, and gelatin from the ban. As long as any rendered animal proteins are fed to food animals, there will always be the possibility that a new prion epidemic will endanger humans. If a spongiform-producing agent does end up infecting chickens or pigs, the dangers could very well escape notice for a long time. The disease was detected in British dairy herds in part because dairy cows are allowed to live somewhat longer (about one-fourth of their natural lifetime) than most food animals. A few of these older animals showed the symptoms that gave farmers and veterinarians the first clue that something was wrong. Most pigs and chickens are killed very early in their lives, before symptoms would show.

In a meat-eating culture, chicken, pig, and beef by-products have a useful place—in pet food (dogs and cats are naturally carnivorous and require specially supplemented food if they are to be fed a vegan diet). But to feed meat by-products back to farm animals is to take a chance on an American spongiform epidemic. Taking such a risk with the American public cannot even be justified financially. In terms of revenue, the rendering industry is relatively small—generating less than 2 percent of the revenue produced by the beef industry.[35] Now that the dangers are so very clear, there is no reason to put Americans at risk in order to protect the rendering industry.

As long as livestock-to-livestock feeding continues, the possibility of a spongiform epidemic will remain. Eating meat will always carry health risks. Livestock producers can do little to reduce meat's link to heart disease, cancer, and obesity. They can, however, all but eliminate the risk of a spongiform disease epidemic.

But even if a blanket livestock-to-livestock feed ban is never passed, Americans can still protect themselves from the possibility of contracting a BSE-related disease. While it may never be possible to know the prion status of meat, it is definitely possible to abstain from eating meat in the first place. The catch is that you've got to avoid meat *before* the supply becomes contaminated. The lesson from Britain is that by the time the dangers were understood, millions of people had already been exposed. Americans have had enough advance warning that they can probably still avoid personal risk by not eating meat or meat by-products.

PART II

The truth about food animals

"If man aspires
towards a
righteous life, his
first act of
abstinence
is injury
to animals."

— *Leo Tolstoy*

With the decline of the family farm, animals that used to be cared for with kindness and a general regard for their welfare now live and die in unconscionable conditions. On a farm in upstate New York and another in California, however, farm animals live out their days without the traumas of crowding, confinement, or transport to the slaughterhouse.

Rescued!

I walk around the barn just in time to see it. Lorri Bauston— not even 120 pounds—approaches a young steer. Without a moment's hesitation, she secures the animal's head with a rope halter and pins him along the side of a corral. She does this so gently and expertly that she's quickly able to immobilize this steer who is many times her weight. In another second, she deftly gives him a shot for worms. She releases him, patting his neck and praising him, then walks to the next animal.

Lorri is one of the founders of Farm Sanctuary, a 175-acre haven for rescued animals in upstate New York. Farm Sanctuary occupies a beautiful piece of rural land outside the tiny town of Watkins Glen. Its dozen barns, built on a gently sloping hill, shelter farm animals of all kinds—veal calves, chickens, milk cows, goats, pigs, sheep, turkeys, even rabbits. When Lorri finishes her work, she gives me special permission to visit the barns by myself—cautioning me to shut all gates after I open them.

I start by exploring the chicken barn. As I open the gate and walk inside, about fifty chickens approach me. I sit on a piece of lumber and feel as though I'm surrounded by curious children. The chickens are timid and while most don't want to be touched, they seem to want to stand near me.

After five minutes or so, the flock gets used to my presence and begins to disperse. But a few hangers-on seem more curious than the others. My attention keeps returning to one bird. He's smaller than the others, and he keeps approaching me with a nervous don't-want-to-be-seen step like a boy trying to sneak into a movie theater. After a few minutes of this, he sits next to me and lets me stroke his wings.

The next barn is about fifteen meters away. As I walk up to it, I hear pigs grunting inside. This barn is twice the size of the chicken barn and houses forty pigs. I always thought pigs were medium-sized animals, maybe 150 or 200 pounds. The pigs in this barn are *enormous*— the largest weigh around 800 pounds. I later learn that, when allowed to live out their lives, this is the size mature pigs attain. Most pigs in this country are slaughtered at around 220 pounds.

Heat lamps ring the inside of the pig barn, and the ground is covered ankle-deep in straw. Most of the pigs are asleep beneath the lamps. Many are snoring. Two or three pigs seem curious about my arrival. Fortunately, they approach me one at a time—I would be nervous if three 800-pound animals surrounded me at once.

Gene Bauston, Lorri's husband, told me there is a saying about pigs: "Dogs look up to people, cats look down on people, but pigs—they look straight at you." Here with these pigs, I realize how true this is. I think of the disdainful looks the family cat sometimes gives my father, while the dog behaves like an adoring vassal. There's none of that with these pigs. They look you **right in the eye** and make you aware that, while they can't do math or speak English, they are quite conscious about what's up. I'm surprised to discover that they are also very gentle. After petting the three pigs who sought my attention, I circle the barn and venture to rub the warm bellies of the sleeping animals. With some, the snore is barely interrupted. But others open their eyes and look up at me. They sigh and do a little stretch as I scratch their ears.

Pigs look
you right in
the eye.

Up the hill a little way is the veal barn. Most of its animals came from veal operations. A plaque on the door reads, "in appreciation to Tom Scholz for the commitment to the veal calf refuge." I walk into the barn. If I felt tiny next to the pigs, I feel completely dwarfed by the cattle around me. Rescued as calves, all but a few of the dozen animals in the barn are now full grown. Here, the variety of responses to my presence is the greatest. A couple animals come up to me and let me stroke their faces. Others stand stock-still the entire time I'm in the barn and show little reaction to being petted. There is one steer who wants nothing to do with me at all. I approach him three times, but each time he nervously avoids me. It's quite strange to have an animal seven times your weight fearing to stand within three paces of you. (This steer, I later learn, is "Alby," rescued several years ago from a veal farm that had neglected its animals so badly most died of starvation.) Stroking the cattle, I'm awed by their size. Their shoulders are as rock-hard as a body-builder's and several times more massive.

> I felt a presence and a consciousness that ran very deep.

Farm Sanctuary's animals, while calm and for the most part trusting, rarely behave toward humans the way dogs or cats do. I found no exaggerated affection, no equivalent of purring or wagging tails. My dog Heather, I remember, was almost a little sister to me. When I wanted to take our family's rowboat for a ride she would follow as I dragged the boat to the river and then jump inside, ready to share my adventures. My morning at Farm Sanctuary left me with no wonderful stories, no touching anecdotes—but I saw something deeper by far. When I walked into the sheds full of chickens, pigs, and cows, **I felt a presence** and a consciousness from these animals that ran very deep.

None of the animals went out of their way to gratify me, and I felt no deep sentiment toward them, which makes it difficult to express why they moved me so. But, standing quietly among them, with no purpose other than to be there, I gained the unmistakable impression that at least some of these animals were as aware of themselves and their surroundings as my beloved and intelligent dog. I don't spend a lot of time around animals, and I didn't feel particularly sentimental toward the animals I met at Farm Sanctuary. Instead, I felt respect, and a sort of humility. When I think about the searching looks of the pigs or their grunts of pleasure at having their bellies stroked, I have to believe that these animals are as conscious of their bodies as I am of mine. I have to believe the knife is as sharp to them as it is to us.

A COMPASSIONATE CAUSE

Later in the day, when I accompany Lorri on her rounds, I see another side of the animals. In Lorri's presence, they become far more trusting and friendly. If the animals treat me with the cautious interest that young children give a visitor, they flock around Lorri like she's a beloved old friend. They know her well, and their affection toward her is unmistakable. Cows lick her, pigs nuzzle her, and roosters strut around proudly in front of her, showing off.

"Up until the 1950s," Lorri says, "most farms in the country looked a lot like Farm Sanctuary. This is in every respect a working farm, resembling traditional family farms before large-scale agriculture took over. The only difference is that we don't slaughter the animals, milk the cows, or collect the eggs for humans. **Everybody who lives and works** here is vegan, since we think raising animals for meat, milk, and eggs is unnecessary."

"Everybody who lives and works here is vegan, since we think raising animals for meat, milk, and eggs is unnecessary."

None of the animals will ever provide meat for a dinner table—they will all be allowed to live out their full lives. Gene and Lorri collect the eggs from the chickens, hard-boil them, and feed them back to the birds. The cows on Farm Sanctuary rarely provide milk because they are not impregnated. The males are neutered. In the rare cases when Farm Sanctuary adopts a pregnant cow, the cow is never milked for human use. Instead, the newborn calf nurses from his mother until the end of the milk cycle. Animals get plenty of space, no hormones, and—because they are living in healthful conditions—

much less medication than is commonly dispensed at commercial farms.

The idea for Farm Sanctuary arose in 1986. Lorri and Gene already knew that working to improve the conditions of animals raised for food was going to be a big part of their lives. From their home in Delaware, they had been making regular trips to stockyards and slaughterhouses to provide aid to injured animals and to document inhumane conditions or practices. In late summer, they drove to a large stockyard in Lancaster, Pennsylvania. The weekly livestock auction had taken place the day before and litter from the event was strewn about the grounds.

All stockyards have "dead piles," where the carcasses of animals who don't survive the auctions are thrown. Lancaster kept theirs in the back of the stockyard. As Lorri and Gene approached it, they were sickened by the putrid odor, and they steeled themselves against the scene they knew they would encounter. Sheep, pig, and cow carcasses had been thrown on a cement slab in a cinder block enclosure. Some of the animals had obviously been dead for weeks, their bones and skulls jutting up from rotting carcasses. The animals from the most recent auction had been dead less than 24 hours, but they were decaying rapidly in the morning heat. Swarms of green-backed flies buzzed around them.

Gene asked Lorri for her camera. "I'll get a picture of this and then we can get out of here." If Lorri had brought her cheap point-and-shoot instead of her good 35-mm camera, what followed would probably never have happened. As Gene snapped the photograph, the camera's internal mirror clunked up and down loudly and its motor drive whined noisily to advance the film. Suddenly, **one of the sheep in the pile** lifted her head, wheezed, opened and closed her eyes, and then dropped her head back down.

Gene and Lorri stared in shocked disbelief, and then hurried over to the sheep. She was lying on her side, breathing shallowly. As carefully as they could, the couple pulled the sheep off the pile and out of the enclosure. Then Gene went back, holding his breath, and prodded the other bodies to see if any were alive. None were.

Gene went back to their van and brought it to the yard's gates. They carried the sheep to the van and drove to a veterinary clinic about

Suddenly, one of the sheep in the dead pile lifted her head.

ten miles away. By the time they arrived, the sheep's breathing was almost undetectable.

"We pulled this animal off a dead pile at the stockyard," Lorri told the veterinarian, "Somehow, she stayed alive all night. We know you probably can't save her, but we wanted her to at least be humanely euthanized."

The veterinarian checked the animal briefly and said, "Looks like not much more than heat exhaustion and severe dehydration. I think she can pull through." He offered the sheep some water and gave her a vitamin shot. His diagnosis proved correct. Twenty minutes later, the animal stood up. Gene and Lorri named her Hilda and began to realize they needed to provide her with a home.

HILDA

Hilda, who needed not much more than a drink of water to be revived, was a throw-away—an animal that just became too much trouble for her handler to bother with. She was the first farm animal the Baustons rescued and has become symbolic of much that is wrong with the way "food animals" are treated.

Hilda had been crowded onto a truck with dozens of other sheep, a standard practice to save money in transporting animals to market. Under these stressful conditions, some animals don't make it. By reviewing stockyard records, the Baustons discovered that Hilda had arrived at the Lancaster Stockyards unable to walk. The driver handling the load had dragged her out of

Courtesy of Farm Sanctuary

Hilda, on the far right, was dumped with the dead animals behind a stockyard in Pennsylvania.

Why would somebody throw this animal away when some shade and water were all she needed? Wouldn't they want to care for her, if only to make money by selling her for slaughter? Not necessarily. On any given day, I learned from the Baustons, you can go to a stockyard and see sick, injured, and downed animals. Some are so sick they are just hours or even minutes from dying, and not much can be done for them. But others—like Hilda—could easily recover with the proper attention. Auction day is a day of economic efficiency, however. When livestock producers arrive at these shows, they bring dozens or even hundreds of animals to sell, and it's not worth their time to tend to the needs of a few sick individuals. The money is in selling animals who are on their feet. Sick or hurt animals are seen as an expected loss, and the producers often throw them on the dead pile where many who could have been saved die of thirst or heat exhaustion.

Lorri and Gene took Hilda the sheep home with them, and realizing that there was a need for a refuge for animals like her, they soon incorporated Farm Sanctuary. They continued making their trips to slaughterhouses and stockyards. On almost every visit, they found at least one animal in distress, abandoned and dying from neglect. Their yard became home to more animals every month. Not just sheep like Hilda, but also chickens, turkeys, a young pig, and a calf rescued from a veal farm.

Hilda at Farm Sanctuary, where she still lives.

the truck and dumped her on the dead pile. She had been on the pile about 16 hours when Gene and Lorri discovered her.

The Baustons felt certain that this act of neglect would be enough to convince local authorities to take action against the trucker and the stockyard for cruelty to animals. They soon learned, however, that in Pennsylvania and many other states, farm animals are exempt from animal cruelty laws. The Baustons were told that leaving live animals on dead piles is considered a normal agricultural practice.

Hilda, the first Farm Sanctuary animal, has been joined by scores of others rescued from cruel or inhumane situations.

"Rescuing animals helps us as well," recalls Gene. "To watch what goes on in slaughterhouses is heartbreaking. Each animal we could rescue gave us a sense of hope. The rescued animals really helped us keep our emotional health, in light of what we saw over and over at the stockyards, slaughterhouses, and factory farms."

As the animals kept coming in, the couple saw that they would soon run out of space, and they began to dream of building a farm animal sanctuary large enough to take in hundreds of rescued animals. By 1990, the Baustons' efforts had attracted dozens of volunteers and thousands of supporters and, after visiting several sites, they purchased the farm near Watkins Glen. They constructed eight animal barns, and set up a visitors' conference center. To raise additional funds, and to give people the opportunity to stay overnight and spend the next day getting to know the animals, they also built three "bed and breakfast" cabins. The barns were soon filled with rescued animals who would have died from injury, illness, neglect, or slaughter if the Baustons had not provided a home.

School buses began to roll into Farm Sanctuary, giving hundreds of children at a time a chance to meet the animals. Families on vacation would stop in to visit. The organization's adopt-an-animal campaigns helped to bring in much-needed funds. **Television programs** and national magazines began highlighting the Baustons' efforts, and Farm Sanctuary's membership swelled into the tens of thousands.

ANIMAL HUSBANDRY BECOMES ANIMAL SCIENCE

Until about fifty years ago, most farmers treated animals much as Farm Sanctuary does today. A farmer's trade was called "animal husbandry," which suggests a duty to provide care. Bernard Rollin, professor and director of bioethical planning at Colorado State University, writes: "In traditional agriculture, if one did anything to violate the animals' natures or systematically harm them in any way, one was acting foursquare against one's own interests, as well as against the ingrained ethic of husbandry."[1]

Rollin writes that over the past fifty years, "animal science," has replaced the term "animal husbandry." The two terms differ profoundly. Animal husbandry reflects the farming ethic of the first half of the 1900s, when farmers strove to provide an ideal environment for their animals. Farmers provided such care not necessarily out of generosity, but because it was the only way to make the animals thrive sufficiently to generate profits. Today's farmers have no need for this ethic. Fifty years of animal science have developed an arsenal of drugs, hormones, systematic mutilation techniques, and specially bred farm animals. Together, these developments let farmers raise animals more profitably—but under harsh and crowded conditions that would have killed earlier farm animals. The result is that every farm animal is worse off as a result of the animal science revolution.

Since their marriage in 1986, Lorri and Gene Bauston have lived modestly. They met while working on a Greenpeace boat, and both chose environmental activism over employment that would support a more lavish lifestyle. But as the Baustons continued to rescue more animals, they realized they needed to increase their income to pay for animal food and veterinary care.

A friend who sold T-shirts at concerts gave them an idea. Soon, whenever a well-known rock group held a concert in the Northeastern U.S., the Baustons loaded their van with tofu hot dogs and drove to the show. Their stand was a huge success and generated enough money to feed and care for the animals they were adopting.

They established Farm Sanctuary in upstate New York in 1990, and in 1993, the Gene and Lorri traveled to California to create a second sanctuary. They acquired a beautiful 300-acre site in Orland, California. On the new farm, they constructed five barns and fenced over 100 acres for animals. By the end of its first year, the West Coast Farm Sanctuary had adopted hundreds of cows, sheep, pigs, and chickens.

As Gene worked on cruelty investigations around the country, Lorri spent much of her time at the new West Coast facility and used it as a base to launch dozens of animal rescue efforts. Farm Sanctuary won its first animal cruelty case against a Pennsylvania stockyard in 1993—the same stockyard where they had picked Hilda off the pile.

Courtesy of Farm Sanctuary

Gene and Lorri Bauston with rescued Farm Sanctuary animals, Spike, Sparky, and Toby.

Meanwhile, Lorri and Gene developed an internship program for people to volunteer full-time at Farm Sanctuary. Each year, Farm Sanctuary grants internships to more than fifty people. Interns help care for the animals, and participate in Farm Sanctuary's day-to-day operations. For many interns, working at Farm Sanctuary brings their first taste of vegan activism, and marks the beginning of a part-time or full-time career helping animals.

Animal rescue activist Lorri Bauston has observed that chickens raised in modern facilities suffer the most inhumane conditions of any of the food animals. So little is made public about these facilities that few people know what the life and death of an egg-layer or a broiler is really like. For an unforgettable "tour," read on.

Chickens and eggs

In modern egg houses, a shed filled with 100,000 birds may be staffed by one or two attendants. The attendants' job is to make sure that automated feed and egg collection machinery is working. Attendants also must remove dead birds from the cages.

Lorri Bauston has visited over a hundred factory farms, stockyards, and slaughter facilities. She has witnessed the standard living conditions for every kind of domesticated animal. I expected her to call veal farms the worst animal confinement systems. I was surprised to hear her say she thinks that egg farms are even worse.

Lorri says, "In both duration of confinement and intensity, there is nothing that approaches 1990s egg farms. I've visited dozens of different egg farms by now, and they are all practically identical, from the battery cages to the facility's design to the treatment of the animals. Birds collapse in their cages on a daily basis. Since an aging, sick layer hen is worth next to nothing, it's never worthwhile to call in a veterinarian to correct the problem. The typical response to a sick bird is to just throw the animal on the floor where it will die from its affliction or from thirst. Other times, the bird dies in its cage and remains there for hours or days until attendants come by to dispose of the bodies."

Previously, farmers had relied on environment and good treatment as a way of keeping chickens healthy.

In the early 1900s, assembly lines transformed production for all manufactured products. But farmers saw no way to apply mass production to farm animals. Little changed in animal agriculture for several more decades. Farmers kept chickens in indoor-outdoor coops, where each bird had plenty of room to walk around and socialize with other birds. When a group of chickens are put together, they quickly create a pecking order, which helps them interact socially and avoid fighting. If two chickens arrive at a feeder at the same time, the bird higher on the pecking order eats first. Each chicken in the flock memorizes which chickens are above and which below its place in the pecking order. Chickens can only remember the status of about fifty birds. Whenever a farmer tried to exceed this limit, he would start having birds die in fights. Additionally, the flock would suffer increased rates of disease.

Bernard Rollin, a bioethics researcher at Colorado State University, writes: "No nineteenth-century agriculturalist would have ever dreamed, for example, of keeping thousands of chickens in one building—that would be a rapid path to ruin, eventuating in quick spread of animal disease, death, and financial disaster."[1] Nonetheless, it began to dawn on poultry producers that if chickens *could* be kept by the thousands in a single building, the cost advantages would be immense.

During the 1940s, animal husbandry—the task of fitting the barnyard environment to meet the needs of an animal—came to be perceived as obsolete. Rollin notes that university livestock departments started changing the name of their degrees from "Animal Husbandry" to "Animal Science." These animal scientists wanted to overcome the pecking order and disease problems of chickens and increase the size of flocks dramatically. Previously, **farmers had relied on environment** and good treatment as a way of keeping chickens healthy. Now, they began to rely on a growing arsenal of powerful medications. Newly developed drugs and antibiotics could let chickens survive the kinds of crowded conditions that would wipe out unmedicated flocks. As Rollin puts it: "No longer are we constrained by the animals' evolved nature in our production practices. . . . Antibiotics, vaccines, hormones, and other drugs, for example, have allowed us to go beyond helping the animals to use their natural powers to thrive—we can [now] raise thousands of chickens in one building without their succumbing to disease."[2]

KEPT OR DISCARDED, ACCORDING TO SEX

While some of the new crop of animal scientists were busy developing drugs, another group, with training in genetics, tried to breed a more profitable chicken. These geneticists began by dividing the chicken species in two. No longer would a single type of chicken be raised for both meat and eggs. Instead, scientists developed a "broiler" strain which would grow quicker and bigger than ever. Next, they developed a "layer" strain, that produced far less meat but many more eggs.

Each year, over 400 million "layer" chicks are born in the U.S.—and half of these are male.[3] Male layer chicks are worthless. They do not produce meat nearly as efficiently as broiler-strain chicks, so raising them for slaughter is unprofitable. What becomes of these 200 million newly-hatched baby chicks? Almost as soon as they finish pecking their way out of their shells and begin to chirp and

LILLY

In 1989, Gene and Lorri visited an egg farm in central Pennsylvania. The cages were suspended so that machinery could drive underneath them to remove litter, manure, and dead birds. As Gene waited alongside the cages on an employee walkway, Lorri walked in the space below the cages. Crusted manure and the bones of dead birds crunched beneath her shoes. It was so dark that she almost didn't notice a discarded hen: "In the corner was a little hen hunched over, as hopeless-looking as any animal I've ever seen."

The trembling little bird had been pulled from her cage and thrown to the floor, probably a day or two before. She had almost no feathers and ▶

Courtesy of Farm Sanctuary

Lilly, on the mend at Farm Sanctuary. Like most battery hens, her feathers were sparse and her skin rubbed raw.

Laying hens are typically kept five to a cage. Each cage has a floor space smaller in size than two pieces of typing paper

◄ was covered with filth. Lorri picked her up and held her. The hen was too weak to move and her head sank down and pushed her beak into her breast, leaving an indentation.

Lorri took the hen back to Farm Sanctuary, named her Lilly, and spent half the night feeding her by hand in her kitchen. By the kitchen lights, Lorri saw bruises covering half of Lilly's little body and confided to Gene that she didn't know if Lilly could survive, and that perhaps bringing her home and caring for her was only prolonging the suffering.

The next morning Lilly seemed just as close to death, but by the afternoon she looked a little better. Lorri stayed with her for hours, feeding her with an eyedropper. One morning, after a week of care, Lorri went downstairs to feed Lilly and found her on her feet. Lorri sat down a few steps away. Lilly walked over to Lorri and hopped into her lap.

Chickens rarely jump into people's laps. "Perhaps," Gene told me, "Lilly wanted to express her gratitude to Lorri, and jumping into her lap was the one way she could communicate this to her. It's something I almost never see a chicken do, especially one that has just spent a week fighting for her life."

Within a few days, Gene and Lorri moved Lilly out to live with the other chickens in the chicken shed. She still lives there today.

blink in the light of the world for the first time, they are thrown away or ground up.

The sexing process takes place at the hatchery. A worker sits in a room with a tray full of newly hatched baby chicks and, taking each one in turn, rubs a finger between its legs to determine sex. All males are disposed of.

The egg industry doesn't advertise how it kills male chicks. The most humane of the methods used is to put the birds under a stream of carbon dioxide gas where they die rather quickly. A more convenient and widely practiced method is to toss the chicks into plastic garbage bags where they slowly smother under the weight of other chicks. Disposing of male chicks is an everyday practice—there are at this moment dozens of hatcheries in the U.S. with trash bags full of struggling, suffocating baby male layer chicks.

Other hatcheries don't even bother to kill the chicks before making use of their bodies. The most common use for discarded chicks is fertilizer, a process

that requires grinding. In some hatcheries, as each male chick is identified, it is tossed—alive—into a grinder. Some chicks are thoroughly
ground almost immediately while others float around in eddies and
are only gradually pulled into the gears. For the chicks, this can
mean a tortured mangling as they gradually swirl into the grinder.
One study reported that: "Even after twenty seconds, there were
only partly damaged animals with whole skulls."[4]

DEBEAKING

After the male chicks are disposed of, attention turns to the females. To help them survive crowding, they receive medicines in
their food throughout their lifetimes. But there is still the social
aspect to control. Lacking a social order and under enormous
stress, they will still tear each other apart. Chicken growers handle
this crowding-related problem simply. The main weapon a stressed
chicken uses is its beak. Get rid of the beak and, no matter how
stressed, the chickens' ability to kill each other will diminish.

Lorri Bauston says, "We get discarded chicks all the time
at Farm Sanctuary and we never debeak them. Commercial chicken
houses debeak their chickens because they keep the birds un-
naturally stressed and confined."

The person doing the debeaking job cuts hundreds of chicks
an hour. You take a chick, put its beak into the guide, and press
down on the blade. The blade is electrically heated and cauterizes
the blood vessels as it snips off about one-fourth of the beak.[5] The
chicken industry characterizes this procedure as "beak-trimming,"[6]
as if it's **little more than a manicure**.

Although the inside of the beak is filled with nerve endings,
some studies seem to validate the industry's claim that the procedure causes little pain—initially. The cutting/burning is so sudden
that, as with the hours following a severe human burn, there seems
to be comparatively little pain. But, again like severe human burns,
the real pain from debeaking begins about twenty-four hours later, and

The chicken
industry
characterizes
beak-trimming
as if it's little
more than a
manicure.

persists for at least six weeks.[7] No pain-killers are used during debeaking or for that matter at any time during a chicken's life, in part because scientists haven't bothered to test pain-killers on chickens.[8]

Bernard Rollin has surveyed the veterinary results of debeaking and writes:[9] "After hot-blade trimming, damaged nerves develop into extensive neuromas, known to be painful in humans and animals.[10] Furthermore, these neuromas show abnormal discharge and response patterns indicative of acute and chronic pain syndromes in mammals.[11] Behavioral and white-cell responses to beak trimming confirm this conclusion.[12] There is also evidence that the pain of debeaking may ramify in pain in eating, weight loss, and 'starve-out' in chicks."[13] Starve-out is the industry term for chickens who die from starvation, often because debeaking has left them unable to eat.

After debeaking, the chicks settle in for the least uncomfortable time of their lives. Their bodies require about twenty weeks to mature and start laying eggs. So for the next twenty weeks, the birds grow bigger until they are old enough to be shipped to an egg farm. The conditions are relatively crowded, but nothing like what the chicks will soon experience. Since hatcheries sell their chicks to egg farms, it's relatively cheap to maintain a clean, uncrowded environment for the few weeks before sale.

Conditions change totally once the birds arrive at the egg farm. They are crowded into cages arranged in "batteries," or long rows, where they are kept for the rest of their lives.

A VISIT TO AN EGG FARM

Michael Greger, a medical student who spends much of his spare time researching the effects of animal foods on human health, recounted the following story from his undergraduate years at Cornell University in Ithaca, New York:

"I had seen the animal-rights pictures of what goes on in egg farms. But I never actually went inside one of those places and I didn't know how credible those pictures were. There is a large chain-grocery store not far from my apartment. I found out that they own the egg farm that produces their eggs. So I wrote them a letter asking them how they treated their chickens.

"They wrote back that everything's completely modern. They even offered to let me bring three acquaintances for a tour. I invited my dad, who's a professional photographer. I also invited Gene Bauston from Farm Sanctuary. We all went down there one morning.

"Before we could enter the layer house, they had us put on jumpsuits. They told us that the jumpsuits were required for cleanliness, but none of the other workers in the plant wore them, so we think it was to keep our status as visitors highly visible so that employees wouldn't do anything embarrassing in front of us.

"Then they took us into the layer house, and it was the last thing I'd expected. I mean, yeah, the birds were super crowded in the cages. But they looked great. They were clean, had nice feathers, and they all appeared healthy. Even the cages were shiny and practically spotless. Nothing like those pictures the animal rights movement puts out of all those tattered, scraped-up chickens. I couldn't figure out how the birds could be so crowded but look so good. I started **wondering if I'd been brainwashed** by staged photos and propaganda.

"But Gene Bauston knows the industry inside out, and he wasn't at all fazed. He gives the egg farm guy this sly, knowing look, and then says, 'Tell us, when did these chickens come in?'

"The egg farm guy looks at the floor kind of nervous and there's this pause. He looks caught and finally just decides to blurt out the truth: 'Last week,' he says. Then Gene asks, 'Can you take us to a shed that holds chickens that have been here for a while?'

"There's some dickering, but finally we're taken to the shed holding chickens that had been in the cages for eight or nine months. On the way to the shed, he tells us that these are 'older' chickens, and—just like older men who lose their hair—many of these chickens are bare of feathers. But Gene and I both knew that chickens don't

> "I started wondering if I'd been brainwashed by staged photos and propaganda."

lose feathers because of age. It had to do with their being cramped in the battery cage and constantly rubbing against metal. Farm Sanctuary's birds are often several years old, and they have all their feathers.

"The cages weren't nearly as crowded in this shed. That's because they remove dead chickens from the cages. As the months go by, the surviving birds get more space. But **the birds were a mess**. They walked with this pathetic hobble-hop because their legs and feet were so messed up. They were scraped everywhere, had open sores, and the whole place stunk like concentrated urine.

"My dad takes out his camera and the egg farm guy starts insisting that if we want to take pictures of these chickens, we also have to take pictures of the newly arrived chickens. His logic was that the beat-up chickens represented only *some* of the birds in the factory farm—the ones that just arrived looked great!

"But really he was doing us a favor by insisting we photograph the newly arrived chickens. It meant we could take perfect before-and-after photographs. All the chickens that just arrived from the hatchery looked wonderful—despite the crowded conditions. But any bird that had been there at least a few weeks looked like it had been through hell."

> "The birds were a mess. They walked with this pathetic hobble-hop. They were scraped everywhere."

A SHORT, WRETCHED LIFE

Michael Greger's first-hand account is compelling—and perhaps all the more poignant because he found a typical egg factory right in his own neighborhood—but there's no need to take just the word of visitors about conditions in laying houses. Poultry industry journals thoroughly document most conditions. Today, about 98 percent of layer hens are caged, most for their entire lives, and industry experts predict that even fewer birds will avoid caging in the years ahead.[14] Layer hens are typically crowded five to a cage, and each cage has a floor smaller than two sheets of typing paper.[15] Naturally, this crowding increases mortality and even depresses egg production—but not enough to offset the extra profits that make five birds per cage more profitable than one, two, three, or four.[16] The industry acknowledges that crowding weakens bones,[17] and 44 percent of layer hens suffer from leg abnormalities.[18]

Today's hens, although capable of laying more eggs, are also increasingly prone to attacking their companions, sometimes even to the point of cannibalism.[19] As geneticists breed chickens that lay ever more eggs, the birds become more aggressive because of their increased requirements for food and water.[20] When one bird attacks another, the victim has no opportunity to escape.[21] If things turn bad between two cage-mates, they will still share the same cage 24 hours a day, until one or the other dies. Heat build-up in the egg factories can further aggravate violence among caged hens, or even kill them by the thousands. In the summer of 1995, more than two-and-a-half million layer hens suffocated in their cages from extreme heat that ventilating fans could not dissipate.[22]

When kept under humane conditions that also preserve natural pecking orders, even the most aggressive varieties of chickens behave in a generally docile manner. By keeping their chickens under natural conditions, Farm Sanctuary averts outbreaks of violence in their flocks.

After about a year, a hen's egg output begins to decline. Depending on the practice of the farm, and on the price of replacement hens, the birds are either sent to slaughter or put through a forced molting procedure. The purpose of forced molting is to simulate a tough winter. It resets the hens' biological clocks and they deliver several months' more egg production. **During forced molting**, lights are turned off and food is totally withdrawn for 7 to 14 days (and sometimes even longer).[23] One leading breeder recommends keeping food withdrawn until the birds lose 30 percent of their body weight.[24] Many chickens face an added horror—their cage-mates die and begin to

During forced molting, lights are turned off and food is totally withdrawn for 7 to 14 days.

decay in the cramped cage. The bodies are not removed until after the molting period. By the time the lights are turned back on and food restored, 5 to 10 percent of the chickens will be dead.[25]

Force-molted or not, within two years of first egg production, egg laying declines and most hens are considered "spent." Though they will still produce some eggs, it is cheaper to clear out their cages and bring in a new set of birds. The entire shed's hens are sent to slaughter simultaneously.

A lifetime spent nearly motionless in cages while losing calcium to eggshells leaves their skeletons in wretched condition. Workers who, as the industry terms it, "depopulate" a hen house are usually paid by the bird and not by the hour, ensuring trauma and broken bones as these birds are hurriedly pulled from their cages.[26] The standard method for emptying battery cages is to lift three birds upside down in each hand.[27] Upon arrival at the slaughterhouse, 30 percent of hens have freshly broken bones.[28] Another study showed that simply removing hens from their transport crates and hanging them on the speeding slaughter line increases broken bones by an additional 44 percent.[29] After pre-slaughter stunning, 88 percent of layer hens have broken bones.[30]

Since layer-hens have comparatively little muscle, stringy meat, and bruises, they are nearly worthless. Sometimes their meat goes into the lowest quality processed foods such as **39-cent pot pies**. Because spent-hen meat is worth so little as human food, it's often made into animal food. One company promotes the Jet-Pro system, where slaughterhouses are eliminated entirely. The company visits the layer shed, bringing equipment to grind up the animals on-site into chicken feed.[31]

While today's egg farms crowd chickens to an almost inconceivable degree, they are dwarfed by the farms now under construction. These new farms will raise chickens in larger numbers than ever before. One industry journal predicts that by the year 2000, there

Sometimes their meat goes into the lowest quality processed foods such as 39-cent pot pies.

will be sixty of these egg "mega-farms" scattered around the United States—each with over one million hens.[32]

It takes a chicken living in battery cage conditions about 24 hours to produce just one egg.[33] Supermarket eggs cost about a dime each. There is no scale with which to compare 24 hours of animal suffering and ten cents of your grocery bill other than the scale of human conscience.

FRANKENSTEIN'S CHICKENS

The other type of chicken raised in the U.S. for mass consumption is the "broiler," bred for meat, not egg production. Today's broiler chickens are behemoths compared to traditional chickens. Modern chickens grow twice as big and twice as fast as traditional birds.[34] The age at slaughter has dropped from sixteen weeks in the 1950s to twelve weeks in 1970 to an amazing seven weeks today.[35]

The breast is the most valuable part of the chicken, and geneticists have learned to concentrate most growth in the breast muscle. Today's eight-week old chickens carry *seven times* more breast muscle than nine-week old chickens of twenty-five years ago.[36]

About 90 percent of broiler chickens have trouble walking.

Such fast growth takes a heavy toll on health, and the fastest growing birds have the worst levels of general health.[37] In many cases, accelerated growth causes crippling. A *Poultry Science* article asserts that: "The changes in growth and carcass development have no doubt contributed to the increased incidence of 'leg weakness.'"[38] About 90 percent of **broiler chickens have trouble walking**.[39] Six percent are so badly disabled that, if the cattle laws applied to chicken, their meat could not be sold as human food.[40]

Farmers refuse to switch back to slower-growing, healthier strains. Instead, many of them deprive their young birds of food in an effort to reduce crippling. Food deprivation helps slow the runaway growth that would cripple or kill an even larger number of birds than are affected today.[41] One poultry study informs farmers that feeding chicks every other day significantly reduces leg deformities.[42]

As growth and leg problems continue to surge, researchers fear that chickens will lose their ability to reproduce naturally.[43] This has already happened with turkeys. Thanks to genetic manipulation emphasizing ever-bigger turkey breasts, domestic turkeys cannot mate naturally—turkey growers now have to rely on artificial insemination.[44]

Rapid growth also undercuts the immune system's ability to fight off disease.[45] As odd as it may sound, chicken producers don't *want* their birds to have normally functioning immune systems.[46] They would rather administer drugs to keep infection at bay. By combating disease through drugs, the animals' metabolic energies fuel growth instead of normal immune response. If geneticists bred chickens to have normally functioning immune systems, the reduction in animal growth would cause chicken industry revenues to drop by several hundred million dollars annually.[47]

Broilers live in huge sheds with up to twenty

BUEFORD

Gene Bauston found Bueford at a broiler chicken slaughterhouse. Lorri stayed to guard the car, while Gene entered the slaughterhouse to check the conditions. Lorri always feels nervous when Gene goes into slaughterhouses undercover. The minutes crawl by and there's no way of knowing if everything is okay. Finally, Gene emerged from the slaughterhouse's side exit with a lump underneath his shirt.

Courtesy of Farm Sanctuary

Now a mature rooster, Bueford is sleek and well-fledged.

Gene carried a filthy, trembling chicken that had fallen out of a crate in the area where broilers are loaded onto the slaughter line. Nervous and frightened, the chicken was attempting to stay out of the way of the heavy machinery that was unloading the enormous crates. His feathers were matted or missing, and he was flecked with blood. Lorri named him Bueford and they took him home to Farm Sanctuary.

While he recovered from his injuries, Bueford lived in the Baustons' office. Generally chickens prefer the company of other chickens. But Bueford didn't seem to know this—he made himself right at home with the Baustons and all their animals. Following the night they brought him home, they awoke in the morning to find Bueford and their dog Whiskey snuggled together asleep.

It wasn't long before Bueford discovered that the refrigerator was a source of treats. He knew that if he just walked up to the refrigerator every ten minutes he wouldn't get anything. But several times a day, he stood by the refrigerator ▶

thousand other birds on the floor. They are incredibly crowded—stocking density averages sixteen birds per square meter.[48] Still, this isn't quite as crowded as the confinement egg layers endure inside a battery cage. Poultry scientists have yet to figure out how to make battery cages profitable for broilers—but they're working on it. William A. Dudley-Cash, a columnist for *Feedstuffs* (one of the most widely read journals in agribusiness), writes: "The cage growing of broilers has been a fantasy of mine for some time."[49]

Bueford, barely seven weeks old, fell out of a crate at the slaughterhouse.

◄ door and waited for a serving of cranberries, grapes, or lettuce.

Farm Sanctuary's philosophy dictates that once an animal is healthy, he should be placed with other animals of his kind. When animals need human attention for medical problems, the Baustons love to spend time with them, but the ultimate goal is to keep the animals with members of their own species. When Bueford's health returned and they tried introducing him to the flock, he squawked and ran back to Lorri. But within a few days Bueford found his way into the pecking order and started getting used to the other chickens. After a week he seemed happiest with other birds.

Broiler houses have surprisingly little in common with layer houses. A layer house has an atmosphere more like a sick ward—the birds have persistent health problems, and while misery is chronic, there is a sense of order. But in a broiler house, commotion and hysteria rule. The birds are very young—under seven weeks of age—and in their excitability, they kick huge amounts of dust, excrement, and bacteria-covered bits of feathers into the air.

With twenty thousand chickens confined to one building, broiler houses have air that borders on being unbreathable. Animal scientists have failed to find an effective way to improve the air quality.[50] Poultry house workers have been shown to inhale dust at levels twice that permitted by government regulations,[51] and they suffer abnormally high rates

Blanche Johnson, courtesy of Farm Sanctuary

of bronchitis, pneumonia, and lung damage.[52] The temperature can also reach deadly extremes. Over four million broiler chickens died during a 1995 U.S. heat wave.[53]

THE RUSH TO SLAUGHTER

At the age of six or seven weeks, producers rush their chickens to slaughter even though they could grow even bigger.[54] Why slaughter a bird before it stops growing? Because around the sixth week, mortality rates begin to surge.[55] **The birds start dying** of heart attacks, infection and other diseases brought about by rapid growth. Many of the chickens slaughtered today are on the brink of heart failure, even though they are only seven weeks old. One study postponed slaughter to sixteen weeks—still a relatively young age since chickens can live several years. Even so, 26 percent of the chickens died from heart failure, and an additional 10 percent were at risk.[56]

Food is cut off twelve hours before slaughter, since anything eaten beyond this point will not be converted to chicken meat. A team of "catchers" then enters the broiler house. The first birds are easiest to catch—the floor is so crowded that the chickens have no place to run. Workers pack the birds into transport crates, which are stacked in trucks and driven to the slaughterhouse.

The ride to the slaughterhouse can inflict fatal trauma, especially on hot days. Chickens, like dogs, cool themselves by panting. As the chickens try to cool themselves by panting, the air inside the crates grows hotter and increasingly unbearable.[57] The vibration and motion during transport puts additional stress on the birds.[58] For chickens who have already endured seven weeks in a broiler house, the stress of transport can be too much. In an examination of 1,324 chickens that had died during transport, 47 percent died from congestive heart failure.[59] The report comments that: "Pre-

> Around the sixth week, the birds start dying of heart attacks, infection and other diseases brought about by rapid growth.

sumably in all the deaths from congestive heart failure, the physiological responses associated with the stress of catching, loading and transport had been too much for the cardiovascular system to cope with."[60]

Bueford the chicken somehow survived his adventure of tumbling out of a crate and then dodging slaughterhouse machinery, without succumbing to a heart attack. Bueford now struts his stuff in the chicken yard at Farm Sanctuary, having escaped his status as "broiler." No longer identified by a method of cooking, Bueford will live out his life in safety.

8

Commercially raised pigs bear little resemblance to the old-fashioned image of barnyard behemoths dozing in mud wallows or patiently foraging for acorns. Today's pigs are crowded into tight quarters with concrete floors and dust-filled air, fed their daily dose of protein concentrate, and kept as immobile as possible until they can be herded off to slaughter at little more than four months of age.

Pigs

Before the 1980s, pigs offered one of the few dependable sources of income for farmers. When a young farmer started out, he could keep a few pigs in a barn. They took some work to look after, but raising pigs would provide a farmer with a good profit. After just a few years of raising pigs, a farmer could earn enough to buy more land and get into the more desirable and potentially more profitable areas of farming, such as growing wheat or soybeans.

But in the 1980s, big corporations stepped in and took over the pig industry with the same large-scale systems applied to poultry. Among other things, these new pig farms have unbreathable air, unhealthy animals, almost unimaginable crowding, and razor-thin profit margins. To keep ahead of costs, the rules of the game are simple: create ever-larger operations that require ever-diminishing human labor. As a consequence, the pigs in today's commercial operations receive almost no human attention. Land-O-Lakes, a big operator of these huge new pig operations, estimates that each pig gets just twelve minutes of human care during the four months it spends growing to slaughter weight.[1]

C O N C R E T E   A N D   C R A T E S

Pig sheds are designed to hold the largest number of animals at the lowest cost.[2] Concrete slats are the standard flooring in commercial pig operations.[3] Slats reduce labor requirements for cleaning because the excrement falls between the slats and into an underground collection area. In fully slatted pens, pigs sleep on the hard slats without bedding materials—because straw would fall through the openings.[4] As these new concrete-floored pig sheds have taken over the industry, the use of straw has diminished, despite the fact that repeated studies demonstrate that straw improves the pigs' psychological and physical well-being.[5]

Sleeping on concrete is more than uncomfortable—over time, it creates serious health problems. Joints swell, skin gets scraped off, and the feet get serious abrasions and infections.[6] This adds to the pigs' stress and increases rates of fighting and cannibalism.[7]

In the past, farmers made sure their sick or injured animals received proper veterinary care, if not on ethical grounds then at least to protect their investment. Today, this is no longer the case. Large farms may deliberately withhold veterinary care when treatment is too expensive or conflicts with the schedule of workers. Bioethics expert Bernard Rollin has written about a veterinarian who, when visiting a large hog operation, noticed that one of the pregnant sows in a farrowing crate had a broken leg. Nobody had contacted him about this pig, so the vet approached the farm's manager and offered to put the leg into a splint.

The manager said that they intended to let the sow give birth, and then send her to slaughter. He told the vet they did not want to pay for treatment because it would be cheaper to slaughter the sow after she gave birth and replace her with a new sow.

The veterinarian thought about the situation. He decided that, ethically, he could not leave the shed without treating the sow. So he went back to the manager and offered to set the sow's leg for just the cost of

Sleeping on concrete creates serious health problems.

the splint. Once again, the manager declined, telling the veterinarian that the facility lacked the workers to look after the sow once her leg was in the splint.[8] This story is not unusual. One in every four commercial pig operations surveyed in 1990 went the entire year without requesting the services of a veterinarian.[9]

A recent examination of 6,000 slaughtered pigs revealed 71 percent suffered from pneumonia.[10] A cause for this high rate of respiratory disease may be the air quality that pigs endure 24 hours a day. When entering a commercial pig shed, you instinctively start breathing shallowly and never through the nose. The air is heavy with dust and reeks of ammonia. As you breathe, urine vapor coats your tongue and leaves your lungs with a sickly, full feeling. Pig producers have tested all kinds of ideas to improve air quality, but have made little progress.[11] The industry rejects the idea of ventilating the buildings with fresh air from outside as too expensive, especially in cooler climates.[12]

The air inside pig sheds is so thick that some areas harbor cloud-like pockets of gases, dust, and pollutants. Industry journals recommend mixing these stagnant air pockets more thoroughly with the rest of the inside air.[13]

Pig workers can develop severe respiratory problems, even though they spend only a part of each day in the buildings. Sixty percent of pig workers in the U.S., Canada, and Sweden have reported breathing problems.[14] One report on air quality ends by stating: "We have concluded that, pending further research in this subject, the most effective means of minimizing inhaled dust is to wear a suitable mask at all times in hog facilities."[15] No mention is made of the pigs' health.

In nature, and even in indoor conditions with plenty of straw, pregnant pigs prepare for birth by building a nest. Outdoors, sows may walk miles in order to find the best possible place to give birth and to nurse.[16] After selecting a site, the sow spends hours constructing her nest in preparation for the piglets.

The air inside pig sheds is so thick that some areas harbor cloud-like pockets of gases, dust, and pollutants.

All this changed when farmers moved their sows to indoor operations. If farmers were going to force sows to give birth indoors, farrowing crates seemed a good and possibly even humane solution. Unlike cows, who have only one calf at a time, a sow gives birth to a litter of around ten piglets. Crushing is a constant danger during suckling, since a sow can easily lose track of newborn piglets, which are so tiny you can hold them in the palm of your hand. Without the opportunity to build a nest, sows have almost no margin for error in shifting their weight. Indoors, if a piglet slips underneath the sow, there is no natural cushioning of mud or straw—the piglet gets crushed or smothered against concrete, wood, or metal.

Farrowing crates were designed to keep the sow almost motionless for the first critical days of nursing. The idea was that, after the piglets grew big enough to avoid crushing, the sow would be moved to a larger pen. But over time, pig farmers found sows could survive in crates year-round.[17] Keeping sows permanently in crates reduces building and labor costs,[18] and today it's common practice **to keep sows in crates** for almost their entire lives.[19] The crates are now used by 86 percent of commercial pig operations.[20]

Farrowing crates force the sows in most U.S. pig facilities to live under confinement almost as intense as a layer hen or veal calf. The crates are so narrow that, like veal crates, the sow is unable to turn around.[21] One typical crate design is just 24 inches wide (these are especially cramped dimensions, considering that the sow can weigh over 400 pounds).[22] The crates permit almost no movement—a sow can take only one or two steps backward or forward.[23] This total confinement angers and confuses sows so much that they sometimes attack their crates.[24] Health problems stemming from crate confinement send up to a third of sows to early slaughter.[25]

Yet nobody has proven that the crates avert piglet-crushing

> Today it's common practice to keep sows in crates for almost their entire lives.

deaths. Two extensive studies have compared crates to more spacious pens. One study found crates offer only a slight improvement in piglet survival, while the other shows crates confer no piglet survival advantages at all.[26] The real motivation for using crates now is that they boost profits by allowing each building to hold more sows.

THE LIFE OF A PIG

Shortly after birth, workers snip notches out of each piglet's ear for identification purposes. No anesthetic is used.[27] To reduce injuries caused by fighting, their "needle" teeth are clipped, again without anesthetic.[28] Male pigs are castrated, usually without anesthetic. The authors of a 1995 *Journal of Animal Sciences* article felt it necessary to castrate a group of test pigs in order to investigate whether a local anesthetic applied before castration reduces suffering. Not surprisingly, they found that without anesthetic, pigs scream more during castration and have higher heart rates.[29]

Pigs are raised in as little space as possible. For young 250-pound pigs, operators are advised to allow a little more than one square yard of floor space for each animal.[30] The crowding is not just to save space—crowding

DAWN

Anybody who spends time around pigs will see how they love to get a rise out of people. The most mischievous of all the pigs at Farm Sanctuary is a big, golden-pink sow named Dawn. Dawn's ears perk up and her tiny eyes level an expectant gaze at any human who approaches. When visitors enter Farm Sanctuary's pig barn, Dawn often sidles up to them and casually unties their shoelaces. Then she walks away, stealthily casting sidelong glances until the visitor notices the untied shoelaces. Dawn loves to tease people with tricks like this, but she is also very affectionate. Just touching her belly makes her instantly flop over for a belly rub.

Dawn's mischievous and spunky character is remarkable ▶

Courtesy of Farm Sanctuary

Dawn was starving and emaciated when she and her pen-mates were discovered. Many had already died.

Blanche Johnson, courtesy of Farm Sanctuary.

A robust, affectionate and responsive pig, Dawn now lives at Farm Sanctuary.

◄ given the factory farm she came from. It is sometimes the case that pig and other animal production facilities will deprive unprofitable animals of food and allow them to starve. This happened to Dawn when, as a young pig, she appeared sickly and wasn't growing normally. She was dumped in a shed with other sickly pigs and left to die. A neighbor heard the animals screaming repeatedly and called the police. (Many animals are brought to Farm Sanctuary following neighbors' concerns about sounds made by abused or neglected animals.) When the police arrived, they found a dozen or so pigs who weren't receiving food or veterinary attention. Emaciated and crusted with filth, they wandered aimlessly among the corpses of dead and decaying pen-mates.

Dawn's bleak future took an immediate upturn when Lorri and Gene Bauston adopted these unwanted pigs. She recovered her health, and it wasn't long before she started behaving with all her current cheerfulness, affection and mischief.

also reduces feed costs. What most people would consider healthy and natural movement is, to today's pig farmer, expensive and undesirable. A modern pig farmer wants his pigs to stay as motionless as possible—when a pig walks, the farmer sees costly feed wasted to provide the energy for movement instead of being stored as flesh. Keeping pigs under crowded conditions decreases activity and increases profits. When researchers cut floor space given to piglets from .22 to .14 square meters, feed expenses dropped by 10 percent.[31] *National Hog Farmer* summed up the incentive to squeeze pigs into tight quarters with an article headlined: "Crowding Pigs Pays—If It's Managed Properly."[32]

While occasional scuffles are normal in any group of pigs, tail-biting is not. Stressed, confined pigs will bite each others' tails. Like pecking among hens, tail-biting gets worse as conditions grow more crowded and stressful.[33] Pig producers reduce tail-biting by cutting off their piglets' tails. Again, no anesthetic is used.[34] Raising pigs under less crowded conditions would also reduce tail-biting, but producers reject this as unprofitable. Cutting off pigs' tails is just like debeaking chickens—the farmers are uninterested in reducing the crowding that causes the violence, and instead handle the problem by mutilating the animal.

Another common practice that almost guarantees tail-biting and fighting is mixing groups of unfamiliar animals in cramped areas.[35] Like chickens, pigs participate within a family-like hierarchy, which gives them a social order and eliminates fighting.[36] When groups of unfamiliar pigs are mixed together, the established orders break down. Fights occur because individual animals cannot know which pigs are dominant. Yet producers frequently mix unfamiliar pigs, especially during stressful situations involving transport and slaughter.[37]

In more humane conditions, unfamiliar pigs mixed in with others quickly settle their differences. Lorri Bauston of Farm Sanctuary says, "Every once in a while we have to introduce a new pig into the barn. There's inevitable conflict when this happens, but we've never had a serious injury. Pigs seem to hate fighting, and the weaker pig generally backs down quickly. Since we provide plenty of space, one pig always has plenty of room to back away and avoid a fight."

But in commercial pig operations, **fights become vicious** and deadly because when two pigs come into conflict, there is insufficient space for the weaker pig to retreat.[38] With no means to signal surrender, a confrontation that would otherwise be quickly resolved can turn deadly.[39]

Another natural activity of pigs that is subverted by modern production methods is the way they eat. The main activity of a wild pig is eating and looking for food. In nature, pigs spend about half their waking hours eating everything from seedlings to tree leaves to insects to an occasional small animal. This instinct is thoroughly frustrated in the factory farm. Farmers make only one kind of feed available: a protein-rich feed concentrate, formulated to encourage rapid weight gain.[40] With modern feeding practices, pigs consume an entire day's worth of food in just twenty minutes.[41] Although these concentrates provide the pig with abundant calories, such feeds do a poor job of satisfying hunger.[42]

While leaving the pig in a chronically hungry state,[43] feed concentrates also frustrate even deeper instinctive needs. One researcher writes: "Concentrated feeds may frequently fail to satisfy hunger while fulfilling nutrient requirements. . . . It is evident that the strong and

In commercial pig operations, fights become vicious and deadly because there is insufficient space for the weaker pig to retreat.

inherent drives to select feedstuffs amongst alternatives, to forage for feed, and to manipulate feed and non-feed matter with the jaw, are all left entirely unsatisfied in modern production systems"[44]

There's no question that the concentrates work wonders in adding profitable flesh to the pig. But concentrates are so unsuited to the pig's nutritional needs that they may actually damage the pigs' internal organs. When researchers examined 6,000 slaughtered pigs, they saw that 51 percent had liver abnormalities[45]—a condition caused by feed concentrates.

DEAD ON ARRIVAL — DOES IT MATTER?

At about six months of age, **pigs go to slaughter**. Pig producers have three objectives in transporting pigs: keep costs down, move the pigs as quickly as possible, and get the pigs to the slaughterhouse alive. Having every pig reach the slaughterhouse alive is not paramount—reducing transportation costs is worth a few dead pigs. Transportation begins in a furious rush to get every pig on the truck, and workers often panic the pigs during loading in an effort to save time. Swine specialist Kenneth B. Kephart writes, "Far and away, the obvious weakness most producers exhibit during the moving and load-out process is a lack of patience. The shouting, the swinging, the shocking, the slapping, and the whipping often serve only to excite the hogs."[46]

Producers reduce transportation costs by overloading trailers. The extra heat, fighting, and stress caused by overloaded trailers kill a great many pigs. Every day more than 250 pigs die during transport to the slaughterhouse.[47] Kephart explains the industry's reasons for overloading trailers: "Even with a zero death rate that might be associated with providing more space on the truck, the hogs that we save would not be enough to pay for the increased transportation costs of hauling fewer hogs on a load. So it becomes a moral issue."

At about six months of age, pigs go to slaughter.

Much of what is done to pigs and other food animals is a moral issue. If an animal is raised with killing in mind, does it matter if that animal suffers during his life or dies short of the ultimate goal? Many animal industry standards indicate that suffering and premature death don't matter as much as profits.

9

As large corporations take over milk and meat production, cows and cattle are treated with less concern for their health, comfort and natural life functions. Veal calves stand chained in crates, and many dairy cows rest no more than three months between pregnancies. Beef cattle live under the best conditions of any food animals until they hit the feedlots to be fattened on feed combinations that may include chicken bedding and manure.

Milk and beef

In 1954, over two million U.S. farms kept dairy cows, with an average of about ten cows each.[1] Only 275,000 dairy farms remained by 1982; 200,000 by 1990; and 155,000 by 1992.[2] As small dairy farms have declined, the surviving dairies have grown larger. This massive consolidation has put America's milk supply increasingly in the hands of large corporations and has degraded the everyday care of the dairy cow.

Large dairies save money by using fewer employees to care for more cows. Clyde Rutherford, the president of a Syracuse, New York dairy cooperative, predicts that dairies will soon produce over a million pounds of milk annually for each employee.[3] As fewer employees tend ever greater numbers of cows, the living conditions for the cows have rapidly transformed.

Traditional milking by hand permitted a twice-daily inspection of the cows' udders. Today's milking machines, when properly maintained, inflict no pain or injury, but the speed with which the machines are used does not allow for much time to notice mechanical malfunctions or other problems. Cows spend about five minutes twice a day in the milking parlor, hooked up to the milking machines. This means that, twice each day, malfunctioning machines can aggravate chronic udder injuries.[4]

Almost any kind of rhythmic tugging causes a cow's udder to release milk. Abnormally hard tugs will hurt the cow, but the milk will still be released. There is often no sign when a milking machine malfunctions—it may be sucking on the teat much too hard, but the machine will still extract the milk. Veterinarian N. Bruce Haynes writes that malfunctioning milk machines on U.S. dairies are ". . . a constant source of udder injury leading to a high incidence of clinical mastitis."[5] Haynes continues that: "Trouble arises when dairy farmers forget that the milking machine operates more hours than any other machine on the farm and therefore requires periodic maintenance. All too often it is forgotten until it quits."[6]

Thanks to the work of geneticists, modern dairy cows are very efficient producers but are also **much more prone to disease**. In 1967, a typical cow produced less than 9,000 pounds of milk per year. Today, a cow averages close to 16,000 pounds of milk.[7] This nearly-doubled milk yield puts enormous stresses on the animal.

As blood circulates through the cows' milk ducts, protein and other components are removed to create milk. It is the blood that provides all of the protein and other nutrients that go into cows' milk. About 300 to 500 pounds of blood circulate through the milk ducts to produce each pound of milk.[8] The huge volume of milk yielded by today's dairy cows can leave the cow lacking enough protein for her own health. When this happens, the cow can suffer serious deficiency diseases like ketosis, a condition that impairs metabolism. The milk industry is well aware that by breeding high-yielding milk cows, they have created animals prone to such deficiency diseases. One headline in *Dairy Today* reads: "Ketosis: The Disease of High Producers."[9]

Modern dairy cows are very efficient producers but are also much more prone to disease.

Mastitis, an inflammation of the udder, afflicts more than one in five cows.[10] The swollen, overworked udders of today's dairy cows offer an ideal setting for infection. Dairies legally sell Grade A milk taken from cows with "subclinical" mastitis infections (i.e., those not showing obvious symptoms). Farmers want to keep infection levels as low as possible because cows suffering subclinical mastitis produce about 20 percent less milk.[11]

To combat infections, it's important to keep the udders clean by trimming away all the hair. Veterinarian Andy Johnson advocates burning away udder hair with a blowtorch. He's demonstrated the procedure's supposed safety by using a blowtorch to burn the hair from his own arm.[12] Obviously, Johnson faced less risk because he was in control of the torch and could react to any indication of pain. But to advocate routine use of blowtorches on the nation's dairy cows is to guarantee mistakes and burns.

About 95 percent of dairies de-horn their cows.[13] While a minority of operations use an electric de-horner, the most common removal methods involve scooping, gouging, or cutting the horns from the cow's head.[14]

C O W S   A N D   C A L V E S

Within 24 hours of birth, more than 90 percent of calves are taken away from their mothers forever.[15] At some milk-producing farms, the calves are removed immediately following birth. This happens in about one in five cases.[16] Most other newborn calves spend only a few hours with their mothers, and less than half get to suckle from the udder since modern dairy udders are so enlarged and fragile.[17] Several times, Lorri Bauston has watched at commercial dairies as less than day-old calves are pulled away from the mother cows. She reports that both appear to be in obvious distress.

The newborn calf drinks a special milk called colostrum that the mother produces right after giving birth. Colostrum has no commercial value, but it helps calves' immune systems develop. In most cases colostrum is milked by hand, and then fed to the calf.[18] Soon after, the calf is fed a milk-replacer, which usually contains antibiotics and other drugs. Milk replacers are made from the cheapest possible ingredients: 93 percent contain animal fat or coconut oil as primary ingredients.[19]

Cows have a natural life span of over twenty years.[20] But starting around age three, they produce progressively less milk after each pregnancy. At about five years of age, cows are sent to slaughter and replaced with younger cows. Slaughtered dairy cows have tougher, older flesh than beef steers. So the flesh from dairy cows ends up as **fast-food hamburgers** and other cheaper ground-meat products.

Shortly after giving birth, the cows' milk yields begin a gradual decline. To keep milk yields as high as possible, the modern dairy cow is almost constantly pregnant. Dairy cows have just two or three months to recover from the birth of a calf before they are again artificially inseminated. On average, U.S. dairy cows deliver a new calf every thirteen months.[21] A string of pregnancies in rapid succession may provide the dairy farmer with more milk, but it puts the cow at great risk. Pregnancy complications cause nearly one in every five health-related deaths in cows.[22]

The almost constant pregnancies and unprecedented milk yields keep today's dairy cows on the brink of serious illness. Each year, tens of thousands of dairy cows become too ill to stand. When they collapse, the industry calls them downed cows (or "downers") and writes them off. Any extra care given to a downed cow only adds to the financial loss. Since animals unable to stand can legally be slaughtered for human food as long as they are still breathing when they arrive at the slaughterhouse, downers are often dragged onto a truck and driven to the plant for slaughter.

Sometimes, after a cow goes down, it is left unattended for several days, even though many downed cows could be nursed back to

> Flesh from dairy cows ends up as fast-food hamburgers and other cheap ground-meat products.

health with attention and proper veterinary care. Dairies are generally unwilling to provide this care, knowing that it's cheaper to send the animal off to slaughter and to replace her with a maturing calf.

Because a cow bears from three to six calves during her life, the dairy industry generates more calves than it needs. As with the egg industry, half of the dairy industry's offspring is unwanted. The egg industry tosses male chickens into plastic trash bags; the dairy industry sells its unwanted offspring to the veal industry.

VEAL CALVES

Veal calves suffer greater mistreatment than any other kind of cattle. Those that are not killed immediately after birth to make "bob" veal become expensive "milk-fed" veal. They are separated from their mothers, sometimes immediately and almost always within a day of birth. To achieve the tenderness that makes veal a more expensive and coveted meat, the calf cannot be allowed to move normally or exercise its muscles. To keep the calf from moving, producers chain him inside a wooden crate scarcely wider than his shoulders. White, milk-fed veal may conjure images of a calf blissfully drinking milk from his mother until his unfortunate end. This is not the case. The calves are fed a cheap milk-replacer

ALBY

In Bradford County, Pennsylvania, a center for milk-fed veal, neighbors reported the constant sound of calves' bawling coming from a veal barn on a local farm. Acting on the complaint, the police went to the farm to investigate. What they found was a barn full of dead and rotting veal calves, still chained in their crates, along with a few survivors on the brink of starvation.

Neighboring farms took in the surviving calves until Farm Sanctuary could arrive to adopt them. Of all the calves, Alby was in the worst shape. The chain around his neck ▶

Veal calves spend their whole lives chained in narrow crates, subsisting on an iron-depleted milk formula to keep their flesh pale.

Blanche Johnson, courtesy of Farm Sanctuary

Alby was rescued from among dying and rotting calves after a veal farmer decided to stop feeding them.

had not been opened up as he got bigger, so it grew into his neck. Gene Bauston remembers that, "For three days Alby wouldn't lie down because he knew if he went down he wouldn't get back up. He couldn't hold down solid food. We had to boil alfalfa and he drank alfalfa tea."

Why would any farmer starve his calves? Many veal calves today are owned by big corporations. The farmer who raises them neither owns the calves nor pays for their food. He receives a payment to raise the animals on his property, and the feed company provides the animals, their food, and supplies. This particular veal farmer was unhappy with his feed company. He felt that they had cheated him, so to retaliate he stopped caring for the animals he had under contract. By the time the police arrived to investigate, 51 of the barn's 64 calves had died of starvation.

With a lot of treatment, Alby survived. The scars from his neck chain are still visible, and he's the most wary of any of Farm Sanctuary's grown veal calves. But once he decides a visitor won't hurt him, he acts like the world's biggest puppy dog. I found that he loves belly rubs and chest-scratching. Although he is upwards of 800 pounds, he is one of the gentlest animals I've ever seen.

Once Alby and the other calves began to recover their health, the Baustons turned their attention to prosecuting the farm's owner. The veal industry rallied behind him and none of the many other veal producers in Bradford County would go on record to say the farmer deserved a conviction. With the Baustons' perseverance, however, the veal farmer became the first U.S. factory farmer to be convicted of cruelty to animals. He was fined $1,000 and sentenced to 30 days in jail.

that often contains powerful antibiotics. This "milk" diet is deliberately iron-free, since in order to produce the desired pinkish-white meat, the calf must be forced into anemia.

At sixteen weeks of age, the veal calf is taken from his crate. He takes his first steps outside the crate since the day he was born—as the producer leads him onto a truck bound for the slaughterhouse.

The life of a veal animal is nothing like the traditional image of the wobbly-legged calf gamboling in a grassy pasture under the protective gaze of the mother cow. Interestingly, veal calves accept their imprisonment without protest. While caged or crowded chickens may exhibit hysteria and pigs will fight viciously when confined to too-tight quarters, the reaction of the veal calf to lifetime confinement is quite different. When you walk by a row of veal crates and look inside one, the impression you get is that the calf is not afraid or angry, merely despondent. The veal calf stands in his crate, his unexercised body growing more anemic each day, appearing to bear his condition with confusion and a tangible sadness.

BEEF CATTLE

"Shoe-leather-on-the-hoof," people sometimes call them. Beef cattle, raised for meat and by-products, are generally perceived as rugged but stolid creatures who must be herded and prodded through life until they are finally of some use to humans. They live on rangeland and in many ways are treated much as they were in the days of the overland cattle drives. Cattle ranchers have a history of disregarding the animals' ability to feel pain, often using the most quick and brutal methods for handling them.

This mindset can carry over into government regulations. Until 1994, the U.S. Department of Agriculture required that all cattle imported from Mexico have an M-shaped symbol branded onto their cheeks. Face-branding causes much more pain than branding on other body parts because the face has many nerve endings, little protective hair, and thin skin. When the USDA attempted, in 1993, to expand face-branding to other categories of cattle, activist Henry Spira led a campaign to expose the face-branding ordeal in full-page newspaper advertisements. Spira suggested several identification alternatives that made face branding unnecessary. The Colorado Cattlemen's Association agreed and the USDA soon scrapped their plans to expand the program. In early 1995 Spira persuaded the USDA to phase out all government face-branding requirements.

Spira's campaign set an important precedent. But it has done nothing to reverse the three major traumas inflicted on young U.S. cattle: branding, de-horning, and for males, castrating, all of which usually occur within the first few weeks after birth.

Gene Bauston has observed cattle being castrated, and he asserts that anesthetic is almost never used. "The calves are usually confined in 'squeeze chutes' to immobilize them during the procedure but on some ranches, castrating and branding are done much as they were a hundred years ago," Gene adds.

On such ranches, cowboys on horses herd, rope, and throw the calves one by one, pinning each animal to the ground while knives and branding irons are applied. As cowboys crouch around the roped calf, one cuts into his scrotum and rips out his testes, another cuts a chunk out of his ear with a sharp knife, and a third sears an identifying marker into the calf's thigh with a blowtorch-heated branding iron.

The burned and cut calves bellow in unmistakable outcries of pain and fear, spreading panic to the other calves. The sounds and movements of the calves become more frantic until finally the last calf is chased and caught.

Regardless of the way in which the animals are controlled, most ranchers use no anesthetic when they castrate cattle despite the fact that the method is deliberately injurious. One time-tested method is to cut the scrotum open and rip the testes out as roughly as possible. The following instructions were given at a prestigious U.S. agricultural college, as a student was about to castrate his first calf: "Remember, Josh, you got to rip 'em off. That causes trauma, and the swelling shuts off the blood. If you cut 'em off, you could get some serious bleeding."[23]

Most cattle are also de-horned.[24] De-horning involves either sawing away the horns or applying a caustic paste that dissolves them. Although horns may appear dead and insensitive on the outside, inside they are laced with nerves and blood vessels.

After these mutilations are completed, the calves are left to grow into adulthood. Over the next year, they graze the land. As range environmentalist Lynn Jacobs has demonstrated, the presence of cattle on the land means the extermination of great numbers of America's wild animals. But as far as the cattle's welfare is concerned, their conditions as they age into maturity are often quite good, much better at any rate than for any other type of commercially raised farm animal. In many cases, the cattle don't even see humans for days or weeks at a time.

A drawback to the cattle's isolation is that veterinary care is sparse. This is particularly critical as females approach calving time. Since a newborn beef calf can weigh around 100 pounds, labor can take many hours and has all the complexity and hazards of human birth. Most beef producers don't maintain facilities to help pregnant cattle.[25] A 1994 USDA report states: "Over half of producers (57.2 percent) only check their heifers one to two times per 24-hour period. This means that heifers having trouble calving may be undetected for up to 12 to 24 hours. . . . Only 32.8 percent of cow/calf operations have specialized calving facilities that allow increased observation or shelter."[26]

Too often, this lack of facilities and veterinary attention means the painful death of mother and calf on the range. "If you're walking around the range," says Gene Bauston, "particularly in the spring, you'll sometimes see a swollen cow

KEVIN

Kevin, who never grew as large as most beef cattle, is very affectionate toward humans.

In January 1992, Lorri Bauston was told about a very sick three-week-old beef calf who was not receiving veterinary care. Lorri drove to the beef ranch in question and found the calf hunched over on the floor and shaking from cold in a dilapidated shed. It was the middle of winter, and ice ringed the shed's water trough. Lorri asked the rancher to call a veterinarian. When the rancher protested that he could not afford the fee, Lorri asked for permission to take the calf to Farm Sanctuary.

The rancher agreed, and in less than two hours, the calf was bedded down in a warm stall and was being examined by a veterinarian. The vet was pessimistic—the calf was severely dehydrated and showed signs of serious vitamin deficiencies and several other symptoms of neglect. Most dangerous of all was an infection between his ribs. Using anesthetic and a scalpel, the veterinarian cut a hole in the calf's chest, and then instructed Lorri and Gene on how to flush the infection twice daily with penicillin. She then set up intravenous feeding tubes to rehydrate and nourish the animal.

Lorri named the calf Kevin, after the former *Saturday Night Live* star Kevin Nealon, who actively promotes veganism. A week passed, and Kevin was ▶

◄ still too sick to stand. Lorri knew that if he didn't get on his feet soon, new complications would make recovery impossible.

As a last-ditch attempt to save Kevin, Lorri told Gene, "Let's put him in the cattle barn. Maybe being around other cattle will make a difference."

That afternoon Lorri and Gene loaded Kevin onto a cart and wheeled him into the corner of the cattle barn to a pen designed to isolate and protect injured animals. They could scarcely believe what happened next. Other cattle in the barn came over to the pen, some stretching their heads over the pen's rails to try to reach Kevin. They made soft, comforting moos—a sound similar to those mother cows use around their calves. For over an hour, the twenty cattle in the shed gathered around Kevin's pen and did not leave him. Then Kevin started slowly improving. Within a couple days he stood on his own, and it was clear he would recover.

Kevin's multiple health problems severely stunted his growth—he is only about half the size of any other steer at Farm Sanctuary. He is very gentle and because he is so comfortable around humans, is a favorite of many Farm Sanctuary visitors.

Blanche Johnson, courtesy of Farm Sanctuary

Kevin had been severely neglected and was very sick when the Baustons rescued him.

lying dead amongst some bushes. Often, she has died in the process of giving birth."

After the cattle have reached their full size, they can still gain several hundred more profitable pounds by eating concentrated protein sources instead of grasses. Much rangeland is in barren, out-of-the-way places many miles removed from productive agricultural regions. A steer can eat a small mountain of feed concentrates—some 4,500 pounds—during the weeks of fattening prior to slaughter,[27] so it's much less expensive to bring the steer to the grain than the grain to the steer.

The steer is loaded onto a truck or train bound for a feedlot. The journey to the feedlot can last over 18 hours, cover more than a thousand miles and pass through several states. Crowding on the trucks can resemble conditions in a broiler house, with animals packed shoulder-to-shoulder. The difference is that cattle on their way to the feedlot weigh about 600 to 900 pounds[28] and the transport floor may pitch violently. When one steer falls down, the consequences can be horrendous. One industry article notes that: "The major risk in cattle transport is that of cattle going down underfoot. This risk is greatly increased at high stocking density. . . . When cattle went down at high stocking density, they were trapped on the floor by the remaining cattle 'closing over' and occupying the available standing space. Several unsuccessful attempts by fallen animals to stand up were observed."[29]

Such tramplings happen often. The authors of the above passage note that: "It is not uncommon for transport conditions to deteriorate to such an extent that considerable suffering and economic losses occur."[30]

The trip to the feedlot **marks the end** of the steer's life in a natural setting. Temple Grandin, who owns a company that makes slaughter devices, has been outspoken in protecting livestock from brutal handling. Grandin estimates that only 20 to 40 percent of U.S. feedlots have excellent handling.[31] Worse, she estimates, "About 10 percent are chronic abusers who allow overt cruelty to occur such as throwing calves, abuse of cripples or the use of brutal restraint methods where live cattle are hung upside down prior to religious slaughter."[32] The remaining 50 to 70 percent of feedlots subject animals to abuse or neglect stemming from incompetent or uncaring management. Grandin explains: "When management relaxes their vigilance, handling quality will usually deteriorate. The employees behave properly because they know that they may be instantly fired if they deliberately abuse an animal. Every facility visited by the author that has excellent handling has this tough policy. In operations where I have observed gross animal abuse there was no management supervision or the manager participated in the abuse."[33]

> The trip to the feedlot marks the end of the steer's life in a natural setting.

GROUND NEWSPRINT AND TABLE SCRAPS?

Feedlots are enormous fenced areas. It can take up to an hour to walk from one end to the other of the biggest of these lots. Large feedlots keep over ten thousand cattle at one time. Occasionally, uncastrated males arrive at the feedlot. More than one-third of feedlots castrate arriving bulls,[34] although the animals are now close to a year old and the procedure probably causes more pain than in younger animals. As usual, no anesthetic is used.

Feedlots exist because ranchers get paid by the pound, not by the animal. Cattle have an instinctive drive to eat almost constantly—they must, since they evolved to eat fibrous, low-calorie foods like grasses, leaves, and shrubs. Feedlot owners take advantage of this natural hunger drive by giving the cattle access to nothing but concentrated feeds that contain far more calories than grasses. Within weeks, the animals swell to hundreds of pounds above their natural weight. Feed concentrates may fatten profits, but these foods are inappropriate for the animals' digestive system with its four-part stomach designed to digest grasses.

Feedlot owners do everything possible to give the cattle the most protein and calories at the least expense. Some researchers advocate feeding feather meal and blood to cattle,[35] and this may be among the more palatable of the alternative feeds. Broiler litter—the **manure, bedding, and other waste** from chicken facilities—is digestible by cattle and far cheaper than feed grains.[36] Feeding broiler litter to cattle has grown increasingly common over the past several years.[37] Some feedlots give cattle a mixture of 50 percent grain and 50 percent broiler litter.[38] Meanwhile, Illinois State University is promoting the concept of feeding cattle a combination of ground newsprint and table scraps from university dining halls.[39] On the grounds that their animals are ruminants (mammals of the suborder Ruminantia, including cattle, sheep, goats, deer, and giraffes), cattle producers are legally entitled to feed their animals garbage and other products generally banned as food for pigs and other animals.

To increase growth further, feedlot cattle are implanted with hormone pellets which can incite abnormally violent behavior. If the implants get crushed, a surge of hormones floods into the bloodstream, and can cause an aggressive sexual behavior called bulling.[40] The affected steer attempts to sexually mount other steers, causing the victims severe muscle injuries and subsequent infections.[41]

The dust that is kicked up into the air causes widespread respiratory problems in feedlot cattle.[42] Two of every three animals dying on

> Broiler litter—the manure, bedding, and other waste from chicken facilities—is digestible by cattle and far cheaper than feed grains.

cattle feedlots succumb to respiratory diseases.[43] But unless cattle are dying in droves, feedlot owners aren't interested in determining the cause of death. When a steer dies on the feedlot, chances are less than one in five that the management will ask a veterinarian to determine what caused the death.[44]

After about two months at the feedlot, the animals are sent to the slaughterhouse where a swift but brutal death awaits.

Many of the facts detailed in this chapter were not easy to write about, and for most, they will not be easy to read. And yet, here is the truth, presented clearly and without exaggeration. It is not necessary to use overblown language to suggest that assembly-line killing of animals debases both the slaughtered and the slaughterers.

The killing business

The most noticeable feature of a chicken slaughterhouse is the shackle conveyer, which snakes from one end of the building to the other. Picture one of those automated conveyer belts at a dry-cleaner's, with chickens hanging from the line instead of shirts. Stand at a point on the line for one minute and up to two hundred chickens will glide past you to their deaths.

Chicken slaughter lines run at several thousand birds an hour.[1] Stunning, bleeding, and even feather-plucking is done mechanically, but people are still needed to put the birds into shackles. When birds are taken to a poultry plant, six or seven employees are responsible for hanging the birds onto the shackles.

Shacklers are predominantly women. The job causes all sorts of injuries. One internal memo circulated at a Perdue plant indicates that 60 percent of the plant's employees visit the company's nurse every morning for painkillers or to have bandages applied to their hands.[2]

To keep their jobs, the shacklers must work fast. Their main job requirement is to keep up with the line speed. Each shackler has from two to four seconds to lift a chicken, grasp its legs, and insert both feet in a shackle.[3] Although it may sound impossible to grab a chicken and shackle its legs every three seconds, shacklers are able to work at this rate.

Because of the rapid pace shacklers must maintain to keep their jobs, they have no time to give injured birds any special attention. Many of the chickens, fresh from transport, have broken bones or some other painful condition. A report in *World's Poultry Science Journal* acknowledges that any time taken to aid an injured bird would force the other shacklers to work even more quickly.[4] The report's researchers observed a shackling team for three days, and in all that time watching thousands of birds shackled, they never saw even one injured bird get a moment's special attention.[5] After slaughter, the researchers found that many of these birds had severe and painful injuries before shackling, "typified by green legs and/or visibly broken bones."[6]

The panicked cackling is silenced at the water bath.

Once shackled, the birds are pulled to slaughter. They do not go gently. They flap their wings and try to kick themselves from their shackles. A panicked cackling coming from all the birds is **silenced at the water bath**, which is intended to stun them before slaughter. The problem is that chicken producers are often reluctant to run enough electricity through these baths.[7] Higher stunning voltages markedly increase broken bones or cardiac arrest,[8] which can lead to downgraded carcasses and less revenue for the slaughterhouse. Even with a perfect stun, many birds regain consciousness before slaughter. In one study, the average hen could respond to a threat less than one minute after being stunned.[9] Some hens regain consciousness within half a minute.[10]

The killing blade is the next stop after the stun. It's all done mechanically, with the same blade cutting several thousand birds per hour. The bird is pulled into a tunnel, and, if he moves like most birds do, the neck will come in contact with the blade and a clean slash will be made through one of the bird's two carotid arteries.

The next stop on the line is a scald tank of boiling water. The dead birds are dropped into this boiling water to prepare for feather removal. But not all of the birds are dead when they're dropped into the boiling water. The cutting of the neck has an expected rate of failure. Sometimes the cutting tool misses, and in most cases it is not designed to cut both carotid arteries,[11] so some birds are still alive when they are dropped into boiling water. If the animal is alive, his skin turns to a reddish hue as he is boiled to death.[12]

Although few articles have been written about these "redskins," a study detailed in the *British Veterinary Journal* examined over a thousand chicken carcasses from a large slaughterhouse. The data suggests that one in five chickens were still alive when dropped into the scald tank.[13]

Down the line, the chickens' feet are trimmed off, and they are beheaded, eviscerated and packed whole or in pieces for wholesale merchandising. Within a very short time, the meat appears, neatly placed in plastic foam trays and covered with shiny plastic, in supermarket cases.

CATTLE SLAUGHTER

Cattle slaughter has become less brutal during the 1990s, thanks largely to the efforts of Animal Rights International's Henry Spira, who pressured slaughterhouses to adopt new equipment, and Temple Grandin, president of a slaughter equipment company that developed alternatives to the "shackle and hoist" method.

Through the 1980s, one common method of killing cattle involved shackling a rear leg and lifting the animal into the air before cutting its throat. Cattle are so heavy that they would often suffer breaking bones and popping ligaments prior to being slaughtered. This method is still used on about 4 percent of U.S. cattle, mainly to supply the market for kosher beef. Even though the ASPCA promotes a kosher slaughter pen that provides an alternative to shackle-and-hoist,[14] the method is still legal in the U.S. and continues in slaughterhouses that don't want to replace their equipment and retrain workers.

The new slaughter systems use a restrainer box that keeps the animal from thrashing around. If all goes perfectly, the animal will voluntarily place his head in the restrainer box, showing few signs of fear or excitement as his throat is cut and bleeding begins.[15]

Most cattle are stunned before slaughter. Unlike pig and chicken stunning, in which electricity or carbon dioxide may be used, cattle slaughterhouses typically use a "captive bolt" system. The animal, often in the restraining box, will be shot in the skull with a compressed-air gun. If the stunning equipment malfunctions, the animal may be shot repeatedly until a blow connects that knocks him out. As one slaughterhouse employee reported: "I was knocking—killing—cows. They run cattle through like a revolving chute, a restrainer, and the animals weren't being cleaned and the gun kept misfiring, so it bounced off most of the time. Instead of knocking them once, you had to knock them two or three times."[16]

Even when it goes right, the slaughter is tough to witness. Larry Gallagher, a writer who spent a month working in a slaughterhouse writes: "When a cow's head emerges into the light of the kill floor, it is greeted with a blast from the gun, which shoots a bolt of steel into its forehead, stunning it in a single mechanical blow. **'Stunned' is the appropriate word** to describe the expression on the animal's face: eyes and mouth frozen open, tongue sticking out, teeth biting into tongue—an expression which, were it human, would be asking 'How could it all come to this?' The pathos of that look catches me by surprise. I thought that a few weeks of gut-cutting had numbed my feelings. I know I am anthropomorphizing, but I still have to bite down on my own tongue to keep the tears from welling."[17]

Fear expressed by one animal during slaughter can be infectious. Temple Grandin writes: "If an animal becomes very agitated and frenzied during restraint, subsequent animals often become agitated. An entire slaughter day can turn into a continuous chain reaction of excited animals. The next day after the equipment has been washed, the animals will be calm. The excited animals may be smelling an alarm pheromone from the blood of severely stressed cattle. . . ." [18]

After the stunning, the throat is cut. The man with the knife is known as the sticker. He makes two cuts. The first cut just barely slashes the hide along the steer's neck. Then he reaches in with his fingers, exposes the jugular, and slits it open.[19] Steers are enormous animals and they bleed profusely. The animal takes several minutes to bleed to death, as over thirty pounds of blood pours from his throat.[20]

Amidst the sights of the kill floor, Gallagher recalls seeing "the unmistakable shape of a mammalian fetus moving down the conveyor belt. . . ."[21] As if it were so much intestine or spinal cord, the now lifeless fetus is dropped down the chute and trucked to the renderer.[22] Such sights are common when the market fluctuates—ranchers often send their pregnant cattle to slaughter when feed prices rise. During the 1996 Great Plains drought, feed prices rose enough to make it unprofitable to fatten cattle on grains. All across the plains states, ranchers started sending their herds to slaughter. The logic was to sell the cattle immediately, since every day feeding them newly expensive grain would add to the rancher's losses. In South Texas, 80 percent of the female cattle sent to slaughter were pregnant.[23]

WORKING AT A SLAUGHTERHOUSE

In some ways, the conditions cattle face at slaughter have improved during the 1990s. Conditions for slaughterhouse workers, however, have deteriorated. The consolidation of power in the beef industry has meant steadily more hazardous conditions to the people—mostly minorities[24]—who work in slaughterhouses. Every year, the "Big Three" slaughter companies gain greater control of the industry and either buy smaller packers or drive them out of business. Over 70 percent of cattle raised in the U.S. end up in slaughterhouses owned by ConAgra, Excel, or IBP.[25] These three companies also slaughter 34 percent of all U.S. pigs.[26]

As the Big Three companies strengthen their grip on the slaughter industry, they compete for the highest worker productivity. Increasing worker productivity is easy: it goes up every time line speeds are raised.[27] Steve Bjerklie, editor of *Meat and Poultry*, writes: "In the meat and poultry industry, the search for faster and better ways to slaughter and process meat and livestock is relentless, and has resulted in line (or "chain") speeds of unimaginable rapidity in packing houses. . . ."[28]

Foremen may prowl the lines looking for workers who aren't keeping up. One worker says: "They tell you, if you can't do it, I'll get somebody else who can."[29] Even the workers who manage to keep pace don't usually last long—turnover has been calculated at 12 percent per month.[30]

OCCUPATIONAL INJURY AND ILLNESS RATES

A comparison of meat and poultry workers to other U.S. manufacturing workers, 1980–1990, shows a high rate of injury and illness.

(number of injuries per 100 full-time workers)

Year	Meatpackers	Poultry Workers	Other Manufacturing Workers
1990	42.4	26.9	13.2
1989	35.1	22.8	13.1
1988	39.2	19.4	13.1
1987	38.4	19.0	11.9
1986	33.4	18.5	10.6
1985	30.4	18.3	10.4
1984	33.4	18.8	10.6
1983	31.4	18.7	10.0
1982	30.7	17.9	10.2
1981	32.8	19.3	11.5
1980	33.5	22.1	12.2

Source: U.S. Department of Labor, Bureau of Labor Statistics

Slaughterhouse workers have higher rates of **on-the-job injuries** than any other profession.[31] Today's meatpackers wear equipment from head to toe: hockey helmets, stainless steel aprons, forearm guards and metal gloves, leather weight-lifters' belts, and shin-guards for the legs.[32] Yet even all this equipment offers inadequate protection on the rushing slaughterhouse lines, which can convey 400 cattle or 1,000 pigs an hour.[33]

As meat-packing plants have steadily increased line speeds, worker injuries have surged. Authors Donald Stull and Michael Broadway have demonstrated how clear the connection is: "As injuries and illnesses rose throughout the 1980s, so too did packer productivity: by 21 percent between 1980 and 1986."[34] From 1979 to 1986, rates of repeated-trauma disorder among slaughterhouse workers rose nearly 300 percent.[35] Stull and Broadway write that "Packers readily admit that injuries cost them money—but the cost is a minor, and an acceptable, one."[36] Workers often come to work with chronic job-related injuries[37] and strain to keep up with the line speed. "They can write you up for any-thing," says one slaughterhouse worker, ". . . three times and you're gone."[38] And once you're gone, there is often no place to go. Slaugh-terhouse workers are among the poorest of the poor—in many cases, their income falls below the poverty line.[39] Meat-packing companies often recruit from immigrant communities, which offer a labor pool willing to perform hazardous work at low pay. Workers often cannot afford a proper diet, nor can they pay for proper medical treatment when they get sick or injured.[40] When the company does pay for medical costs, the workers are often forced to go to company doc-tors instead of a private physician.[41]

If they are hurt on the job and unable to work, slaughter-house workers and their families often have no financial safety net. Meat industry lobbyists have successfully persuaded many states to weaken worker compensation laws.[42] Kansas, for instance, has repeatedly enacted laws that limit financial settlements to workers suffering the most common slaughterhouse injuries.[43]

Safety laws to protect slaughterhouse workers are similarly lacking. In 1983, two employees died at a slaughterhouse owned by National Beef. They collapsed while breathing toxic fumes as they cleaned a blood storage tank. After investigating the fatali-ties, the federal Occupational Safety and Health Administration fined National Beef $960 and requested safety measures be added to the cleaning procedures. In 1991, three more workers died while attempting to scrub out the same tank.[44] In 1992, a worker at a California slaughterhouse got pulled into a grinder.[45] The same ac-cident occurred again in 1993, this time to an Alabama worker.[46]

The federal government charged one of the Big Three slaugh-terhouse companies with "willfully failing to record 1,038 job-related injuries and illnesses in 1985 and 1986."[47] Government prosecutors showed the company failed to report such major injuries as burns, head injuries, knife wounds, hernias, broken bones, and carpal-tunnel syndrome.[48] In 1991, the U.S. government fined another company 1.1 million dollars for "egregious violations of safety laws."[49]

Slaughterhouse
workers have
higher rates of
on-the-job
injuries than
any other
profession.

Why have slaughterhouse injury rates continued to rise? One answer is that, unlike manufactured goods, the size of animals can never be standardized. Cattle coming down a slaughterhouse line can vary by 300 pounds,[50] so there is no way to put in place standardized protective devices like those used in most assembly lines.

The constant stress endured by employees also has an effect on the welfare of the animals. A 1990 article in Meat & Poultry warns: "Good handling is extremely difficult if equipment is 'maxed out' all the time. It is impossible to have a good attitude toward cattle if employees have to constantly over-exert themselves, and thus transfer all that stress right down to the animals, just to keep up with the line."

George Eisman, a registered dietitian who promotes vegetarian eating and who has written about the horrors of slaughterhouse conditions for both the animals and the people, suggests: "A society that demands meat for its tables creates a group of people who are either miserable and hate their jobs, or are somewhat demented and dangerous because they like what they are doing. In either event we lose because we have an **alienated set of individuals** who are certainly not at peace with society."

> "We have an alienated set of individuals who are certainly not at peace with society."

LAWS THAT HELP AND LAWS THAT DON'T

The Europeans are ahead of the U.S. in legislating humane animal production. The United Kingdom has banned the veal crate[51] and by 1999 will also forbid keeping sows in farrowing crates.[52] In the European Community, the veal crate will likely be banned; a European Commission report recommends banning the crates by 2008.[53] The Swiss have outlawed battery cages since late 1991, and other European countries are showing similar inclinations.[54]

As Europe moves forward, the situation for U.S. farm animals is much less promising. The U.S. Animal Welfare Act protects animals from severe crowding, deliberate cruelty, and other abusive situations. Yet farm animals are **specifically excluded from protection** under the

Act.[55] The only federal laws covering farm animals apply to transportation and slaughter, not how they are raised. Most state laws covering animals on the farm are either minimal or nonexistent.

Federal law requires that animals must be given a rest period after 28 hours of transport, but only if the animals cross state lines. Vermont's transport laws are more stringent than any other state, yet it still allows animals to spend up to 18 hours in transport without water or food.[56] Many states allow animals to be shipped for up to 28 hours without water, food, or rest. And in the rare cases in which violators of state or federal transport laws are prosecuted, the fines average only about $500.[57]

The federal government does have a Humane Slaughter Act which, however, exempts all chickens. Additionally, the Humane Slaughter Act covers only federally inspected slaughterhouses. Chickens and animals in non-inspected slaughterhouses have only state laws to protect them. Twenty-three states have no humane slaughter laws on the books: Animals can be killed however the slaughterhouse management pleases.[58] Nine states even allow a sledgehammer to be used as the means of stunning before slaughter.[59] Breaking state slaughter laws—when they exist at all—brings only minor penalties. The penalty averages about $500 in most states and in some states there is no recommended fine at all.[60]

Attorney David Wolfson spent four years reviewing U.S. animal laws. It appears that agribusiness lobbyists won an unpublicized campaign to rid state law books of legislation protecting farm animals. Wolfson discovered that a variety of statutes have recently been amended to exempt farm animals from protection. Between 1986 and 1996, 17 states amended their cruelty laws.[61] The amendments all accomplished the same purpose: they exempted all routine livestock practices from cruelty statutes.

Today, 22 of 50 states do not allow cruelty prosecution when the condition in question is "accepted," "common," "customary," or "normal."[62] The issue has become not whether the act is cruel, but whether it is common. No matter how cruel the act may be, it will not

Farm animals are specifically excluded from protection under the federal Animal Welfare Act.

violate state cruelty laws so long as it is practiced widely. Says Wolfson: ". . . who decides what is considered an 'accepted,' 'common,' 'customary' or 'normal' practice? . . . The agribusiness community has been delegated the entire authority over what is, and is not, cruelty to animals in their care."[63]

Even when cruelty laws are violated, detection is difficult and prosecution sometimes impossible. In the United States, all factory farms are private property. People who suspect that a given operation is abusing animals may not be given access to the farm to investigate. Those who get into the farm and witness cruelty violations in progress often discover that local police are unwilling to file charges. Gene Bauston says, "There have been times at slaughterhouses where we've seen outrageous cruelty going on. We would call the police and ask them to address the problem. When the police arrived, they would threaten to charge *us* for trespassing, and at the same time turn their backs on what's happening at the facility."

The trend toward ever-weaker animal protection laws helps to explain the prevailing conditions in the American livestock industry—it explains why chickens have their beaks seared off, why bulls and pigs are castrated without anesthetic, and why most farm animals are housed in confinement and discomfort. U.S. livestock interests can put animals through all this without breaking a single law.

GENE BAUSTON TALKS ABOUT FARM ANIMALS

The evening of my visit to Farm Sanctuary, I had dinner with Gene Bauston, one of the founders of the farm, in his home. As we talk, Gene busies himself at the stove, cooking us a simple yet delicious dinner. I am awed by his presence—several people in the vegetarian movement tell me he's a genuine saint. Certainly, few people witness so much suffering with so much compassion as Gene. He has visited hundreds of stockyards and slaughterhouses, keeping himself receptive to each animal's pain. Each chicken with a deformed leg, each cow prodded onto the kill floor, each pig he sees castrated makes him wince.

"Going to these places is so painful, Erik," he says. "For every animal we rescue, I watch tens of thousands continue on down the line to the blade. And every year, with the corporate consolidation of this industry, the conditions the animals endure get worse."

He puts our meal on the table—an all-vegan meal which offers a stark contrast to the violence we have just been discussing. It is a simple but absolutely delicious dinner—pasta in a peppery tomato sauce topped with vegetables. I ask him, "In all that you see in these factory farms, what bothers you the most?"

"It's that with all these animals killed, none of these deaths need to happen. *Not one.* I mean, if people ate dinners like this, not one animal would ever go to slaughter. If the human body needed meat, milk and eggs to survive that would be one thing. But there's no need to eat animal products—and there's now so much evidence that vegan foods are the healthiest choice. So we're killing **eight billion animals** in the U.S. every year with no reason whatever.

"It's easy to say eight billion," Gene continues, "but it's impossible to grasp the enormity of the suffering. Eight billion means one animal raised under harsh conditions and then slaughtered, then a second animal, then a third animal, and on and on until you reach eight billion. And none of these animals suffers for any purpose.

"And yet, I'm hopeful. People are starting to realize that instead of eating a chicken's wing, they can eat any number of delicious vegan foods from burritos to rice dishes to potatoes. It doesn't take long before people actually start preferring vegan foods to what they grew up on. Despite all the suffering I see, I keep my hope. On every level—health, the environment, and the animals—people are starting to understand what a world of difference there is between a burger and a plate of spaghetti."

> "So we're killing eight billion animals in the U.S. every year with no reason whatever."

Beyond the dinner table

"Veganism is not passive
self-denial. On the contrary,
it instills active and
vibrant responsibility for
initiating social change by
presenting a constant
challenge to consistently
seek out the highest ideal."

— *J o a n n e   S t e p a n i a k*

C   H   A   P   T   E   R

The world's population is growing, and may expand to catastrophic proportions. Many who now inhabit the earth already live in marginal conditions, and some experts warn that we are depleting the resources needed to feed the added billions. A widespread shift to a vegan diet could help to offset current and future problems with world hunger.

World hunger

In Genesis 9:7, which describes the events after the Great Flood, God tells Noah and his sons: "Be fruitful, then, and increase in numbers; people the earth and rule over it."

From Old Testament times and beyond, the prevailing desire across many cultures has been to expand the human population and to establish dominion over the earth. And for much of history, there has appeared to be enough planet to go around. Many think we have reached a point, however, at which we need to limit human population.

Historians estimate that 2,000 years ago, just 250 million people inhabited the entire earth—fewer people than live in the United States today. And in spite of the fact that most societies maintained high birth rates, the world population faltered more than it flourished in the first thousand years after the birth of Christ. Although birth rates were high, death rates were even higher. Many babies died at birth, and many more people died before they reached childbearing age. The first millennium AD contained several centuries during which the world population actually declined. These declines were so substantial that by 1000 AD, the earth's population was 225 million. This shrinkage in population has been largely attributed not to declining birth rates but to a significant portion of people dying before they could become parents.

After the year 1000, however, the earth's population began to slowly increase. Between the years 1000 and 1800, the number of people on earth doubled every 385 years.[1] By 1800, the population had reached nearly one billion.

Then the Industrial Age arrived and with it came improved living conditions and advances in hygiene and disease control. As many nations around the world became industrialized, their mortality rates for babies and children dropped. In just a few decades, more babies than ever before in history were surviving to adulthood and having babies of their own. The practice of having as many children as possible contin-

WORLD POPULATION GROWTH SINCE 1800[3]

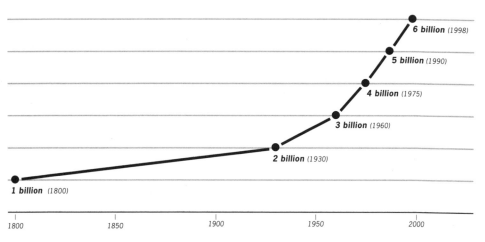

ued, however, without regard to the likelihood that most would grow into childbearing adults. As a result, earth's population hit two billion by 1930, three billion by 1960, four billion by 1975, and five billion by 1990.

As of this writing in 1997, 5.7 billion people inhabit the earth. In 1970, when the population growth rate reached its historical peak, the population was doubling at a rate of once every 34 years.[2] While the growth rate has since declined somewhat (the doubling period is now about 40 years), the world population still increases by *a quarter of a million people every day*.

P L A N E T   X

How much longer will the earth's population continue to grow? The best we can do is make an educated guess. Joel Cohen, the head of the Laboratory of Populations at Rockefeller University, writes: "Here is one of the best-kept secrets of demography: most professional demographers no longer believe they can predict precisely the future growth rate, size, composition and spatial distribution of populations."[4]

One reason population estimates are so uncertain is that no one really knows how future generations will behave. Even if you're predicting just 25 years ahead, you must estimate how many children today's newborns will have upon reaching adulthood. Projecting 50 years ahead means that you must predict the behavior of people whose parents are still unborn.

Nevertheless, virtually every population scientist agrees that our world's population will expand rapidly for **at least 30 more years**. The key to this prediction is the age distribution of the people now living on earth.

To understand why earth's population is almost guaranteed to increase, let's first imagine a simpler scenario on a world we'll call Planet X. Planet X has been colonized by one billion 20-year-olds, half men and half women, all capable of and desiring to produce children. To control population growth, these 20-year olds have agreed to have just two children per couple. Finally, we'll say that everybody on Planet X can expect to die between the ages of 61 and 79.

Here's what would happen. As soon as the 20-year-olds started having children—even though they had agreed to limit family size to two—the population would surge. Remember, Planet X has no older people to die off and balance the increase. By the time every couple had its two children, Planet X's population would have doubled. In an-

> Our world's population will expand rapidly for at least 30 more years.

other 20 or 30 years, assuming the next generation kept the same two-children-per-couple pact, the population would rise to three billion, where it would begin to stabilize as the people who began the story started to die at approximately the same rate that their great-grandchildren were being born.

Why talk about this imaginary place? Strange as it might seem, the current age proportions of the earth are not terribly different from Planet X. Right now, the world's population is massively weighted toward young people. Every third person on earth is under fifteen years old, while only one person in ten is over 60.[5] The average age of the current world population is just 28.[6] This concentration of young people world-wide means that, for at least the next 30 years, birth rates will almost certainly exceed death rates, even if today's parents were to have small families.

The United Nations calculates that if every couple in the world, from 1995 onward, stopped reproducing after the birth of their second child, today's world population of 5.7 billion would still climb to 7.8 billion by the year 2050.[7] The earth's population will level off only when today's mass of young people reaches old age and begins to die. Keep in mind that the U.N.'s calculations are based on a best-case scenario. The population is very likely to grow beyond 7.8 billion, since there is no concerted worldwide movement toward achieving the lowest birth rates in human history. Some researchers think—barring a vast political or social mandate—the number will be closer to 10 billion by the year 2050.

Joel Cohen sums up the issue: "Stopping a heavy truck and turning a large ocean liner both take time. Stopping population growth in noncoercive ways takes decades under the best of circumstances."

STUDYING THE EARTH'S RESOURCES

David Pimentel specializes in studying a very basic question: How many people can the earth support? Pimentel is a Cornell University professor of insect ecology and agricultural sciences. He has studied food and population issues since the late 1960s, and is the author of 19 books and over 450 scientific articles.

I asked Pimentel: "It's been over 25 years since Paul Ehrlich of Stanford University wrote *The Population Bomb.* So far, the book's most dire warnings have not come to pass. Can we therefore find some reason for optimism?"

"I think Professor Ehrlich was correct about the existence of a serious population problem," said Pimentel. "I have little doubt that his general warnings will be proven correct in the future, but I think he was wrong and in a sense misled the public in predicting that there was going to be a bomb or an explosion or a sudden crisis. That isn't the way that population dangers unfold. It's not like everything is fine one year and then you have worldwide famine the next.

"As the population expands," continued Pimentel, "each individual we add uses up a certain amount of resources. The negative effects of population growth don't happen all at once. Instead of a bomb or explosion, what we actually get is a gradual, insidious process."

Pimentel's work in population studies took a giant step forward in 1992 when he accepted an offer from Henry Kendall, a Nobel Prize-winning physicist, to join in a collaboration. Kendall's career has been especially colorful. One of the world's leading physicists, Kendall has also explored such unrelated fields as alternative energy sources and extinguishing oil well fires. Convinced that scientists have a special duty to ensure that their discoveries never be used for harm, Kendall co-founded the Union of Concerned Scientists and today serves as the group's chairman. All this activity has been a mere sideline to his job as an M.I.T. physics professor, where he teaches classes and publishes several of the field's most influential papers each year.

Kendall offered to collaborate with Pimentel to find out whether the world's food supply could keep pace with expected population growth. Although their analysis would be enormously complex, the structure of their paper would be very simple. After mentioning the current trends in population, they would analyze the earth's capacity to grow crops. They would base their analysis on the three main items that determine crop yields: farmland; water; and energy.

FARMLAND

The most obvious way to supply food for an expanding population is to cultivate additional land. So Kendall and Pimentel began their research by assessing how much land could still be converted to farmland. The findings were not encouraging. They wrote that, "Most of the unexploited land is either too steep, too wet, too dry, or too cold for agriculture."[8]

Kendall and Pimentel found that 30 percent of the earth's total landmass is frozen, desert, inaccessible, or otherwise unsuited for farming.[9] An additional 10 percent of the earth's surface has been taken over by humans for non-farm needs: houses, roads, industry, cities, etc.[10] **For every person added** to the U.S. population, another acre of land is devoted to housing, pavement, industrial or commercial use. Although people born in poorer countries use up less land than their American counterparts, the impact is still felt. Kendall and Pimentel calculated that if the world population expands by 2.5 billion by the year 2020, the world will have 1 billion fewer acres available for farmland.[11]

Even more alarming was the discovery of how much farmland is undergoing massive erosion. Topsoil is critical to farmers' ability to grow crops. Unfortunately, topsoil levels on much of the earth's farmland are currently in decline. Worldwide, topsoil is being eroded at rates 16 to 300 times faster than it can regenerate.[12] Kendall and Pimentel wrote that "Almost all arable land that is currently in crop production, especially marginal land, is highly susceptible to degradation."[13]

When erosion on farmland continues unchecked, so much topsoil can disappear that the land can no longer be used to grow crops. Much of the farmland around the world is on the brink of becoming useless to farmers. To prevent the most fragile farmlands from turning into desert, Kendall and Pimentel concluded that one-fourth of current farmland should be removed from cultivation.[14]

For every person added to the U.S. population, another acre of land is devoted to housing, pavement, industrial or commercial use.

Taking into account the above limitations, Kendall and Pimentel calculated that the earth's available farmland can increase by no more than a third.[15] This has troubling implications if the population doubles over the next 50 years.

W A T E R

Kendall and Pimentel next investigated the future supply of water. They found that vital water supplies, both in the U.S. and abroad, are in decline. One of the worst cases of depletion of an irreplaceable water supply is going on in our own country's central plains.

When settlers began farming the Plains States over a hundred years ago, what seemed like an endless supply of water lay beneath their feet. The Ogallala aquifer extended from South Dakota to Texas, stretching so wide and deep as to appear infinite. In his book on the Ogallala, John Opie reports that, "The original myth told of a grand underground river that swept down from the snowfields of the Rocky Mountains as far away as Canada."[16]

Soon after American farmers settled the midwest, scientists became aware that the Ogallala was not some inexhaustible river, but rather an underground fresh water lake, hundreds of feet deep, that had slowly built up over hundreds of thousands of years. The limits of nineteenth-century technology would have let the Ogallala's supply last practically forever. "If you sank a well and erected a windmill-driven pump," writes the noted water expert Marc Reisner, "you got enough for a family and a few head of stock."[17]

But the introduction of the diesel-powered centrifugal pump doomed the Ogallala. Delivering 800 gallons of water every minute, centrifugal pumps turned Ogallala's mosquito bites into ruptured arteries.[18] The farmers who used these pumps had no worries. Enough water existed to supply them for life, but many have treated the Ogallala as if they were draining the last keg at a fraternity party: drink as much and as quickly as possible or somebody else will drink it for you. Now they are extracting the last of her water, and most of the Ogallala will be lost to farmers within 40 years.

As Reisner notes, the Ogallala should have been handled like topsoil—considered a long-term resource to be conserved and passed from one generation to the next. Through planning, the Ogallala could have supplied farmers for hundreds of years, instead of just decades.[19] Instead, Reisner notes that U.S. farmers and policy makers handled the Ogallala like a coal mine: the object being to extract the water for cash crops as quickly as possible.[20] Stephen Reynolds, the chief of New Mexico's Water Administration, says: "We made a conscious decision to mine out our share of the Ogallala in a period of 25 to 40 years."[21] Reisner abstains from commenting on **how conscious a decision can be** that exhausts in 40 years a resource that took a half million years to accumulate.

When Kendall and Pimentel looked outside the U.S., they saw that the water situation is even more bleak. Irrigation vastly increases crop yields, but water shortages are making irrigation increasingly difficult in the world's main grain-growing regions. Major wheat and corn fields in China have seen ground water reserves fall over four meters per year.[22] Similar declines are underway in India and several other countries.[23] This sweeping depletion of worldwide water reserves has already reduced irrigated land per person by 6 percent since 1978.[24] Pimentel predicts this is only the beginning.

FOSSIL FUELS AND AGRICULTURE

Kendall and Pimentel next investigated petroleum. It may not be so obvious that petroleum is an essential factor in farming. I asked Professor Pimentel why petroleum supplies are so vital for food production.

"When I mention petroleum," Pimentel responded, "people usually think of cars and perhaps plastics or factories. What people don't realize is that in modern agriculture, petroleum has become as essential

How conscious can a decision be that exhausts in 40 years a resource that took a half million years to accumulate?

as soil and water. Petroleum-based fertilizers and pesticides are the main reason that the earth's eroding soils are still producing high yields. And on the most productive farmlands, diesel-powered machinery has taken over tilling, plowing, and even harvesting."

"Can you give me some examples to show how much fossil fuels are demanded by modern crops?"

"It takes about 140 gallons of oil equivalent to raise just one acre of corn," says Pimentel. "Some of the petroleum goes to run the tractors, some of it goes for the petroleum that goes into pesticides, and most of it goes into petroleum-based fertilizers. Most modern fertilizers, pesticides, and herbicides are produced from oil. This means that our crops are incredibly dependent upon oil supplies."

In his book *Food, Energy, and Society*, Pimentel found that a year's worth of food for one person in the U.S. requires 400 gallons of oil equivalents. Everything included, 17 percent of the nation's fossil fuel consumption goes to the food system.[25] Fossil fuels are also needed for essentially every step of Western food production: processing, packaging, distribution, cooking.

"So **from start to finish,**" says Pimentel, "we have based our food production system on petroleum and other energy sources that will continue to dwindle. Right now, modern agriculture's high yields come largely from cheap oil. When oil starts getting expensive, and it probably will between 2005 and 2015, we won't have the resources to heavily fertilize our soils."

> "From start to finish, we have based our food production system on petroleum—a commodity that will continue to dwindle."

TECHNOLOGY AND HUNGER

As we've seen, there are numerous constraints on increasing tomorrow's food supply. Some argue that we should rest easy because technology is improving farming methods and yields per acre. But there are diminishing returns in boosting yields, said Pimentel. "It will be very, very tough to dramatically improve crop yields in the coming years. The problem lies in our past success. For 50 years, food production per acre has gone up consistently. Today's wheat varieties produce four times more wheat per acre than varieties from the 1940s.[26] Any plant geneticist can rapidly improve a traditional variety of grain, but it's much harder to continue to improve plants that are already yielding several times more than their predecessors. As a result, we've seen the annual yield-per-acre improvements slip markedly over the past several years."

There's little evidence that crop yields can be boosted much more than they have been.

"You don't think there is still room for improvement?" I asked.

"Of course there is," he said, "but to break even in the next 25 years, we would need biotechnology to double our current yield per acre. **There's very little evidence** that such an improvement could happen. Americans have a real misconception about biotechnology, thinking that it will miraculously boost yields. Most of the new biotechnology crops don't yield substantially more than existing crops. Rather, their special traits involve resistance to pests or the production of crops that can be better harvested with machinery. While these advantages may improve yields a little, we're just not seeing biotechnology produce miracle grains that produce double or triple our current varieties."

"Let's assume you're mistaken on this point," I said. "Imagine for a moment that biotechnology will eventually double our yields of grains and potatoes."

"I don't think that will happen," said Pimentel, "but even if genetically engineered crops met our wildest hopes, it would not transcend our resource limitations. Higher-yielding crops require more water, which is becoming scarce in many agricultural areas. They require more fertilizer, which is about to get much more expensive. If the crops do not get this fertilizer, they take the nutrients from the soil, which reduces yields and eventually leads to desertification. High-yield seeds also require the money to purchase new technology, petrochemicals, and often new machinery—money which is not available to people slipping deeper into poverty."

I responded, "What you seem to be saying is that **biotechnology will benefit some people,** but it doesn't hold much promise for the hungry."

"Exactly," said Pimentel. "We consistently see biotechnology being introduced into wealthy areas with the best farmland. Often it's to grow specialty fruits and vegetables for large corporate farms that can afford to pay for extra fertilizers, machinery, and so forth. On the other hand, biotechnology-produced seeds are not being used by impoverished corn farmers occupying poor hill-lands in countries like Mexico."

HOW MANY PEOPLE CAN THE EARTH FEED?

It's clear that the earth can indeed support 6 billion people—albeit badly for a sizable minority—for now. But can the earth support 6 to 8 billion people for 50 or a hundred more years? Scientists use the term "carrying capacity," to reflect the amount of people a planet can theoretically support.

In a 1996 interview, Paul Ehrlich said, "By almost any standard, we are beyond carrying capacity now; but that doesn't mean we can't still go beyond that capacity for some time."[27]

I asked Pimentel how the human population could temporarily exceed the earth's true carrying capacity.

He responded: "We're accomplishing this by depleting oil reserves by using lots of petroleum-based fertilizers. We're switching to high-yield farming practices that often cause massive soil erosion. And we're drying up irreplaceable aquifers by irrigating vast amounts of cropland. By doing this, we're managing to feed growing numbers of people over the short term. But every year we do this, we are reducing the earth's capacity to support its population over the long term."

I then asked Professor Pimentel how many people the earth can support without depleting resources.

"There's no single answer," said Pimentel, "A lot of this relates to what standard of living we want to have."

"Well, suppose society took all the environmental steps you recommend. Suppose we cut fossil fuel use, adopted sustainable agriculture, and took care of other ecological issues. How many people could the earth support?"

Biotechnology will benefit some people, but it doesn't hold much promise for the hungry.

Pimentel responded, "Under those conditions of sustainability, I think we could support a maximum of 2 billion people over the long term."

Two billion people is barely more than one-third of today's population.

PLANT DIETS USE UP FEWER RESOURCES

Producing animal products uses staggering amounts of resources— resources that could easily be used to feed people.

There is a very bright ray of hope in the midst of these dismal predictions. Population control may be a near impossible task but Kendall and Pimentel determined that there exists an immediate way for people to greatly conserve world food supplies. They found that animal products use **staggering amounts of resources**—resources that could easily be used to feed people.

Kendall and Pimentel found that about 38 percent of the world's grain goes to feed livestock.[28] "In the United States, for example, this amounts to about 135 million tons per year of grain, of a total production of 312 million tons per year, sufficient to feed a population of 400 million on a vegetarian diet. If humans, especially in developed countries, moved toward more vegetable protein diets rather than their present diets, which are high in animal protein foods, a substantial amount of grain would become available for direct human consumption."[29]

The National Cattlemen's Association tells the public that it takes 4.5 pounds of grain to produce each pound of beef.[30] It would seem, however, that any rancher who used this ratio to formulate business decisions could face financial ruin. For their business plans, ranchers are supplied a different set of numbers by the beef trade press. *American Agriculturist* tells ranchers that "Feed conversion— or the pounds of feed required to convert to a pound of gain—varies in the literature from a low of four to a high of 30. Assuming a better efficiency than 10:1 is probably risky."[31] This waste of resources is more than doubled after slaughter: just 35 to 40 percent of a steer's body weight ends up as beef for human consumption.[32]

Vegans take a comparatively small bite out of the earth's scarce resources. According to Joel Cohen, vegans consume around 2500 calories of crop production each day, whereas people who eat 30 percent of their food as animal products require crop production of over 9,000 calories.[33]

How is it that the world's scarce grains go to feed farm animals instead of the world's hungry people? Here is what Joel Cohen had to say about the plight of the world's poor: "They cannot compete for grain with the cattle and chickens of the world's wealthy people. The extremely poor are irrelevant to international markets; they are economically invisible. But they are people nonetheless."[34]

If the entire world switched to a well-balanced vegan diet tomorrow, how many people could we expect to feed? "Right now, only 4 billion of the world's 5.6 billion people are adequately nourished," says Pimentel, "but if the entire world switched to a vegan diet, our current food production could properly nourish 7 billion people."[35]

That's not to suggest that if the entire world went vegan, everybody would automatically be properly fed. This is a point that confuses many vegetarian advocates, who often suggest that reducing meat consumption worldwide would in itself guarantee a reduction of world hunger. To get some insight into this frequently misunderstood issue, I contacted Dr. Carl Phillips of the University of Michigan School of Public Health. Phillips received his training in economics and policy analysis at Harvard's Kennedy School of Government, and has spent years looking into the connection between food choices and hunger.

Phillips strongly objects to the frequent assertions in pro-vegetarian literature that if we in the West reduced our meat consumption by a certain percent, enough grain would become available to eliminate starvation in Africa: "The whole idea that reducing meat consumption in the U.S. can prevent starvation overseas is really misleading. While eliminating meat consumption would make us a lot wealthier and thus perhaps more willing to give wealth to hungry Africans, it would not necessarily happen. Starvation is due to local shortages of wealth, not global shortages of food."

Ending or reducing meat consumption would not automatically end world hunger. Instead, doing so would **free up resources** that would give wealthier countries a greater choice in the matter. People and governments would still have to choose to use these freed-up resources to feed areas with shortages. It's with this sentiment—mixed with the fact that present trends are indeed alarming—that Kendall and Pimentel conclude their work:

> "If present food distribution patterns persist, the chance of bettering the lot of the majority of the world's peoples vanishes. The likelihood of a graceful and humane stabilization of world population vanishes as well. Fertility and population growth in numerous developing countries will then be forced downward by severe shortages of food, disease, and by other processes set in motion by shortages of vital resources and irreversible environmental damage."[36]

LOOKING BEYOND HUNGER

Let's turn back to Dr. Carl Phillips, who points out that ever since Thomas Malthus published *An Essay on the Principle of Population* in 1798, there has been round after round of predictions about global food shortages. Phillips says: "The irony about Malthusian predictions is that although they must eventually be correct (assuming the population continues to increase), they have been wrong every time so far, and for that reason are likely to be wrong in the 1990s as well. Each time the world hits the deadline for running out of food, some new technology—unforeseen during the last round of predictions—dramatically increases availability."

Phillips acknowledges the possibility of danger in the years ahead, but thinks that focusing on possible worldwide famine actually distracts attention from the true ecological benefits of plant-based diets: "Wasting resources is bad regardless of whether it leads to famine. Even without the threat of famine, to pump energy, land, and human effort through livestock uses up resources that could improve our lives in any number of ways."

Few decisions will influence life on earth in the coming generations more than the food and reproductive choices we all make today. In

Ending or reducing meat consumption would free up resources.

an ideal world, people might take stock of the current population issues and change their dietary and reproductive patterns accordingly. But this would be a world of robots, not people with individual needs and beliefs.

In his book *How Many People Can the Earth Support?* Joel Cohen puts this confusing matter into perspective with his characteristic insight:

"The fertility evolution represents a new step in human consciousness, a step that places humans in the forefront of all species that have ever lived on the earth. Changes in billions of beds and byways gave humans conscious control of their own fertility. Of course, not all humans have taken this forward step in consciousness."[37]

As out of our hands as the population issue may appear, it is in reality an issue that is completely determined by individual choices. It was once right and good for the majority of couples to have large families. Today, however, the situation has clearly changed.

As population pressures mount in the years ahead, we will doubtless witness a profound re-assessment of values regarding childbirth and food choices. In relatively recent history, for example, societies around the world have changed their code of what constitutes proper behavior regarding the environment. It's no longer socially tolerable to pour motor oil into storm drains, or to drive a vehicle that's belching huge clouds of smoke. We're probably going to see a similar redefinition of what constitutes responsible family planning and food choices.

For each of us today, this is a time of transition in which people need to decide how to handle this changing set of social priorities. Somewhere in this mix, it all comes down to **personal responsibility**. Clearly there is no "one-size-fits-all" approach. We cannot expect everyone to make identical decisions about family size or food choices, nor should we. In the future, there will probably be a redefinition of what constitutes responsible behavior. But for now, childbirth and food issues are still a matter of personal conscience. Perhaps humanity's main hope is that enough people will act according to their conscience on these issues, without waiting to see what the rest of society does.

It all comes down to personal responsibility.

Speaking out against the powerful National Cattle-men's Association requires courage. The associa-tion's lobbying influence, battery of lawyers, and deep-seated heritage of ruling America's range-land make it a formidable adversary. But Lynn Jacobs says it's time to set aside the Cattlemen's litany and understand the facts about cattle ranching's devastating effects on the environment.

American rangeland

Although surrounded by plants and animals, I find it's the air that first draws my attention. It carries a complex, sweet odor rising from the soil's rich upper layer—a litter of decomposing grasses, leaves, twigs, and flowers. Insects buzz around the nearby plants, and when I listen carefully I can hear several different pitches at once. Delicate, many-hued wildflowers flourish in the open areas between the scattered stands of shrubs and trees. Bushes shake as we pass and I see quail hopping inside. Lizards scurry out of our way, and rabbits bound ahead of us.

This is American rangeland, and it is not—as I had imagined it would be—dull and vacant. Instead, it's the kind of natural para-dise many people dream of visiting; yet except for a few backcountry hikers, most of us never see land so bountiful and unscarred.

I am nearly overwhelmed by the power of being radiating from this land. Lynn Jacobs, who has brought me here, senses my wonder and pauses while I drink it all in. Two hundred years ago, land this saturated with life stretched unbroken across what has become the western United States.

Lynn and I are standing in a small relic of the past, a patch of ungrazed "desert grassland" near Tucson, Arizona called Page Experimental Farm. Lynn, a leader in the movement to abolish ranching on public lands, tells me this is one the best places in the Tucson area to compare grazed land to ungrazed land.

"This square-mile enclosure has seen almost no grazing in the last half-century," he tells me. "Most people don't appreciate America's rangelands because they never see them in their natural state. The rangeland that forms our mental picture is a vampire's victim, regularly bled of life beyond the minimum needed for regeneration."

I say, "I always pictured Arizona as mainly desert."

"We only average about 14 inches of rain here each year," says Lynn, "but it's amazing how a complex ecosystem like this can thrive in almost desert dryness."

We walk on through the grass and bushes, serenaded by bird calls and the buzz of the insects. Thick bunchgrass sticks up in clusters. Lynn points out several different species of this plant. Now I can see a barbed wire fence up ahead. We clamber over it to arrive in a relative moonscape. We trudge a few yards in silence and I let my senses explore these very different surroundings.

PARADISE LOST

It's much quieter here. The sound of birds has been left behind. The sweet smell in the air has vanished, replaced by a flat, dusty odor. There are far fewer wildflowers, tall grasses, insects, or lizards. The bunchgrass clusters are about a third as frequent as those on the ungrazed side of the fence, and Lynn tells me there are about two-thirds fewer species here. Many of the clusters have been leveled, chomped almost to the roots.

The other main visible lifeforms are sparse forbs and knee-high shrubs, and a few scattered and stunted mesquite trees. Many of these plants are bad-tasting or poisonous to cattle, which helps them survive in an overgrazed landscape. **The desolation extends** to the horizon, and the few cows roaming it look as out of place to me as the truck-driving cows in a Far Side cartoon. What is left for them to eat? I think.

I point to a surviving weed and say, "Here's something that can live here."

"Yes, but that's not a native plant," says Lynn. "It's an exotic that originally came from Asia. These and other thorny or poisonous plants have taken over, since practically everything else gets eaten or trampled.

"But don't let this land fool you," he continues. "It has the same potential as the spot we just left. The only difference between this side of the fence and the other is that this land is grazed by cattle. Without cattle, this land would support the same amount and variety of life."

"Why do cows cause more harm than wild animals?" I ask. "After all, everything they eat goes back into the soil, doesn't it?"

"Not at all," says Lynn. "For one thing, the hundreds of pounds a cow gains while grazing represents thousands of pounds of consumed biomass that never gets returned to the land. The food is gone and the meat gets trucked away. For another thing, a cow eats far more biomass than almost any animal native to this area. Cattle are also far less selective about what they eat, and are capable of stripping the land of almost every kind of plant."

Lynn walks over to one of the many cow pies that dot the ground here. He kicks it, and it tumbles a few feet but does not break apart.

"See that?" he says. "Cow pies are vastly different from the feces left by wildlife. Animals native to these parts produce small, pellet-like feces that quickly break up and return to the soil, even under dry conditions. Cattle excrement is a moist, sludgy mass that hardens quickly in the sun and often doesn't break down for months or sometimes years. Paul Ehrlich, a prominent ecologist at Stanford, calls cow pies 'fecal pavement.' Whatever they cover up usually dies."

Further ahead, Lynn shows me a natural drainage in the land that has eroded into a yawning gully. Grazing causes this kind of erosion largely

The desolation extends to the horizon.

because there are fewer roots to anchor the soil during heavy rains.

As we walk back through the devastated rangeland, I comment again on the vast difference between this landscape and that of Page Experimental Farm. Lynn says, "Remember that everything we've seen today is public land."

PUBLIC LAND FOR PRIVATE USE

Federal public land is managed mainly by the Bureau of Land Management and the U.S. Forest Service, while state public land is administered by state land departments. Altogether, 306 million acres of public land is used for private ranching.[1] This is 41 percent of the land in eleven Western states, or 25 percent of the total acreage of the lower 48 states. Including private land, cattle graze about 70 percent of the West.[2]

"Do U.S. citizens want their public land devastated by cattle, or do they want it filled with diverse plant and animal life?"

"The grazing is relentless," says Lynn. "The range becomes more barren and eroded each year. The question I keep asking over and over is: Do U.S. citizens and taxpayers actually want their public land devastated by cattle, or do they want it to be as it should be, filled with **diverse plant and animal life**?"

Lynn Jacobs has many questions about the fate and future of public land in the American West. We sit in his living room that evening and talk about it.

The precedent for putting vast expanses of public rangeland under the control of one industry lies in frontier history, Lynn explains. "Back in the 1800s, ranchers bought land from the U.S. government for just a few dollars per acre. The government practically gave land away because settlement helped drive out Native American and Mexican powers. But the deal didn't end there. After buying a relatively small amount of land, a rancher often gained exclusive grazing privileges to thousands or even tens of thousands of federally-owned acres adjacent to his property.

"Today most grazing permits are technically up for renewal every ten years, but renewal is essentially automatic. Once a rancher obtains a permit, it's almost as though the public land becomes his property. So today, when a rancher boasts about 'his' 14,000-acre spread, he may actually own just 40 or 80 acres, while all the rest is public land that he is allowed to use."

An irony in the history of cattle ranching in the U.S. is that while the image of the grizzled, tough and self-reliant cowboy prevails, the ranch owners have been treated to generous government handouts. "The myth is at odds with reality," says Lynn. "Ranch owners are the original welfare kings. Every step of the way, the government has given them a free ride."

Writer James Michener arrived at a similar conclusion in his book *Centennial*. Michener mocks the early rancher's supposed independence: "All he wanted from Washington was the free use of public lands, high tariff on any meat coming from Australia and Argentina, the building and maintenance of public roads, the control of predators, the provision of free education, a good mail service with free delivery to the ranch gate, and a strong sheriff's department to arrest anyone who might think of intruding on the land. 'I want no interference from the government,' the rancher proclaimed, and he meant it."

Lynn continues, "In the century or so that has passed since those first ranchers arrived, the welfare has only gotten sweeter. This year [1997], the fee for grazing a steer on government land for a month is just $1.35.[3] Think about that: $1.35 to fatten an 800-pound steer for an entire month—that's less than what it costs to feed a house cat!"

"How do you respond," I ask, "to the National Cattlemen's Association's claim that 'Cattlemen pay a fair value for the public lands they use?'"[4]

"The fees are so low," says Jacobs, "that the entire federal grazing program costs the government much more money than it generates. None of this is any secret, by the way. A 1991 report by the U.S. General Accounting Office [a watchdog agency of the federal government] says that reformers still haven't made progress on issues they fought for in the 1930s." Lynn is right. The report criticizes the pricing structure, saying: "It does not achieve an objective of recovering reasonable program costs because it does not produce a fee that covers the government's cost to manage the grazing program."[5]

Lynn goes on to explain that cattlemen benefit from many other government supports and free services: "Low grazing fees are actually a relatively minor part of an overall system of welfare. The government pays for ranching roads, barbed wire fences, gates, cattle crossings. When ranchers complain that certain wildlife are threatening their cattle, the Animal Damage Control Bureau kills that wildlife.[6] And these are just a few examples."

THE LOSS OF WILDLIFE

"What do you think happened to the grizzly bear, the wolf, the antelope, and many of the other animals that once roamed the open land in the West?" asks Lynn. "They started to disappear over a century ago, when cattle ranching became widespread. We understand now how important it is to preserve our wildlife, but an elite handful of special interests keeps these species from repopulating. This suppression of wildlife is directly related to cattle ranching."

The invention of barbed wire in 1874 was a boon to the cattle ranchers who rapidly adopted it to fence in their herds. It was cheap, and easy to keep in reasonably good repair. Ranch hands could clamber over it while the cattle were completely stymied. Over the decades, miles and miles of this fencing were strung across the hills and plains. "By 1900 it criss-crossed and strangled most of the West," says Lynn.

Barbed wire is an effective barrier, not just for livestock but for wildlife as well. Certain large mammals cannot find a way through it, and animals that migrate over large areas may face starvation. Fenced from their winter feeding grounds, several species have experienced periodic die-offs. "Most people think barbed wire is just a way of keeping livestock enclosed," says Lynn, "without considering its role in facilitating destructive livestock grazing and its potential as a weapon against wildlife."

To many in the **cattle business**, most wild animals are enemies. The frontier cattlemen's war on sheep is still well known. At the same time—in a less obvious manner—cattle ranching has killed off vast numbers of elk, pronghorn, bighorn, and dozens of other species. "I've seen many places where entire landscapes have been stripped of nearly all edible vegetation," says Lynn. In cold areas, stockmen usually feed their livestock hay through the winter. Nearby wildlife sometimes starve during these cold months because the cattle have eaten so much of the edible forage during the summer and fall.

"Cattlemen have attacked any animal they thought competed with their cattle," Lynn says. The holes and tunnels made by prairie dogs cause trouble for cattle whose hooves can suddenly plunge into a hole, trapping them or causing broken bones. Ranchers have poisoned or shot tens of billions of prairie dogs in the last hundred years, and the killing continues today.[7]

"Wilderness biologists call prairie dogs a 'keystone species,'" Lynn tells me. "The metaphor refers to architecture, where the keystone at the top of an archway holds all the other stones in place. Take away the keystone and the arch collapses. As the prairie dog is killed off, hundreds of other animals woven into the ecosystem—hawks, mice, coyotes, bison—have all declined as well."

> To many in the cattle business, most wild animals are enemies.

WILDLIFE KILLED BY THE FEDERAL GOVERNMENT IN 1988[10]

The U.S. Animal Damage Control Bureau, which often acts in response to ranchers' complaints, regularly eradicates animals that are seen as threats to human activities. Perceived threats to cattle and sheep grazing public lands account for most of the kills. These numbers for 1988, the most recent available, have been identified by the bureau as typical of its activities.

Black Bear	275
Bobcat	1,158
Coyote	75,869
Gray Fox	669
Red Fox	4,057
Mountain Lion	192
Prairie Dog	124,292
Timber Wolf	53

The ranchers' war on wildlife has remained steady. For example, in the mid-1990s, ranchers have been key promoters of a California ballot initiative to remove protection for mountain lions.[8] In 1996, ranchers went to court in an unsuccessful attempt to keep wolves from being reintroduced into Yellowstone National Park.[9]

The federal government's wildlife killing program exists mostly for the benefit of cattle and sheep ranchers. The Animal Damage Control Bureau kills a wide range of wildlife, including birds, all at taxpayer expense. In 1994 the program called 1988's numbers, the most recent available, a "'snapshot' year" typical of the bureau's activities.

No record is kept of wild animals poisoned, shot, or trapped by ranchers. Lynn says ranchers undoubtedly kill far more than the government. Wildlife control is the main reason ranchers often carry guns on "their" public land. Richard Lessner, deputy editor of the *Arizona Republic*, sums it up:

"Although they love to dress up like Gabby Hayes, ranchers are businessmen, and like all businessmen, they want to maximize profits. If bears or lions take a few calves, that is an economic loss, one which is most easily avoided by killing the predator. But those are **my lions and bears**. They belong to the public just as surely as does the land. I object to the wholesale slaughter of the public's wildlife so that a few dozen ranchers can sustain an uneconomical 'lifestyle' that became an anachronism 50 years ago."[11]

THE MAKING OF AN ACTIVIST

In 1977, Lynn had just completed building a small adobe house in southwestern New Mexico. His family's new home, in the Gila National Forest, was adjacent to public land administered for grazing by the U.S. Forest Service. Lynn frequently took hikes with his dog Mishka on the public land. Each hike revealed another impact of cattle ranching. Several times, Lynn came upon dead cattle in streams—bloated, rotting, and polluting downstream water. Sometimes he found wild animals impaled on or entangled in barbed wire fences. The bodies of shot coyotes hung on fence posts where ranchers had put them as a warning for other coyotes to stay away.

> "Those are my lions and bears. I object to the wholesale slaughter of the public's wildlife."

Lynn began compiling a list of things he had seen, and then he began to think about all the other places in the West that are dominated by cattle ranching. He started to research the bigger picture. Through his studies, Lynn calculated that U.S. ranching requires a half million miles of fence and another half million miles of dirt ranching roads.[12] He found out that the federal government pays for most of this. He also learned that the U.S. government has paid for hundreds of thousands of water tanks built on public lands. The tanks encourage overgrazing, and although they are said to benefit wildlife as well as cattle, in reality wild animals do not approach very often. Cattle dominate the tanks, trampling the surroundings into a vegetation-scourged wasteland.[13]

Lynn had traveled extensively throughout the West for years and he had seen first-hand the condition of public lands in all of the western states. He added these observations to the list. He still didn't know what he would do with the list or the results of his research, but he was coming to the irrefutable conclusion that livestock ranching in the U.S. West results in destructive land-use practices.

Meanwhile, the ranchers he talked with seemed to see everything other than grass and cattle as valueless unless it could generate a profit.

One day he mentioned his concerns to a rancher's wife, who declared, "I believe **grass was put here** by the good Lord for us to raise livestock. If you don't graze this public land's grass, what are you going to do with it?"

Lynn answered, "Not much; I'd leave it mostly for wild animals and the rest of nature."

To which she replied, "Now, what are you going to *do* with all those wild animals?"

Two different ways of looking at the earth were colliding, and Lynn felt a need to speak out for what he believed was right. "I needed a way," says Lynn "to show the big picture to the general public."

In 1980, Lynn and his family moved to central Arizona, where

"I believe grass was put here by the good Lord for us to raise livestock."

they bought an acre on a creek and built a small house. As in New Mexico, their land was bordered by thousands of acres of federal land used for grazing. Lynn and his family had moved 500 miles, but the ranching destruction he encountered was the same as in New Mexico.

Lynn continued to investigate the deleterious effects of cattle ranching and to record more and more of his own observations. Turning to his pile of notes and literature, Lynn resolved to distill its hundreds of pages into something that would be concise and readable. He wrote up several years' worth of his rangeland observations, now in narrative form instead of as a list. The result was a hefty 48-page tabloid, which he titled "Free Our Public Lands!" It was illustrated, entertaining, and readable in one sitting. Best of all, Lynn had just inherited enough money to print 100,000 copies.

Lynn circulated the tabloid as widely as possible. He sent it to the media, to politicians and government officials, to friends, and to members of environmental and vegetarian organizations all over the country. The cost of mailing out the copies used up most of the rest of Lynn's inheritance. It took months to mail them out, but even before he was done, letters began arriving. People wanted to become involved in Lynn's fledgling effort to end public lands ranching.

Lynn soon became a player in the movement to abolish grazing on public lands. He was invited to speak to numerous groups throughout the Western states, advancing awareness of the need to stop public lands ranching. He made the people with the power— big ranchers and the congressional representatives who support them—nervous.

A DANGEROUS PATH

Some ranchers feel so threatened by change, they allude to violence against those they perceive as dangerous to them. In 1990, compelled by destructive overgrazing, Idaho District Ranger Don Oman sought a 10 percent reduction of cattle in the allotment he supervised. *The New York Times* quoted rancher Winslow Whitely as saying: "Either Oman is gone or he's going to have an accident. Myself and every other one of the permit holders would cut his throat if we could get him alone."[14]

Some range officers seeking to enforce the law on public lands in Idaho have felt uneasy in the last several years. In 1995, the Bureau of Land Management in Idaho began instructing rangers to never travel alone and to stay in frequent radio communication.[15] Meanwhile in Nevada, Michelle Barret of the BLM says, "There are some areas we won't go into anymore."[16]

Lynn Jacobs says he has suspected for some time that his presence was growing increasingly irksome to ranchers. While he and his family were still living in New Mexico, someone shot his dog Mishka and dumped the skinned body on the side of the road near Lynn's house. On two different occasions in Arizona, lug nuts on a wheel of his van appeared to have been loosened, causing the vehicle to suddenly veer from side to side. Both times, Lynn's children were riding with him.

After he released the tabloid, harassment took another form. In one week, a flood of requests for materials arrived; an editor for a ranching newspaper suggested readers inundate Lynn with information requests to deplete his resources.

PUTTING A CAUSE FIRST

Courtesy of Lynn Jacobs

Like many people in rural areas and small towns throughout the West, Lynn Jacobs makes his living with his hands. He might dig post holes for a few days, then find a two-week house painting job, then help a friend plant trees. Between jobs, he works around his own place, and spends time with friends, family, and nature. His greatest avocation, however, is environmental work.

Lynn has spent 20 years compiling information and writing about the destruction of Western rangeland by cattle. He was first able to reach the public with his discoveries in 1985, when a distant relative died and left him a modest inheritance. The money was completely unexpected. Lynn talked it over with his family and they agreed that he should use the windfall to publish his environmental work.

Lynn put his information into a thick tabloid that cost 15 cents each to print. But instead of attempting to sell the tabloids, Lynn mailed them free to as many people as he thought would pay attention. People did pay attention and Lynn became known as a key figure in the public lands abolition movement.

The tabloid was effective, but Lynn felt the need for a ►

◄ more substantial and lasting format for his environmental work. He set about writing a book and handled every task in the project, from research to copy editing and page-layout. He worked on a small, slow personal computer that could barely run his desktop publishing software.

For three years, Lynn—who loves the outdoors—worked on the book from eight to sixteen hours a day, six days a week. He spent so much time hunched over his computer, a disc in his spine became compressed, causing pains and numbness in his left arm. At last, *Waste of the West* was finished, a 600-page book that Lynn proceeded to publish himself. It has sold 5,000 copies so far.

Despite this, Lynn's work was gaining momentum. With his tabloid's success, environmental groups began funding Lynn's projects. The grants totaled less than half an Arizona teacher's salary, but these grants and continuing private donations allowed Lynn to devote much of his time to ranching issues.

While the "Free Our Public Lands!" tabloid publicized the effects of ranching, it only skimmed the surface. So Lynn began to write a book which gradually evolved into a kind of *War and Peace* of public lands ranching. Of course, as Lynn has said, "relative to the dimensions of the issue—hundreds of millions of acres of degraded land in the U.S. alone, even a book this size is small."

THE TRUTH ABOUT GRAZING

One of the most significant facts Lynn Jacobs has uncovered is how little grazing contributes to our country's beef supply. The National Cattlemen's Association promotes grazing as an efficient way to maximize food production: "Only through ruminant [four-stomach] grazing animals can we harvest food from most of the more than 800 million acres of range and pasture land in the U.S."[17]

This assertion is at once correct and deceptive. A more important question is: How much beef does rangeland produce? Lynn dug through countless documents looking for the answer and finally found a 1986 government report that states that federally owned land produces just 2 percent of the feed that is eaten by U.S. cattle.[18] And yet to obtain that 2 percent, 70 percent of the land in the West is exposed to destruction and depletion.

Similarly, ranchers are right when they contend that farming is more destructive than grazing. Grazing does cause less soil erosion than farming. But farm land is replenished with fertilizers, and grazing is done on land with far less topsoil that is therefore more seriously damaged by erosion. Also, farming produces much more food per acre than grazing (just one irrigated acre, for example, can produce nineteen tons of tomatoes per year).[19] As long as this country raises cattle for beef, it's better to nourish them with feed grown on Eastern farms than to turn them loose to ravage public lands in the west.

In 1991, public land grazing fees for the entire U.S. raised just under 30 million dollars.[20] Think of it: what the federal government charges for allowing 41 percent of land in the West to be grazed wouldn't buy even one fighter plane. The beneficiaries of this government bonanza are a relative handful of elite range ranchers. Research by *Fortune* magazine reveals that the nation's 28,700 livestock permits are controlled by **only 2.5 percent** of all American ranchers, and half of the permits go to just a quarter of a percent of all ranchers.[21] These permit holders pay one-quarter the price they would pay for comparable leases on private land.[22] It is no exaggeration to label this small group elite. All this has lead *Fortune* to editorialize: "Why shouldn't private citizens who are profiting from the use of public land—and possibly putting the resource in peril—at least pay a market rent? The answer is they should."[23]

> Public land grazing permits are held by only 2.5 percent of all American ranchers.

LYNN JACOBS'
WASTE OF THE WEST

Few people are more eloquent and earnest in defending the future of Western rangeland than Lynn Jacobs. These selected excerpts from *Waste of the West* ring with Lynn's voice and vision:

"You and I and all Americans are joint land owners. Together as 'the public' we own almost half of the land in the 11 Western States. . . . This public land encompasses an incredible amount and variety of country—some of the most diverse and beautiful in the world, including the Grand Canyon, Yellowstone, Death Valley, the slickrock country of southern Utah. Few other countries have so much land open to all people. . . . As collective public land owners, we have relied largely on various government agencies to implement our wishes for wise use and protection of the land. But our governments have not done, are not doing, and even refuse to do their job. In fact, with our government's help, a small sector of the business community has continuously manipulated and exploited public land for personal gain for more than 100 years. . . . Unfortunately, the most harmful land use in all history is also one of the most subtle and least recognized—livestock production. The seemingly benign act of raising livestock has caused more environmental damage than any other land use, not only in the western U.S., but throughout the world."

Lynn's statements cut to the heart of ranching mythology, and a deep and widely believed mythology it is. The Cattlemen's Association perennially publicizes claims such as: "Cattle production is compatible with, and in many cases essential to, sound and beneficial environmental stewardship."[24] "Crops raised for cattle production are not responsible for significant amounts of soil erosion."[25] "U.S. Cattlemen were the original ecologists and environmentalists before it was in vogue."[26]

Waste of the West counters the Cattlemen's claims of responsible stewardship with an exhaustive description of livestock ranching impacts. Lynn shows how fenced domesticated cattle wipe out wildlife. He devotes pages to describing how non-native grasses like cheatgrass move into grazed areas.[27] And he tells stories drawn from personal experience revealing the reckless disregard many cattlemen have for public land.

As Lynn continues educating the public, the movement to abolish public lands ranching is attracting unlikely supporters. The business community is now joining the movement to end special treatment for ranchers.

Lynn Jacobs has devoted most of his adult life to defending the

West's public land on behalf of its owners—the American people—and along with staunch opposition, he has found many willing and sympathetic listeners. He has shown people how to use factual arguments and the political process to influence change. It is possible, however, to support the preservation of western land, water, and natural fauna and flora without ever attending a meeting or writing a letter to your congressman, and that is by reducing the demand for beef. As more people make a personal decision to eliminate this resource-gobbling food from their diets, fewer acres of western land will be given over to cattle production.

When I met my first vegetarian in 1987, he told me he had not eaten meat for fourteen years. I looked at him as if he had managed to hold his breath the entire time. Today I know there is nothing rigorous or strange about eating a diet that excludes meat. For more than ten years now, I have lived happily and healthily on an all-plant diet.

Awakening

Like most Americans, I grew up eating an abundance of animal products. But I was raised to be vegan. Let me explain. My parents taught me to value my health, and to take care of my body so I would live a long, happy life. They taught me to try to live in balance with the environment. And they taught me that it was wrong to ever hurt an animal, especially without a compelling need. But as I moved into adolescence, I started to realize that the food my parents put on my plate did not square with the values they taught me.

When I was seventeen, I mentioned to a friend's mother that I was thinking of giving up meat. "Oh, no," said Mrs. Neumann, who "knew" about food because she had studied nutrition in college twenty years earlier. She told me in no uncertain terms that human beings definitely need meat to be healthy. She was so adamant in her warnings that I believed her, imagining vegetarians to be sickly and emaciated creatures. Still, while I went on eating hamburgers, I switched to canvas shoes because I knew that my health didn't depend on wearing leather.

During my freshman year in college, I encountered two things that finally convinced me to give up meat. The first was an image I stumbled across quite by accident. I was living in a dormitory, and the guys in the next room had a VCR and frequently rented movies. I dropped in on them one day while they were watching a movie that contained footage taken inside a slaughterhouse. The shot I saw was of a dying calf, looking right into the camera. I felt as if this animal, who was rapidly bleeding to death as the film rolled, were looking directly at me. I left the room deeply shaken.

Nevertheless, I ate a hamburger for dinner that night, and I continued eating meat for several more months. But at the same time, I was growing uneasy and even a little angry as I tried to reconcile the general thinking—that we need meat to be healthy—with the image I had seen of the calf in the slaughterhouse. I found **I wasn't very happy** with a world in which a healthy diet required that we brutalize animals.

A few months later, the second thing happened, and again, it sprang from popular culture. I was a big fan of the band, Boston, and had just bought a copy of their third album. Glancing through the liner notes, I found a paragraph that announced that Tom Scholz and others in the band were vegetarians and advised anyone interested in learning about vegetarianism to contact the Farm Animal Reform Movement (F.A.R.M., which these days can be reached by calling 1-888-FARM USA).

I couldn't believe it. Tom Scholz—over six feet tall and a powerhouse of energy on stage—was a *vegetarian*? Maybe Mrs. Neumann had her facts wrong. I remember just sitting and staring at nothing for about half an hour as I tried to sort things through.

I can't say the idea of changing my diet excited me. It sounded like work and also like I was going to have to join some weird club or cult. I didn't want to become a vegetarian—whatever that was. All I wanted to do was stop eating animals! And what exactly was I going to eat, I wondered? Iceberg lettuce and tofu?

I was almost 20, and my personal spiritual and philosophical convictions were forming. As I thought about how I wanted to live my life, I realized that one of my priorities was to cause as little suffering as possible. I realized that if I wanted to prevent more suffering than I created, I had to stop eating animals. I knew I could never directly harm an animal,

I wasn't happy
with a world
in which a
healthy diet
required that
we brutalize
animals.

so how could I allow one to bleed to death on my account? And yet that was exactly what I was doing—because it was culturally sanctioned and because I was uncertain about how to break a habit.

A 1995 article in *The Economist* put the point perfectly: "Few people would themselves keep a **hen in a shoe box** for her entire egg-laying life; but practically everyone will eat smartly packaged, 'farm fresh' eggs from battery hens."[1]

I sent Farm Animal Reform Movement a short letter requesting more information. The next week, a flyer arrived in my mailbox. It claimed that vegetarians could be as healthy as non-vegetarians, and that it really wasn't so hard to quit eating meat. The flyer reminded me of how many of my everyday foods were already vegetarian—things like bagels, vegetable soup, oatmeal mixed with fruit, and dozens more.

The F.A.R.M. flyer also contained information about the conditions under which most food animals are raised and killed. I began to own up to the reality behind the burger patties and chicken I ate regularly. I did a little math and saw that if I ate the standard American diet, I'd go through 2,000 chickens, seven cattle, and twelve pigs in my lifetime. Each of these animals would likely be raised in confined and inhumane conditions on factory farms and eventually be stunned, cut, and then bled to death. I decided that I didn't want to particate in that chain of events. I didn't want any action of mine to cause animal suffering.

My next realization was that it wasn't going to be enough to drop meat. Eggs and dairy products had to go, too, because anything but a total vegan diet still creates a great deal of suffering. If I ate just one egg every other day for 70 years, my egg consumption would require the slaughter of 30 chickens, since a chicken usually lays less than 500 eggs before being slaughtered and replaced with a younger bird. The time these birds would be cramped in cages to supply my eggs would total 35 years. Each single egg I ate would require a hen to live in a battery cage for about 30 hours.

I resolved to make vegetarian foods a bigger part of my meals, although I still ate meat occasionally, especially if I were travelling or

"Few people would keep a hen in a shoe box, but practically everyone will eat a 'farm fresh' egg."

having dinner at a friend's house. One thing I quickly realized was that my old meat-centered diet was pretty boring. As a non-vegetarian, I had spent my life eating the same foods day in and day out—hamburgers, chicken breasts, rice puddings, yogurt, pot pies. I didn't eat those foods because they tasted especially wonderful. I ate them because I was brought up eating them.

As I discovered the great variety of pastas, grains, vegetables, beans, sauces, fruit dishes, nuts, spices, and more that I could enjoy as a vegan, I was well on my way to giving up animal products altogether. I located some good natural foods groceries that had bulk food sections, fabulous locally-baked breads, and a variety of packaged vegetarian dinners—a boon for the busy student.

With time, even the occasional piece of chicken or fish became distasteful. I learned to bring food with me when I took a trip, and to patronize restaurants that offered a salad bar or good vegetarian menu options. I bought a stack of vegetarian cookbooks, and kept finding great new foods that I liked. The process of switching my diet had become exciting—and not at all what I expected. Instead of limiting my food choices, my meals became tastier and more varied than ever before.

Perhaps if I had focused my energy on what I was giving up, I would have felt hungry and deprived. Instead, I concentrated on expanding rather than contracting my diet—taking joy in finding new favorites rather than lamenting the losses. Becoming vegetarian requires not willpower but willingness—a willingness to try new foods.

Could life be worth living without cheese pizza?

As my diet became more vegetarian, I decided I was ready to begin the last step: breaking the milk and egg habits. Cutting out eggs was fairly easy for me. But the dairy—**could life be worth living** without cheese pizza?

Around this time, I moved into a new house, and I resolved to have an all-vegan kitchen: I would never bring any food into my house that wasn't vegan. However, I did allow myself to buy and eat a slice or two of pizza when I was downtown. I knew I'd never go back to the standard pizzeria after I invented my own "cashew cheese" pizza recipe. One non-vegetarian friend called it "the pizza that sounds like it would be horrible but tastes even better than cheese pizza." With the cashew pizza break-through, I had become exclusively vegan.

It had been two years since I first realized I wanted to change my diet. And it had been hard at first—because I had to give up a lot of foods I loved. To become a vegan, I had to say: no more ice cream, no more pancakes (I thought), no more pudding, no more cheese pizzas. But then vegan products began to appear, including desserts like "ice cream" cookie sandwiches, puddings, brownies, donuts. Vegan cookbooks started to show up and I found vegan recipes for all my favorite foods. Muffins, pancakes, cakes, and pies could all be made totally vegan.

Nowadays, as increasing numbers of people move toward vegetarian and vegan diets, dozens of companies have started to develop tasty and nutritious vegan foods. It's no longer uncharted territory, and every new vegan helps the natural foods market grow, making things easier for everyone else making the switch.

> The lack of worry about heart disease and cancer is invigorating in itself.

Although I originally became a vegan for ethical reasons, I have experienced a number of unexpected benefits.

I had gained over twenty pounds during my freshman year of college. But as a vegan, the extra weight came right off, and today I weigh exactly what I did when I graduated from high school. My general health also improved. I had always suffered frequent colds. Today, I get less than one cold a year, and they are much milder than before. I also used to get hay-fever attacks twice each year; they stopped as soon as I gave up dairy products. (Scientists have not yet adequately studied the connection between veganism and colds, but almost all the vegans I've spoken with tell me that their colds and allergies became less frequent and less severe after they stopped eating meat, eggs, and dairy products.) A year after I became a vegan, I had my cholesterol tested and it was 128. My worry about one day developing heart disease has been virtually erased. I also worry less about developing cancer or other diseases. The **lack of worry** is invigorating in itself.

Terry Shintani, who created the vegan weight-loss diet described in Chapter Three of this book, was 26 when he switched to a vegan diet. "I still believe it set the stage for an intellectual and spiritual awakening," he says.

Until he changed his diet, Shintani had earned mediocre grades. During his first year of law school, he complained to a friend about how he lacked the energy and motivation to put time into school.

"Of course you're doing poorly," said the friend, "look at what you're eating. Look at all the meat, milk, eggs and junk food you eat. How could you possibly perform to your potential?"

Shintani listened to his friend talk about the importance of diet. Although very skeptical, Shintani decided to give veganism a try:

"The transformation in me was astonishing, and happened almost overnight. I had more energy than ever before in my life, my thought processes became crystal clear, my grades improved and I published in the law review. I also (incidentally) lost 35 pounds in four months and felt better than ever before in my whole life."

Upon completing law school, Shintani realized that diet was so important that he wanted to become a medical doctor. In medical school, he was named outstanding first year medical student, and he maintained a 4.0 grade point average.

"I couldn't believe the change," says Shintani, "Going vegan made me feel as though I had lived my first 26 years in a fog. For the first time in my life, I tapped abilities I never even knew I had."

Is it reasonable to assume that the human brain—by far the most complicated biological organ—functions identically no matter how it is nourished? Is it logical that a diet of beef and chicken and ice cream will produce the same thoughts and emotions as a diet of fruits, vegetables, and whole grains?

Some people like to label vegetarians as sissies or freaks. I'll concede the point that it's possible to find strange vegetarians, just as it is easy to find strange people who follow any other diet. But what some hold as sissified is really the starting point of a new way of looking at the world. At the core of vegetarian philosophy is a concern for personal health, for the environment, for world hunger, and for animals. And it hinges on what veteran animal rights activist Henry Spira calls the "non-violent dinner table."

The Economist editorializes: "To see an animal in pain is enough, for most, to engage sympathy. When that happens, it is not a mistake: it is mankind's instinct for moral reasoning in action, an instinct that should be nurtured rather than mocked."[2]

History's list of famous vegetarians reads like a roll call of the greatest thinkers and gentlest souls civilization has yet produced—Leonardo Da Vinci, George Bernard Shaw, Isaac Bashevis Singer, Mahatma Gandhi, Leo Tolstoy, and dozens more. Society's best and brightest have been attracted to this diet for 2,000 years, even when society at large dismissed vegetarianism as dangerous or odd.

Today it's not just eminent people who follow a vegetarian diet. People of all ages and all walks of life are becoming vegetarian and vegan. Perhaps it's because people are better informed about health than ever before. Or perhaps we are gradually learning to value compassion.

The typical American diet puts us at war with animals, the environment, even our own bodies. Whatever one's reason for becoming vegan, it is at bottom **an act of compassion**, and compassion can become an act of deep transformation. If you are what you eat, switching your diet remarkably changes who you are. After becoming vegan, many people find their health improving over the months and years. Perhaps this improved health sets the stage for a spiritual awakening that often follows. This awakening may take years, but ultimately you are likely to find yourself a different being than the one you were before you changed your diet. This awakening is, I believe, open to anyone.

> Whatever one's reason for becoming vegan, it is at bottom an act of compassion.

There are few choices as vital as what to eat, and yet many people still don't make the connection between what they eat and what they believe. A person can become a teacher or social worker in order to make the world a better place, without considering that dining on animals three times a day is doing just the opposite. Other people plan fitness programs without first making the decision to keep their systems free from dietary cholesterol, saturated fat, and animal protein.

It was once mainly the greatest thinkers in history who weighed the consequences of their diet. Today, almost everyone has the resources to reconsider their food choices. It is an awakening whose time has come.

The New Four
Food Groups

The following is reprinted, with permission, from the "Vegetarian Starter Kit," produced by the Physicians Committee for Responsible Medicine.

Many of us grew up with the USDA's old Basic Four food groups, first introduced in 1956. The passage of time has seen an increase in our knowledge about the importance of fiber, the health risks of cholesterol and fats, and the disease-preventive power of many nutrients found exclusively in plant-based foods. We also have discovered that the plant kingdom provides excellent sources of the nutrients once only associated with meat and dairy products—namely, protein and calcium.

The USDA revised its recommendations with the Food Guide Pyramid, a food grouping plan that reduced the serving suggestions for animal products and vegetable fats. PCRM, determining that regular consumption of such foods—even in lower quantities—poses serious, unnecessary health risks, developed the New Four Food Groups in 1991. This no-cholesterol, low-fat plan supplies all of an average adult's daily nutritional requirements, including substantial amounts of fiber.

The major killers of Americans—heart disease, cancer, and stroke—have a dramatically lower incidence among people consuming primarily plant-based diets. Weight problems—a contributor to a host of health problems—can also be brought under control by following the New Four Food Group recommendations.

Try the New Four Food Groups and discover a healthier way to live!

VEGETABLES
3 or more servings a day

Vegetables are packed with nutrients; they provide vitamin C, beta-carotene, riboflavin, iron, calcium, fiber, and other nutrients. Dark green, leafy vegetables such as broccoli, collards, kale, mustard and turnip greens, chicory, or bok choy are especially good sources of these nutrients. Dark yellow and orange vegetables such as carrots, winter squash, sweet potatoes, and pumpkin provide extra beta-carotene. Include generous portions of a variety of vegetables in your diet. Serving size: 1 cup raw vegetables, ½ cup cooked vegetables.

WHOLE GRAINS
5 or more servings a day

This group includes bread, rice, pasta, hot or cold cereal, corn, millet, barley, bulgur, buckwheat groats, and tortillas. Build each of your meals around a hearty grain dish—grains are rich in fiber and other complex carbohydrates, as well as protein, B vitamins, and zinc. Serving size: ½ cup hot cereal, 1 ounce dry cereal, 1 slice bread.

FRUIT
3 or more servings a day

Fruits are rich in fiber, vitamin C, and beta-carotene. Be sure to include at least one serving each day of fruits that are high in vitamin C—citrus fruits, melons, and strawberries are all good choices. Choose whole fruit over fruit juices, which do not contain very much fiber. Serving size: 1 medium piece of fruit, ½ cup cooked fruit, 4 ounces juice.

LEGUMES
2 or more servings a day

Legumes—which is another name for beans, peas, and lentils—are all good sources of fiber, protein, iron, calcium, zinc, and B vitamins. This group also includes chickpeas, baked and refried beans, soy milk, tempeh, and texturized vegetable protein. Serving size: ½ cup cooked beans, 4 ounces tofu or tempeh, 8 ounces soy milk.

TO FIND OUT HOW TO RECEIVE A COPY OF THE VEGETARIAN STARTER KIT, an informative booklet on the whys and hows of adopting a vegetarian or vegan diet, CALL (202) 686 2210.

OR WRITE TO: Physicians Committee for Responsible Medicine; 5100 Wisconsin Ave. N.W.; Suite 404; Washington, D.C. 20016

Vitamin B$_{12}$
A Genuine But Simple Issue

(Abridged from the Physician's Committee for Responsible Medicine "Fact Sheet.")

There is one vitamin, called vitamin B$_{12}$, which does present a genuine nutritional issue, although one that is easily solved. B$_{12}$ is important for maintaining healthy blood and healthy nerves. The vitamin is not produced by plants or animals, but rather by bacteria and other one-celled organisms. The body needs only about 1 μg per day.* Since the body can store this vitamin, there is no need to have a daily source of B$_{12}$, but you should include B$_{12}$ at least every few days.

There have traditionally been vegetarian sources of vitamin B$_{12}$. Some evidence suggests that bacteria in the soil can contribute traces of B$_{12}$ to root vegetables, and Asian foods such as miso and tempeh are loaded with the vitamin, due to the bacteria used in their production. But improved hygiene, careful washing, and modern processing destroy the bacteria that make B$_{12}$. Spirulina, which is often sold at health food stores, is not a consistent source of true B$_{12}$.

Some packaged foods, particularly breakfast cereals, are enriched with B$_{12}$, as you will see on their labels. Nearly all common multivitamin tablets, from Flintstones to One-A-Day to Stress Tabs, also contain B$_{12}$. Health food stores carry vegetarian B$_{12}$ supplements, usually made from algae. Look for the words cobalamin or cyanocobalamin on the label, which are the chemical terms for vitamin B$_{12}$.

Deficiencies are quite rare, and you certainly should not include animal products in your diet to get B$_{12}$. But you do need to include a source of B$_{12}$ in your diet. A deficiency is usually manifested by anemia and neurological problems, such as weakness, tingling in the arms and legs, and a sore tongue. Some people experience digestive disturbances. Findings can be subtle. Medical evaluation is essential because problems with B$_{12}$ absorption—which is a digestive tract problem having nothing to do with the amount of the vitamin in your diet—are much more common than a dietary deficiency.

*Herbert V. Vitamin B$_{12}$: plant sources, requirements, and assay. American Journal of Clinical Nutrition 48 (1998):852 8.

Resources

VEGAN.COM

Vegan.com was established by Erik Marcus to promote vegan diets. Continually updated vegan news, resources, and recipes can be found on the World Wide Web at http://www.vegan.com. To learn more about Vegan.com's work, send a blank or very brief e-mail message using your e-mail account as the return address to: info@vegan.com.

To send a longer message to Vegan.com or Erik Marcus, please e-mail to: correspondence@vegan.com, or write to

> *Vegan.com*
> *P.O. Box 1933*
> *Cupertino, CA 95015-1933*

Please enclose an SASE if a reply is desired.

FARM SANCTUARY

For information on visiting, joining, becoming an intern, or attending seminars or events at Farm Sanctuary, call (607) 583-2225 (New York); (916) 865-4617 (California), or write to:

> *Farm Sanctuary—East*
> *P.O. Box 150*
> *Watkins Glen, NY 14891*

> *Farm Sanctuary—West*
> *P.O. Box 1065*
> *Orland, CA 95963*

OPENING YOUR HEART RESIDENTIAL RETREATS

Every year the Preventive Medicine Research Institute offers residential retreats led by health professionals who have collaborated with Dr. Dean Ornish in his work to reverse heart disease. For more information on the retreats, which are currently held in Oakland, California, call (800) 775-PMRI, ext. 21, or write to:

> *PMRI Residential Retreats*
> *900 Bridgeway, Suite One*
> *Sausalito, CA 94965.*

EATING WITH CONSCIENCE CAMPAIGN

Howard Lyman, director of the Eating with Conscience Campaign, Humane Society of the United States, is a national spokesperson for sustainable organic agriculture, family-run farms, and an all-plant diet. Lyman is available to speak to groups anywhere in the country. For more information call (301) 258-3051.

RECOMMENDED READING

Nutrition

Virginia Messina, M.P.H., R.D. and Mark Messina, Ph.D. *The Vegetarian Way*. Crown Trade Paperbacks, 1996.

Mark Messina, Ph.D. and Virginia Messina, M.P.H., R.D. *The Dietitian's Guide to Vegetarian Diets*. Aspen Publishers, 1996.

Suzanne Havala, M.S., R.D., F.A.D.A. *The Vegetarian Food Guide and Nutrition Counter*. Berkley Books, 1997.

Heart Disease

Dean Ornish M.D. *Dr. Dean Ornish's Program for Reversing Heart Disease: The Only System Scientifically Proven to Reverse Heart Disease without Drugs or Surgery*. Ballantine Books, 1990, 1996.

Weight Loss

Terry Shintani, M.D., J.D., M.P.H. *Eat More, Weigh Less™ Diet*. Halpax Publishing, 1993. (P.O. Box 2677, Kamuela, Hawaii 96743-2677)

Terry Shintani, M.D., J.D., M.P.H. *Eat More, Weigh Less™ Cookbook*. Halpax Publishing, 1995.

Dean Ornish M.D. *Eat More, Weigh Less: Dr. Dean Ornish's Life Choice Program for Losing Weight Safely While Eating Abundantly*. HarperCollins, 1993.

Population/Hunger

Joel E. Cohen. *How Many People Can the Earth Support?* W.W. Norton and Company, 1995.

David Pimentel, ed. *World Soil Erosion and Conservation*. Cambridge University Press, 1993.

Rangeland

Lynn Jacobs. *Waste of the West*. Lynn Jacobs, 1991. (P.O. Box 5784, Tucson, AZ 85703)

Ethics

George Eisman, R.D. with Anne Green, Ph.D. and Matt Ball, M.S. *The Most Noble Diet*. Diet Ethics, 1994. (3835 Route 414, Burdett, NY 14818)

Notes

Part One: To your health

CHAPTER ONE:
THE BEAT GOES ON

1. Roger R. Williams, "Diet, Genes, Early Heart Attacks, and High Blood Pressure," in *Nutrition in the '90s: Current Controversies and Analysis*, ed. Frank N. Kotsonis and Maureen A. Mackey (New York: Marcel Dekker, Inc., 1994), 25–44.

2. Ibid.

3. Hans Diehl, "Reversing Coronary Heart Disease," in *Western Diseases: Their Dietary Prevention and Reversibility*, ed. N. J. Temple and D. P. Burkitt (Totowa, N.J.: Humana Press, 1994), 237–316.

4. Ibid.

5. Jay N. Cohn and William B. Kannel, "Cardiovascular Medicine," in *Preventative Cardiology*, ed. James T. Willerson and Jay N. Cohn (New York: Churchill Livingstone, Inc., 1995), 1809–1827.

6. Diehl, "Reversing Coronary Heart Disease."

7. Peter Sleight, "Cardiovascular Risk Factors and the Effects of Intervention," *American Heart Journal* 121, no. 3 (1991): 990–995.

8. Hans U. Kloer, "Diet and Coronary Heart Disease," *Archives of Internal Medicine* 65 (1989): S13–S21.

9. Diehl, "Reversing Coronary Heart Disease."

10. Doralie L. Segal, "The Rationale for Controlling Dietary Lipids in the Prevention of Coronary Heart Disease," *Bulletin of PAHO* 24, no. 2 (1990): 197–209.

11. John C. LaRosa, "AHA Medical/Scientific Statement Special Report: The Cholesterol Facts: A Summary of the Evidence Relating Dietary Fats, Serum Cholesterol, and Coronary Heart Disease," *Circulation* 81, no. 5 (1990): 1721–1733.

12. Cohn and Kannel, "Cardiovascular Medicine."

13. Scott M. Grundy, "Cholesterol," in *Cardiovascular Medicine*, ed. James T. Willerson and Jay N. Cohn (New York: Churchill Livingstone, Inc., 1995), 1846–1865.

14. Diehl, "Reversing Coronary Heart Disease."

15. H. Kesteloot, "Dietary Fat and Health: The Epidemiological Evidence," *Acta Cardiologica* 44, no. 6 (1989): 446–448.

16. Kesteloot, "Dietary Fat."

17. Diehl, "Reversing Coronary Heart Disease."

18. Dean Ornish, *Dr. Dean Ornish's Program for Reversing Heart Disease* (New York: Ivy Books, 1990, 1996), 260.

19. Department of Health and Human Services; Department of Agriculture, *The Relationship Between Dietary Cholesterol and Blood Cholesterol and Human Health and Nutrition*, a report to the Congress pursuant to the Food Security Act of 1985 P.L. 99–198, Subtitle B, Section 1453. (Washington, D.C., 1987).

20. Ibid.

21. Herman A. Tyroler, "Nutrition and Coronary Heart Disease Epidemiology," in *Nutrition and Biotechnology in Heart Disease and Cancer*, ed. John B. Longenecker, David Kritchevsky, and Marc K. Drezner (New York: Plenum Press, 1995), 7–19; H. Kesteloot, "Nutrition and Health: The Conclusions of the B.I.R.N.H. Study," *Acta Cardiologica* 44, no. 2 (1989): 183–194; Segal, "Controlling Dietary Lipids;" Sleight, "Cardiovascular Risk Factors."

22. Department of Health and Human Services; Department of Agriculture, *The Relationship Between Dietary Cholesterol and Blood Cholesterol*.

23. Ibid.

24. Alberto Ascherio and Walter Willett, "New Directions in Dietary Studies of Coronary Heart Disease," *Journal of Nutrition* (1995) 125: 647S-655S; Walter Willett and Frank M. Sacks, "Chewing the Fat," *New England Journal of Medicine* 423: 121–123.

25. Department of Health and Human Services; Department of Agriculture, *The Relationship Between Dietary Cholesterol and Blood Cholesterol*

26. Kesteloot, "Dietary Fat."

27. W.F. Enos, R.H. Holmes, and J. Beyer, "Coronary Disease Among United States Soldiers Killed in Action in Korea," *Journal of the American Medical Association* 152 (1953): 1090–1993.

28. J. Judson McNamara et al., "Coronary Artery Disease in Combat Casualties in Vietnam," *Journal of the American Medical Association* 216, no. 7 (1971): 1185–1187.

29. Elizabeth J. Lipp, Donna Deane, and Nancy Trimble, "Cardiovascular Disease Risks in Adolescent Males," Applied Nursing Research 9, no. 3 (August 1996): 102–107.

30. Scott M. Grundy, "Lipids and Cardiovascular Disease," *Evaluation of Publicly Available Scientific Evidence Regarding Certain Nutrient-Disease Relationships*. Center for Food Safety and Applied Nutrition; Food and Drug Administration; Department of Health and Human Services Under FDA Contract No. 223-88-2124; Task Order #9. Washington, D.C.

31. K. Lance Gould et al., "Changes in Myocardial Perfusion Abnormalities by Positron Emission Tomography After Long-term, Intense Risk Factor Modification," *Journal of the American Medical Association* 274, no. 11 (1995): 894–901.

CHAPTER TWO:
CUTTING YOUR CANCER RISKS

1. R. Doll and R. Peto, "The Causes of Cancer: Quantitative Estimates of Avoidable Risks of Cancer in the United States Today," *Journal of the National Cancer Institute* 66 (1981): 1191–1208.

2. Walter C. Willett, "Who Is Susceptible to Cancers of the Breast, Colon, and Prostate?" *Annals of the New York Academy of Sciences* 768 (Sept. 30, 1995): 1–11.

3. Doll and Peto, "Causes of Cancer."

4. Walter C. Willett, "Diet and Health: What Should We Eat?" *Science* 264 (April 22, 1994): 532–537.

5. Willett, "Who Is Susceptible?"

6. Kurt Kleiner, "Vitamin Pill Fails to Fend Off Cancer," *New Scientist*, no. 2014 (Jan. 27, 1996): 4.

7. Ibid.

8. Cheryl L. Rock et al., "Update on the Biological Characteristics of the Antioxidant Micronutrients: Vitamin C, Vitamin E, and the Carotenoids," *Journal of the American Dietetic Association* 96 (July 1996): 693–702.

9. Ibid.

10. Mark Messina and Virginia Messina, *The Dietitian's Guide to Vegetarian Diets* (Port Townshend, Wash.: Aspen Publishers, 1996), 39.

11. R. L. Phillips and D. A. Snowdon, "Association of Meat and Coffee Use with Cancers of the Large

Bowel, Breast, and Prostate Among Seventh-Day Adventists: Preliminary Results," *Cancer Research* 43 (1983): 2403S–2408S.

12. Ibid.

13. M. Lipkin et al., "Seventh-Day Adventist Vegetarians have a Quiescent Proliferative Activity in Colonic Mucosa," *Cancer Letter* 26 (1985): 139–144.

14. B. S. Reddy and E. L. Wynder, "Large-Bowel Carcinogenesis: Fecal Constituents of Populations with Diverse Incidence Rates of Colon Cancer," *Journal of the National Cancer Institute* 50 (1973): 1437–1442; J. T. Korpela, "Fecal Free and Conjugated Bile Acids and Neutral Sterols in Vegetarians, Omnivores, and Patients with Colorectal Cancer," *Scandanavian Journal of Gastroenterology* 23 (1988): 277–283; A. van Faassen, "Bile Acids, Neutral Steroids, and Bacteria in Feces as Affected by a Mixed, a Lacto-Ovovegetarian, and a Vegan Diet," *American Journal of Clinical Nutrition* 46 (1987): 962–967.

15. J. R. Thornton, "High Colonic pH Promotes Colorectal Cancer," *Lancet*, no. 8229 (1981): 1081–1082.

16. G. J. Davies. "Bowel Function Measurements of Individuals with Different Eating Patterns," *Gut*, 27 (1986): 164–169.

17. G. A. Glober. "Bowel Transit Times and Stool Weight in Populations with Different Colon Cancer Risks," *Lancet* (1977): 110–111.

18. American Cancer Society. *Cancer Facts and Figures* (1984).

19. Antonio Trichopoulou, "Consumption of Olive Oil and Specific Food Groups in Relation to Breast Cancer Risk in Greece," *Journal of the National Cancer Institute* 87 (1995): 110–116.

20. A. Ronco et al., "Meat, Fat and Risk of Breast Cancer: A Case-Control Study from Uruguay," *International Journal of Cancer* 65 (Jan. 26, 1996): 328–331.

21. Patricia M. Madigan et al., "Premenopausal Breast Cancer Risk and Intake of Vegetables, Fruits, and Related Nutrients," *Journal of the National Cancer Institute* 88 (1996): 340–348.

22. Ibid.

23. Keiji Wakabayashi, "Food-Derived Mutagens and Carcinogens," *Cancer Research* 52 (April 1, 1992): 2092s–2098s.

24. H. P. Thiebaud, "Airborne Mutagens Produced by Frying Beef, Pork and a Soy-Based Food," *Food Chemical Toxicology* 33 (1995): 821–828.

25. Ibid.

26. B. Stavric, "Evaluation of Hamburgers and Hot Dogs for the Presence of Mutagens," *Food Chemical Toxicology* 33 (1995): 815–820.

27. M. Thorogood et al., "Risk of Death from Cancer and Ischaemic Heart Disease in Meat and Non-Meat Eaters," *British Medical Journal* 308 (1994): 1667–1671.

28. L. J. Kinlen et al., "A Proportionate Study of Cancer Mortality Among Members of a Vegetarian Society," *British Journal of Cancer* 48 (1983): 355–361.

29. J. Chang-Claude and R. Frentzel-Beyme, "Dietary Lifestyle Determinants of Mortality Among German Vegetarians," *International Journal of Epidemiology* 22 (1993): 228–236.

30. T. Hirayama, "Mortality in Japanese with Life-Styles Similar to Seventh-Day Adventists: Strategy for Risk Reduction by Life-Style Modification," *National Cancer Institute Monograph* 69 (1985): 143–153.

31. H. Halling and J. Carstensen, "Cancer Incidence Among a Group of Swedish Vegetarians," *Cancer Detection and Prevention* 7 (1984): abstract.

32. Marion Nestle et al., "Guidelines on Diet, Nutrition, and Cancer Prevention: Reducing the Risk of Cancer with Healthy Food Choices and Physical Activity." *CA—A Cancer Journal For Clinicians* 46, no. 6 (Nov./Dec. 1996): 325–341.

33. Ibid.

34. Personal communication, November 19, 1996.

C H A P T E R   T H R E E :
E A T   W E L L   T O   W E I G H   L E S S

1. Robert J. Kuczmarski et al., "Increasing Prevalence of Overweight Among U.S. Adults," *Journal of the American Medical Association* 272, no. 3 (July 20, 1994): 205–211.

2. A. White et al., *Health Survey for England 1991* (London: Her Majesty's Stationary Office, 1993).

3. Kuczmarski et al. "Increasing Prevalence of Overweight."

4. F. Xavier Pi-Sunyer, "Health Implications of Obesity," *American Journal of Clinical Nutrition* 53, no. 6 (June 1991) p. 1595S–1603S; F. Xavier Pi-Sunyer, "Medical Hazards of Obesity," *Annals of Internal Medicine* 119, no. 7, part 2 (Oct. 1993): 655–660.

5. Pi-Sunyer, "Health Implications of Obesity;" Pi-Sunyer, "Medical Hazards of Obesity."

6. L. Garfinkel, "Overweight and Cancer," *Annals of Internal Medicine* 103: 1034–6.

7. T. Van Itallie, "Health Implications of Overweight and Obesity in the United States," *Annals of Internal Medicine* 103: 983–988.

8. Martha M. Werler, Carol Louik, and Allen A. Mitchell, "Prepregnant Weight in Relation to Risk of Neural Tube Defects," *Journal of the American Medical Association* 275, no. 14 (April 10, 1996): 1089–1092.

9. Dean Ornish, *Eat More, Weigh Less* (New York: HarperCollins, 1993), 4.

10. Alan S. Levy and Alan W. Heaton, "Weight Control Practices of U.S. Adults Trying to Lose Weight," *Annals of Internal Medicine* 119, no. 7, part 2 (Oct. 1993): 661–666.

11. Ibid.

12. Ibid.

13. NIH Technology Assessment Conference Panel, "Methods for Voluntary Weight Loss and Control," *Annals of Internal Medicine* 119 (1993): 764–770; F. M. Kramer et al., "Long-Term Follow-Up of Behavioral Treatment for Obesity: Patterns of Weight Regain Among Men and Women," *International Journal of Obesity* 13 (1989): 123–136.

C H A P T E R   F O U R :
T H E   P E R F E C T   F O O D   I S N ' T

1. Henrietta Fleck, *Introduction to Nutrition*, 4th ed. (New York: Macmillan, 1981), 385.

2. Ibid.

3. Steve Carper, *Milk is Not for Every Body* (New York: Facts on File, 1995), 11.

4. R. K. Montgomery et al., "Lactose Intolerance and the Genetic Regulation of Intestinal phlorizin Hydrolase," *FASEB J* 5 (1991): 2824–2832; F. J. Simoons, "The geographic hypothesis and lactose malabsorption," *Dig Dis Sci*, 23 (1989): 963–980.

5. Carper, *Milk is Not for Every Body*, 1.

6. Gordon M. Wardlaw and Paul M. Insel. *Perspectives in Nutrition*. (St. Louis: Mosby, 1996), 535.

7. N. Mead, "Don't Drink Your Milk," *Natural Health* (July/Aug. 1994): 72.

8. (June, 1995) *Journal of the American Dietetic Association.* Volume 95, Number 6.

9. H.C. Gerstein, "Cow's Milk Exposure and Type I Diabetes Mellitus," *Diabetes Care* (1993) 17: 13–19.

10. (June, 1995) *Journal of the American Dietetic Association.* Volume 95, Number 6.

11. Osteoporosis Consensus Panel, "Osteoporosis," *Journal of the American Medical Association* 252 (1984): 799–802.

12. Eivind Gudmand-Hoyer, "The Clinical Significance of Disaccharide Maldigestion," *American Journal of Clinical Nutrition* (March 1994) Volume 59, Number 3, 735S.

13. Kimberly Knight, "Dairy Tales," *Essence* (May 1993) Volume 24, Number 1: 30.

CHAPTER FIVE:
HOW NOW, MAD COW

1. Alan McGregor, "WHO Coordinates Responses to New CJD Variant." *The Lancet* 347 (1996): 1036.

2. *BBC Horizon* (television program), Sunday and Monday, Nov. 18, 1996.

3. Paul Brown, et al. "Resistance of Scrapie Infectivity to Steam Autoclaving after Formaldehyde Fixation and Limited Survival after Ashing at 360C," *Journal of Infectious Diseases* 161 (1990): 467–472; S. F. Dealler and R. Lacey, "Transmissible Spongiform Encephalopathies," *Food Microbiology* 7 (1990): 253–279; T.A. Holt and J. Phillips, "Bovine Spongiform Encephalopathy," *British Medical Journal* 296 (1988): 1581–1582.

4. J. Gerald Collee, "A Dreadful Challenge," *The Lancet* 347 (1996): 917–918.

5. *BBC Horizon.*

6. Richard W. Lacey, *Mad Cow Disease: The History of BSE in Britain* (Jersey, Channel Islands: Cypsela Publications Limited, 1994).

7. Mark Caldwell, "Mad Cows and Wild Proteins," *Discover* (April 1991): 69–74; Daniel Pearl, "Beef Disaster in U.K. Raises Oversight Issues," *Wall Street Journal* (March 22, 1996).

8. *BBC Horizon.*

9. Lacey, *Mad Cow Disease*

10. Ibid.

11. Jeremy Cherfas, "Mad Cow Disease," *Science* 249 (1990): 1492–1493.

12. J.K. Kirkwood and A.A. Cunningham, "Epidemiological Observations on Spongiform Encephalopathies in Captive Wild Animals in the British Isles," *Veterinary Record* (September 24, 1994) : 296–304; "Mad Cows and Englishmen." *Economist* (March 30, 1996).

13. "Dangerous Food," *Oprah Winfrey Show,* Harpo Productions, April 16, 1996. (Livingston, N.J.: Burrelle's Information Services).

14. *BBC Horizon*

15. Paul Brown,"Beef Crisis," *Guardian* (March 26, 1996): 7; Luisa Dillner, "BSE Linked to New Variant of CJD in Humans," *British Journal of Medicine* (March 30, 1996); Victoria MacDonald, "CJD Study Casts Doubt on Link to Mad Cow Disease," *Sunday Telegraph* (March 31, 1996): 1.

16. John Collinge and Martin Rossor, "A New Variant of Prion Disease," *The Lancet* 347 (1996): 916–7; "The Link is Unproved, But No Better Explanation is Presently Forthcoming," *British Medical Journal*

(March 30, 1996); "Ten Deaths That May Tell a Shocking Tale," *New Scientist* (March 30, 1996)

17. *BBC Horizon.*

18. C. Arthur and L. Hunt., "Scientists Split Over Dangers of Beef-Eating," *Independent* (March 21, 1996): 2.

19. *BBC Horizon.*

20. William D. Hueston, Anita M. Bleem, and Kevin D. Walker, "Bovine Spongiform Encephalopathy," *Animal Health Insight* Fall 1992: 1–7; R.F. Marsh and R. A. Bessen, "Epidemiologic and Experimental Studies on Transmissible Mink Encephalopathy," *Developments in Biological Standardization* 80 (1993): 111–118; Department of Agriculture, Animal and Plant Health Inspection Service, "Qualitative Risk Assessment of BSE in the United States" (Fort Collins: Centers for Epidemiology and Animal Health, 1991).

21. Ibid.

22. "Apocalypse Cow: U.S. Denials Deepen Mad Cow Danger," *PR Watch* 3.1 (1996): 1–8.

23. Tara Gruzen, "U.S. Never Banned Suspect Feed," *Chicago Tribune,* (March 28, 1996): 19.

24. National Cattlemen's Association, "Questions and Answers About Bovine Spongiform Encephalopathy (BSE)," *Fact Sheet* (November 1996).

25. Ibid.

26. Ibid.

27. "BSE/Scrapie Group Share Research, Debate Feed Bans," *Food Chemical News* (July 5, 1993): 57–59.

28. "Mad Cow Disease Must Be Found in U.S. Cows in Low Levels." *Food Chemical News* (June 3, 1996).

29. D. J. Middleton and R. M. Barlow, "Failure to Transmit Bovine Spongiform Encephalopathy to Mice by Feeding Them with Extraneural Tissues of Affected Cattle.," *Veterinary Record* (May 29, 1993): 545–547.

30. Department of Agriculture, Animal and Plant Health Inspection Service, "Bovine Spongiform Encephalopathy: Implications for the United States" (Fort Collins: Centers for Epidemiology and Animal Health, 1993); M. E. Ensminger, *Beef Cattle Science* (Interstate Printers and Publishers, 1987; Associated Press,"U.S. Inspectors to Increase Testing for 'Mad Cow' Disease" (March 26, 1996).

31. "Hearing before the Subcommittee on Livestock of the Committee on Agriculture, House of Representatives, One Hundred Third Congress, Second Session on HR 559," September 28, 1994. (Washington: U.S. Government Printing Office, 1995).

32. D. J. Middleton, and R. M. Barlow, "Failure to Transmit Bovine Spongiform Encephalopathy."

33. Tam Garland, Nathan Bauer, and Murl Bailey, Jr. "Brain Emboli in the Lungs of Cattle After Stunning," *The Lancet* 348 (August 31, 1996): 610.

34. Joel Bleifuss, "Killer Beef," *In These Times* (May 31, 1993): 12–15.

Part Two: The truth about food animals

CHAPTER SIX:
RESCUED!

1. Bernard E. Rollin, "Animal Production and the New Social Ethic for Animals," *Food Animal Well Being: 1993 Conference Proceedings and Deliberations* (West Lafayette, Ind.: USDA and Purdue University Office of Agricultural Research Programs, 1993), 3–13.

CHAPTER SEVEN:
CHICKENS AND EGGS

1. Bernard E. Rollin, "Animal Production and the New Social Ethic for Animals," *Food Animal Well Being: 1993 Conference Proceedings and Deliberations* (West Lafayette, Ind.: USDA and Purdue University Office of Agricultural Research Program, 1993), 3–13.

2. Rollin, "Animal Production."

3. Rod Smith, "Eggmen Starting to Downsize Flock but Continued Reduction Still Needed," *Feedstuffs* 67, no. 21 (May 22, 1995): 33; Bureau of the Census, *1992 Census of Agriculture* (Washington, D.C.): Table 20.

4. Walter Jaksch, *Int. J. Stud. Anim. Prob.* 2 (1981): 4.

5. *California Poultry Letter,* Department of Avian Science, U.C. Davis (Davis, Cal., March, 1994): 7–8.

6. Ibid.

7. M. J. Gentle, "Pain in Birds," *Animal Welfare* 1, no. 4 (1992): 235–247.

8. Ibid.

9. Bernard E. Rollin, *Farm Animal Welfare: Social, Bioethical, and Research Issues.* (Ames, Iowa: Iowa State University Press, 1995), 119.

10. Joy Mench, "The Welfare of Poultry in Modern Production Systems," *CRC Critical Reviews in Poultry Biology* 4 (1992).

11. Andrew Fraser and D. M. Broom, *Farm Animal Behaviour and Welfare,* 3rd ed. (London: Bailliere Tindall, 1990), 370.

12. Mench, "Welfare of Poultry."

13. Ibid.

14. D. Bell, "The Egg Industry of California and the U.S.A. in the 1990s: A Survey of Systems," *World's Poultry Science Journal* 49, no. 1 (March 1993): 58–64.

15. David Fraser, "Assessing Animal Well Being: Common Sense, Uncommon Science," *Food Animal Well Being: 1993 Conference Proceedings and Deliberations* (West Lafayette, Ind.: USDA and Purdue University Office of Agricultural Research Papers, 1993), 41.

16. Ibid.

17. Allison A. Taylor and J. Frank Hurnik, "The Effect of Long-Term Housing in an Aviary and Battery Cages on the Physical Condition of Laying Hens: Body Weight, Feather Condition, Claw Length, Food Lesions, and Tibia Strength," *Poultry Science* 73, no. 2 (Feb. 1994): 272.

18. Ian Elliott, "McDonald's Libel Suit Continues in London," *Feedstuffs* (July 24, 1995): 17.

19. Chris Sigurdson "Perdue's 'Kinder, Gentler Chicken' Moves into Real World Test," *Feedstuffs* 67, no. 3 (Jan. 16, 1995): 47–48.

20. Ibid.

21. Gentle, "Pain in Birds."

22. Robert H. Brown, "Hot, Humid Weather Kills Millions of Poultry," *Feedstuffs* (July 24, 1995): 5.

23. Taylor and Hurnik, "Condition of Laying Hens," 270; R. J. Buhr and D.L. Cunningham, "Evaluation of Molt Induction to Body Weight Loss of Fifteen, Twenty, or Twenty-Five Percent by Feed Removal, Daily Limited, or Alternate-Day Feedings of a Molt Feed," *Poultry Science* 73, no. 10 (Oct. 1994): 1499–1510.

24. Buhr and Cunningham "Evaluation of Molt Induction."

25. *Journal of Applied Poultry Research* 1 (1992): 200–206

26. T. G. Knowles, "Handling and Transport of Spent Hens," *World's Poultry Science Journal* 50, no. 1 (March 1994): 60–61.

27. Knowles, "Spent Hens."

28. N. G. Gregory and L. J. Wilkins, "Broken Bones in Domestic Fowl: Handling and Processing Damage in End-of-Lay Battery Hens," *British Poultry Science* 30, no. 3 (Sept. 1989): 555–562; Knowles, "Spent Hens."

29. N. G. Gregory, "Pathology and Handling of Poultry at the Slaughterhouse," *World's Poultry Science Journal* 50, no. 1 (March 1994): 66–67.

30. Gregory and Wilkins, "Broken Bones."

31. *Feedstuffs,* October 24, 1994.

32. Bell, "Egg Industry."

33. Carol V. Gay, "Penn State Poultry Pointers: Building Better Bones," *Lancaster Farming* (July 18, 1992): C5

34. J. W. Deaton and F. N. Reece, "Temperature and Light and Broiler Growth," *Poultry Science* 49, no. 1 (Jan. 1970): 44–46; N. Acar, E. T. Moran, Jr., and D. R. Mulvaney, "Breast Muscle Development of Commercial Broilers from Hatching to Twelve Weeks of Age," *Poultry Science* 72, no. 2 (Feb. 1993): 317–325.

35. Deaton and Reece, "Temperature and Light;" H. Xin et al., "Feed and Water Consumption, Growth, and Mortality of Male Broilers," *Poultry Science* 73, no. 5 (May 1994): 616.

36. Acar, Moran, and Mulvaney, "Breast Muscle Development."

37. K. Boa-Amponsem et al., "Genotype, Feeding Regimen, and Diet Interactions in Meat Chickens, Part 3: General Fitness," *Poultry Science* 70, no. 4 (April 1991): 697–701.

38. Michael S. Lilburn, "Skeletal Growth of Commercial Poultry Species," *Poultry Science* 73, no. 6 (1994): 897–903.

39. S. C. Kestin et al., "Prevalence of Leg Weakness in Broiler Chickens and its Relationship with Genotype," *Veterinary Record* 131, no. 9 (Aug. 29, 1992): 190–194.

40. Ibid.

41. Xin et al., "Mortality of Male Broilers."

42. Boa-Amponsem et al., "Meat Chickens, Part 3."

43. F. E. Robinson et al., "The Relationship Between Body Weight and Reproductive Efficiency in Meat-Type Chickens," *Poultry Science* 72, no. 5 (May 1993): 912–922.

44. Robinson et al., "Body Weight and Reproductive Efficiency."

45. Boa-Amponsem et al., "Meat Chickens, Part 3."

46. Sarah Muirhead, "Conference Provides Latest on Feed Energy Values, Immunity, Fats," *Feedstuffs* (May 9, 1994): 12.

47. Ibid.

49. William A. Dudley-Cash, "Commercial Cage Rearing of Broilers Should Not be Ignored," *Feedstuffs* 67, no. 10 (March 6, 1995): 11,19.

50. R. T. Whyte, "Aerial Pollutants and the Health of Poultry Farmers," *World's Poultry Science Journal* 49, no. 2 (July 1993): 139–156.

51. J. R. Mulhausen et al., "Aspergillus and Other Human Respiratory Disease Agents in Turkey Confinement Houses," *American Industrial Hygiene Association Journal* 48 (1987): 894–899.

52. Whyte, "Aerial Pollutants."

53. Brown, "Hot, Humid Weather."

54. Xin et al., "Mortality of Male Broilers."

55. Ibid.

56. R. J. Julian et al., "The Relationship of Right Ventricular Hypertrophy, Right Ventricular Failure, and Ascites to Weight Gain in Broiler and Roaster Chickens," *Avian Diseases* 31, no. 1 (1987): 130–135.

57. M. A. Mitchell and P. J. Kettlewell, "Road Transportation of Broiler Chickens: Induction of Physiological Stress," *World's Poultry Science Journal* 50, no. 1 (March 1994): 57–59.

58. Mitchell and Kettlewell, "Transportation of Broiler Chickens."

59. Gregory, N.G. (March, 1994) "Pathology and Handling of Poultry at the Slaughterhouse," *World's Poultry Science Journal*. Volume 50, Number 1, p. 66–67.

60. Gregory, "Pathology and Handling of Poultry."

CHAPTER EIGHT:
PIGS

1. Scott Kilman, "Iowans Can Handle Pig Smells, But This is Something Else," *Wall Street Journal* (May 4, 1995).

2. C. M. Wathes and D. R. Charles, *Livestock Housing* (Oxon, United Kingdom: CAB International, 1994), 289.

3. Ray Herren, *The Science of Animal Agriculture* (Albany: Delmar Publishers, 1994), 182; Department of Agriculture, *Swine '95: Grower Finisher Part II: Reference of 1995 U.S. Grower/ Finisher Health & Management Practices* (Fort Collins, Colo., June, 1996): 8.

4. Colin Whittemore, *The Science and Practice of Pig Production* (Essex, England: Longman Scientific and Technical, 1993), 256.

5. D. S. Arey, "The Effect of Bedding on the Behaviour and Welfare of Pigs," *Animal Welfare* 2, no. 3 (1993): 235–246.

6. Whittemore, *Pig Production*, 256.

7. Ibid.

8. Bernard E. Rollin, "Animal Production and the New Social Ethic for Animals," in *Food Animal Well Being: 1993 Conference Proceedings and Deliberations* (West Lafayette, Ind.: USDA and Purdue University Office of Agricultural Research Papers), 3–13.

9. United States Department of Agriculture, *Highlights of the National Swine Survey*, (Fort Collins, Colo.: USDA Animal and Plant Inspection Service, March 1992), 1–2.

10. U.S. Department of Agriculture, Animal and Plant Health Inspection Service, National Animal Health Monitoring System, *Swine Slaughter Surveillance Project* (Fort Collins, Colo.), 1–2.

11. W. D. Morrison, R. R. Hacker, and J. H. Smith, "Dust in Hog Growing Facilities: A Research Update," *Highlights of Agricultural and Food Research in Ontario* 14, no. 2 (June 1991): 6–10.

12. John Pickrell, "Hazards in Confinement Housing: Gases and Dusts in Confined Animal Houses for Swine, Poultry, Horses and Humans," *Veterinary and Human Toxicology* 33, no. 1 (Feb. 1991): 32–39.

13. Ibid.

14. *Lancaster Farming* (April 24, 1993).

15. Morrison, Hacker, and Smith, "Dust in Hog Growing Facilities."

16. Per Jensen, "Observations on the Maternal Behaviour of Free-Ranging Domestic Pigs," *Applied Animal Behaviour Science* 16, no. 2 (Sept. 1986): 131–142.

17. P. A. Philips and D. Fraser, "Developments in Farrowing Housing for Sows and Litters," *Pig News and Information* 14, no. 1 (March 1993): 51N–55N.

18. William H. Friday et al., *Swine Farrowing Handbook* (Ames, Iowa: Midwest Plan Service, 1992), 5.

19. Philips and Fraser, "Developments in Farrowing Housing;" Whittemore, *Pig Production*, 249.

20. United States Department of Agriculture, *National Swine Survey*, 1–2.

21. Philips and Fraser, "Developments in Farrowing Housing."

22. Friday et al., *Swine Farrowing Handbook*, 4.

23. Whittemore, *Pig Production*, 151.

24. E. S. E. Hafez and J. P. Signoret, "The Behavior of Swine," in *The Behavior of Domestic Animals*, ed. E. S. E. Hafez (London: Bailliere Tindall, 1969), 349–390.

25. Whittemore, *Pig Production*, 249.

26. Dale S. Arey, "The Welfare of Pigs in Confined and Non-Confined Farrowing Systems," *Pig News and Information* 14, no. 2 (June 1993): 81N–84N.

27. G. J. Noonan et al., "Behavioural Observations of Piglets Undergoing Tail Docking, Teeth Clipping and Ear Notching," *Applied Animal Behaviour Science* 39, nos. 3–4 (March 1994): 203–213.

28. Ibid.

29. R. G. White, et al., "Vocalization and Physiological Response of Pigs During Castration With or Without a Local Anesthetic," *Journal of Animal Science* 73, no. 2 (Feb. 1995): 381–386.

30. Bob Ridgen, *The Economics of Pig Production* (Ipswich, U. K.: Farming Press Books, 1993), 515.

31. Ibid.

32. "Crowding Pigs Pays—If It's Managed Properly," *National Hog Farmer* (Nov 15, 1993): 62.

33. Whittemore, *Pig Production*, 256.

34. Noonan et al., "Behavioural Observations of Piglets."

35. Whittemore, *Pig Production*, 257.

36. Ibid., 145.

37. Ibid.

38. Ibid.

39. Ibid.

40. Ibid., 153.

41. Ibid., 152.

42. Ibid.

43. Ibid.

44. Ibid.

45. U.S. Department of Agriculture, *Swine Slaughter Surveillance Project*, 1–2.

46. Kenneth B. Kephart, "Pork Prose," *Lancaster Farming* (Oct. 27, 1995): D14, D16.

47. Ibid.

CHAPTER NINE:
MILK AND BEEF

1. James R. Gillespie, *Modern Livestock and Poultry Production*, 5th ed. (Albany: Delmar Publishers, 1997), 709.

2. Exact numbers are: 602,093 U.S. dairies in 1950; 277,762 in 1982; 202,068 in 1990, and 155,339 in 1992. Bureau of the Census. *1992 Census of Agriculture*, Table 01.

3. Eleanor Jacobs, "A Future for Northeast Dairy?" *American Agriculturist* 192, no. 10 (Oct. 1995): 6–7.

4. N. Bruce Haynes, *Keeping Livestock Healthy: A Veterinary Guide to Horses, Cattle, Goats, and Sheep* (Pownal, Vt.: Storey Communications, 1994), 146.

5. Ibid.

6. Ibid., 147.

7. Gillespie, *Modern Livestock*, 710.

8. Ray Herren, *The Science of Animal Agriculture* (Albany: Delmar Publishers, 1994), 64.

9. "Ketosis: The Disease of High Producers," *Dairy Today* (Jan., 1993): 30.

10. T. C. White et al., "Clinical Mastitis in Cows Treated with Somctribovc (Recombinant Bovine Somatotropin) and its Relationship to Milk Yield," *Journal of Dairy Science* 77 (1994): 2249–2260.

11. Haynes, *Keeping Livestock Healthy*, 145.

12. Paula Mohr, "Flame Away Dirty Udders," *Dairy Today*, Sept. 1994, 24.

13. U.S. Department of Agriculture, Animal and Plant Health Inspection Service, *Dairy Herd Management Practices Focusing on Preweaned Heifers* (Fort Collins, Colo., July 1993), 10.

14. Ibid.

15. U.S. Department of Agriculture, Animal and Plant Health Inspection Service, *Dairy Heifer Morbidity, Mortality, and Health Management Focusing on Preweaned Heifers* (Fort Collins, Colo., Feb. 1994), 16.

16. Ibid.

17. Ibid., 15.

18. Ibid.

19. USDA, *Dairy Herd Management*, 35.

20. Philip L. Altman and Dorothy S. Dittmer, *Biology Data Book*, 2nd ed., vol. 1 (Bethesda, Md.: Federation of American Societies for Experimental Biology, 1972), 229; Gene Bauston, personal communication.

21. U.S. Department of Agriculture, Animal and Plant Health Inspection Service, *Reference of 1996 Dairy Management Practices, Part I*. USDA, (Fort Collins, Colo., May, 1996), p. 8.

22. Ibid., 33.

23. Jim Doherty, "The Cattle Ranch that Doubles as a School for Doers," *Smithsonian* 26, no. 1 (April 1995): 115.

24. U.S. Department of Agriculture, Animal and Plant Health Inspection Service, *Cattle on Feed Evaluation, Part 1: Feedlot Management Practices*, (Fort Collins, Colo. Jan. 1995), 8.

25. U.S. Department of Agriculture, Animal and Plant Health Inspection Service, *Operations to Improve Calving Management on Beef Cow/Calf Operations* (flyer) (Fort Collins, Colo., March 1994).

26. Ibid.

27. Gillespie, *Modern Livestock*, 303.

28. Ibid., 302.

29. Vivion Tarrant and Temple Grandin, (1993) "Cattle Transport," in *Livestock Handling and Transport*, ed. Temple Grandin (Oxon, U.K.: CAB International, 1993), 109–126.

30. Ibid.

31. Temple Grandin, "Introduction: Management and Economic Factors of Handling and Transport," in *Livestock Handling and Transport*, ed. Temple Grandin (Oxon, U.K.: CAB International, 1993), 1–9.

32. Ibid.

33. Ibid.

34. USDA, *Cattle on Feed Evaluation*, 8.

35. F. M. Pate, W. F. Brown, and A. C. Hammond, "Value of Feather Meal in a Molasses-Based Liquid Supplement Fed to Yearling Cattle Consuming a Forage Diet," *Journal of Animal Science* 73, no. 10 (Oct. 1995): 2865–2872.

36. David D. Kee et al., "Research Stocker Systems: An Economic Evaluation of Parasite Control, Stocking Rate, and Broiler Litter/Grain Supplementation for Stockers on Bermudagrass," *Journal of Production Agriculture* 8, no. 3 (1995): 329–334.

37. Ellis W. Brunton, "Animal Waste Management: An Industry Perspective," *National Livestock, Poultry, and Aquaculture Waste Management: Proceedings of the National Workshop, 29–31 July 1991* (St. Joseph, Mich.: American Society of Agricultural Engineers, 1992), 23–27.

38. David D. Kee, et al., "Research Stocker Systems;" T. A. McCaskey et al., "Feed Value of Broiler Litter for Stocker Cattle," *Highlights of Agricultural Research* 41, no. 2 (summer 1994): 12.

39. Floyd B. Hoelting and Paul M. Walker, "Illinois State University to Recycle Dining Center Food and Paper Wastes into Cattle Feed," *Bioscience Technology* 49, no. 1 (1994): 89–92.

40. T. A. Edwards, "Buller Syndrome: What's Behind This Abnormal Sexual Behavior?" *Large Animal Veterinarian* 50, no. 4 (July/Aug. 1995): 6–7.

41. Ibid.

42. U.S. Department of Agriculture, Animal and Plant Health Inspection Service, *Environmental Monitoring by Feedlots* (Fort Collins, Colo., Jan. 1995), 2.

43. U.S. Department of Agriculture, Animal and Plant Health Inspection Service, *Cattle Death Rates in Small Feedlots* (Fort Collins, Colo., May 1994), 2.

44. USDA, *Cattle on Feed Evaluation*, 16.

CHAPTER TEN:
THE KILLING BUSINESS

1. Steve Bjerklie, "On the Horns of a Dilemma," in *Any Way You Cut It: Meat Processing and Small-Town America*, ed. Donald D. Stull, Michael J. Broadway, and David Griffith (Lawrence: University Press of Kansas, 1995), 41–60.

2. Michael J. Broadway, "From City to Countryside," in *Any Way You Cut It: Meat Processing and Small-Town America*, ed. Donald D. Stull, Michael J. Broadway, and David Griffith (Lawrence: University Press of Kansas, 1995), 17–40.

3. J. M. Sparrey and P. J. Kettlewell, "Shackling of Poultry: Is It a Welfare Problem?" *World's Poultry Science Journal* 50, no. 2 (July 1994): 167–176.

4. Ibid.

5. Ibid.

6. Ibid.

7. N. G. Gregory et al., "Broken Bones in Domestic Fowls: Effect of Husbandry System and Stunning Method in End-of-Lay Hens," *British Poultry Science* 31, no. 1 (1990): 59–69.

8. Ibid; N. G. Gregory and S. B. Wotton, "Effect of Electrical Stunning Current on the Duration of Insensibility in Hens," *British Poultry Science* 35, no. 3 (July 1994): 463–465.

9. Ibid.

10. Ibid.

11. N. G. Gregory, "Stunning and Slaughter," in *Processing of Poultry*, ed. G. C. Mead (New York: Elsevier Applied Science, 1989), 31–63.

12. G. B. S. Heath et al., "Further Observations on the Slaughter of Poultry," *British Veterinary Journal* 139, no. 4 (1983): 285–290.

13. Ibid.

14. Temple Grandin, "Handling and Welfare of Livestock in Slaughter Plants," in *Livestock Handling and Transport,* ed. Temple Grandin (Oxon, U.K.: CAB International, 1993), 289–311.

15. Ibid.

16. Donald D. Stull and Michael J. Broadway, "Killing Them Softly," in *Any Way You Cut It: Meat Processing and Small-Town America,* ed. Donald D. Stull, Michael J. Broadway, and David Griffith (Lawrence: University Press of Kansas, 1995), 61–83.

17. Larry Gallagher, "The Killing Floor," *Details,* March 1996, 152–157, 209.

18. Grandin, "Livestock in Slaughter Plants."

19. Gallagher, "The Killing Floor."

20. Blood loss is calculated based on the total blood volume for each pound of cow, as determined by Reynolds (57 cc's blood per kilogram bodyweight). The slaughtered steer in our example weighs 1200 pounds. The accepted livestock calculation maintains that half the total blood pours from the animal during slaughter, with the rest remaining in the animal's flesh and organs; Monica Reynolds, "Plasma and Blood Volume in the Cow Using the T-1824 Hematocrit Method," *American Journal of Physiology* 173 (1953): 421–427.

21. Gallagher, "The Killing Floor."

22. Ibid.

23. Sam Howe Verhovek, "Worst Drought Since Thirties Grips Great Plains," *New York Times* (May 20, 1996).

24. Lourdes Gouveia and Donald D. Stull, "Dances with Cows," in *Any Way You Cut It: Meat Processing and Small-Town America,* ed. Donald D. Stull, Michael J. Broadway, and David Griffith (Lawrence: University Press of Kansas, 1995), 85–107.

25. Broadway, "From City to Countryside."

26. Ibid.

27. Ibid.

28. Bjerklie, "Horns of a Dilemma."

29. David Griffith, Michael J. Broadway, and Donald D. Stull, "Making Meat,"in *Any Way You Cut It: Meat Processing and Small-Town America,* ed. Donald D. Stull, Michael J. Broadway, and David Griffith (Lawrence: University Press of Kansas, 1995), 1–15.

30. Gouveia and Stull, "Dances with Cows."

31. Stull and Broadway, "Killing Them Softly."

32. Ibid.

33. Bjerklie, "Horns of a Dilemma."

34. Stull and Broadway, "Killing Them Softly."

35. Ibid.

36. Ibid.

37. Gallagher, "The Killing Floor."

38. Griffith, Broadway, and Stull, "Making Meat."

39. Ibid.

40. Ibid.

41. Stull and Broadway, "Killing Them Softly."

42. Ibid.

43. Ibid.

44. Ibid.

45. Gallagher, "The Killing Floor."

46. Ibid.

47. Stull and Broadway, "Killing Them Softly."

48. Ibid.

49. Ibid.

50. Bjerklie, "Horns of a Dilemma."

51. David J. Wolfson, *Beyond the Law: Agribusiness and the Systemic Abuse of Animals Raised for Food or Food Production* (New York: Archimedian Press, 1996), 24.

52. Animal Welfare Institute, Animals and Their Legal Rights: A Summary of American Laws from 1641–1990 (1987), Supra note 8, at 304. No. 2021.

53. Wolfson, *Beyond the Law,* 25–26.

54. Ibid., 25.

55. Animal Welfare Act, Section 2132(g).

56. VT. STAT. ANN. tit. §13, 382 (Supp. 1994).

57. Wolfson, *Beyond the Law,* 9.

58. Ibid.

59. Ibid.

60. Ibid., 10.

61. Ibid., 3.

62. Ibid.

63. Ibid., 19.

Part Three: Beyond the dinner table

CHAPTER ELEVEN: WORLD HUNGER

1. At times the population doubled at a rate faster than once every 385 years and at times the doubling rate was slower. The 385-year figure reflects the average rate of doubling between the years 1000 and 1800.

2. Joel E. Cohen, *How Many People can the Earth Support?* (New York: WW Norton and Sons, 1995), 30.

3. Wolfgang Lutz, "The Future World Population," *Population Bulletin* 49, no. 1 (June 1994): 2.

4. Cohen, *How Many People?,* 109–110.

5. Lutz, "The Future World Population," 29.

6. Ibid.

7. Henry W. Kendall and David Pimentel, "Constraints on the Expansion of the Global Food Supply," *Ambio* 23, no. 3 (May 1994): 198–205.

8. Ibid.

9. P. Buringh, "Availability of agricultural land for crop and livestock production," in *Food and Natural Resources,* ed. D. Pimentel and C. W. Hall (San Diego: Academic Press, 1989), 69–83.

10. Pimentel, David. Personal communication.

11. Pimentel, David. Personal communication.

12. Kendall and Pimentel, "Global Food Supply."

14. H. E. Dregne, *Historical Perspective of Accelerated Erosion and Effect on World Civilization* (Madison, Wisc.: Amer. Soc. Agron, 1982); Kendall and Pimentel, "Global Food Supply."

15. Ibid.

16. John Opie, *Ogallala: Water for a Dry Land* (Lincoln: University of Nebraska Press, 1993), 163.

17. Marc Reisner, *Cadillac Desert: The American West and its Disappearing Water* (New York: Penguin Books, 1986), 453.

18. Ibid.

19. Ibid., 457.

20. Ibid., 456.

21. Ibid., 11.

22. S. Postel, *Water: Rethinking Management in an Age of Scarcity*, Worldwatch Paper no. 62, Worldwatch Institute, Washington. D.C., 1984; S. Postel, *Water for Agriculture: Facing the Limits*, Worldwatch Institute, Washington, D.C., 1989.

23. Worldwatch Institute (1990) State of the World 1990. Washington. A report by The World Resources Institute. 1990. World Resources 1990–1991. Oxford University Press, New York.

24. S. Postel, *Last Oasis: Facing Water Scarcity* (New York: W. W. Norton and Co., 1992).

25. Pimentel, David. Personal communication

26. Kenneth Blaxter and Noel Robertson, *From Dearth to Plenty* (Cambridge: Cambridge University Press, 1995), 124.

27. Jim Motavelli, "Paul and Anne Ehrlich: The Countdown Continues on the Population Bomb," *E-The Environmental Magazine* (Nov./Dec. 1996): 10–12.

28. A. T. Durning and H. B. Brough, "Reforming the Livestock Economy," in *State of the World*, ed. L. R. Brown (New York: W. W. Norton & Co., 1992), 66–82.

29. Kendall and Pimentel, "Global Food Supply."

30. National Cattlemen's Association and Beef Board, *12 Myths & Facts About Beef Production*, (Englewood, Colo.: National Cattlemen's Association and Beef Board, undated, content current to 1995), 3.

31. Michael Baker, "For Livestock Farmers," *American Agriculturist* (Aug. 1995): 15.

32. Ray Herren, *The Science of Animal Agriculture* (Albany: Delmar Publishers, 1994), 76.

33. Cohen, *How Many People?*, 170–171.

34. Ibid., 54.

35. R. W. Kates et al., *The Hunger Report* (Providence, R.I.: Brown University Hunger Project, 1988); R. W. Kates et al., *The Hunger Report: Update 1989* (Providence, R.I.: Brown University Hunger Project, 1989).

36. Kendall and Pimentel, "Global Food Supply."

37. Cohen, *How Many People?*, 56.

CHAPTER TWELVE:
AMERICAN RANGELAND

1. Lynn Jacobs, *Waste of the West* (Tuscon AZ: Lynn Jacobs, 1991), 21.

2. National Cattlemen's Association, *Cattle and Beef Handbook*, 2—Grazing; Lynn Jacobs, *Waste of the West*, 21.

3. "Grazing Fees Drop to $1.61," *Western Livestock Journal* 74, no. 13 (23 Jan. 1995): 1, 7.

4. National Cattlemen's Association, *Cattle and Beef Handbook*, 4—Grazing

5. *Rangeland Management: Current Formula Keeps Grazing Fees Low*, GAO/RCED-91-185BR (Washington, D.C.: U.S. General Accounting Office, June, 1991), 1–33.

6. U.S. Department of Agriculture, Animal and Plant Health Inspection Service, *Animal Damage Control Program Final Environmental Impact Statement* (Washington, D.C., April 1994), 61–63.

7. William K. Stevens, "Prarie Dog Colonies Bolster Life in the Plains," *The New York Times* (July 11, 1995).

8. "Lion Attacks Lead to Vote in California," *The New York Times* (Oct. 18, 1995).

9. "Judge OKs Release of Yellowstone Wolves," *Los Angeles Times* (March 30, 1996).

10. U.S. Department of Agriculture, Animal and Plant Health Inspection Service, *Animal Damage Control Program Final Environmental Impact Statement*, (Washington, D.C., April 1994), 61–63.

11. Richard Lessner, "Dancing with Wolves: Ranchers Should Lose this War," *Arizona Republic* (April 1, 1991).

12. Jacobs, *Waste of the West*, 221.

13. Ibid., 216.

14. Timothy Egan, "Ranchers vs. Rangers Over Land Use," *The New York Times*, (Aug. 19, 1990).

15. "Western Showdown," *Newsweek* (April 17, 1995), 39.

16. Ibid.

17. National Cattlemen's Association, *Cattle and Beef Handbook*, 3—Resource Use.

18. Committee on Government Operations, 34th Report, *Federal Grazing Program: All is Not Well on the Range* (Washington, D.C.: U.S. Government Printing Office, 1986), 3.

19. *Colorado Agricultural Statistics, 1990* (Lakewood, Colo.: Colorado Agricultural Statistics Service), 112.

20. National Cattlemen's Association, *Cattle and Beef Handbook*, 4—Grazing.

21. Andrew Kupfer, "Where's the Beef? Check this Out," *Fortune* 24, no. 3 (July 29, 1991):163–164.

22. Ibid.

23. Ibid.

24. National Cattlemen's Association, *Cattle and Beef Handbook*, 1—Environment.

25. National Cattlemen's Association, *Cattle and Beef Handbook*, 1—Erosion/Soil Conservation.

26. National Cattlemen's Association, *Cattle and Beef Handbook*, 1—Environment.

27. Jacobs, *Waste of the West*, 44.

CHAPTER THIRTEEN:
AWAKENING

1. "What Humans Owe to Animals," *The Economist* (August 19, 1995): 11–12.

2. Ibid., 11.

Index

Dairy farms, 125

Dairy Today, 126

Dawn the pig, 119–120

Dealler, Stephen, 75–77

Debeaking of chickens, 103–104

De-horning, of cattle, 127, 132

Diabetes
  and milk, 60
  and weight, 45

Diet. *See* Animal-based diet; Plant-based diet; Vegan diet; Weight control

Dietitian's Guide to Vegetarian Diets (Messina), 33

Downed cows, 128–129

Downed cow syndrome, 81–82

Dr. Dean Ornish's Program for Reversing Heart Disease (Ornish), 7, 21

Drugs, given to animals, 60, 100–101, 136

Dudley-Cash, William A., 111

Dust
  in broiler houses, 111–112
  in feedlots, 136–137
  in pig sheds, 117

E

Eat More, Weigh Less™ Diet (Shintani), 49

Eat More, Weigh Less (Ornish), 7

Eat More Index (EMI), 47, 49–50

E. Coli, 36–37

Economist, 187, 190–191

Ednie, Jean, 53–55

Eggs, 187
  See also Chickens, treatment of layer

Ehrlich, Paul, 157, 163, 171

Eisman, George, 146

Erosion, 158, 163, 171–172, 181

Essay on the Principle of Population, An (Malthus), 166

Essence, 62

Excel, 143, 145

F

Face-branding, of cattle, 131

Farm Animal Reform Movement (F.A.R.M.), 186–187

Farm animals, lack of protection for, 146–148

Farming, 180–181

Farmland, 158–159

Farm Sanctuary, 89–97, 107
  animals rescued by, 91, 94–95, 101–102, 110–111, 113, 119–120, 129–130, 133–134

Farrowing crates, 118–119, 146

Fat Free and Delicious (Siegel), 23

Fats, 48
  in milk, 60
  saturated, 11–13, 17, 34

Feedlots, 134–137

Fertilizer
  from male chickens, 120–123
  petroleum-based, 161, 162, 163

Fiber, 34

Fitzsimons, Dina, 46

Food, Energy, and Society (Pimentel), 161

Food and Drug Administration
  and cattle-to-cattle feeding, 84
  on cholesterol reduction, 15

Food groups, new, 40, 63, 192–193

Forbes , 20

Fortune, 181

Fossil fuels, 160–161

Slaughter
  of cattle, 83–84, 135, 141–143
  of chickens, 139–141, 147
  of dairy cows, 128–129
  of pigs, 118, 122

Slaughterhouses
  and bovine spongiform encephalopathy, 83–84
  working conditions in, 139–140, 143–146

Southwood, Richard, 70

Southwood Committee, 70–72

Spira, Henry, 131, 141, 190

Starvation, 165

Stress relief, 8, 17

Stull, Donald, 144

Stunning, before slaughter, 83–84, 140, 142, 147

T

Taro, 46–47

Texas A&M, 83

Topsoil. *See* Erosion

Transportation, of animals, 94, 112–113, 122, 134–135, 147

Turkeys, 110

U

Union of Concerned Scientists, 157

United Nations, 156

United States Department of Agriculture, 131, 133

United States General Accounting Office, 173

United States government
  and support of ranchers, 172–174, 177, 181
  and wildlife control, 174–176

Urea nitrogen, 29–30

V

Veal calves, 129–131

Veal crate, 129, 146

Vegan diet
  and cancer, 34, 39–41
  and cholesterol, 22–23
  and overall health, 189–190, 191
  population potentially fed by, 165
  and saturated fat, 10–13, 14, 30
  and weight loss, 51–55

Vegetables, 193

Vegetarians, 32, 39, 190, 191
  and fats, 13, 14

Vermont, 147

Veterinary care, 116–117, 133–134

Vitamin C, 32–33

Vitamin D, 60, 61–62

Vitamin E, 32–33

von Eggers Doering, William, 32

W

Waste of the West (Jacobs), 180, 181–183

Water, 159–160, 162

Weber, Gary, 77–79, 82

Weight control, 43–55, 192

West Coast Farm Sanctuary, 97

Whitely, Winslow, 179

Wildlife, 174–176

Willet, Walter C., 11, 30–31

Winfrey, Oprah, 77–79

Wolfson, David, 147–148

Worker compensation laws, 145

World Health Organization, 67, 74

World's Poultry Science Journal, 140

ABOUT THE AUTHOR

Erik Marcus is a writer and public speaker who is dedicated to the advocacy of vegan and vegetarian diets. Since authoring *Vegan: The New Ethics of Eating*, Mr. Marcus frequently speaks to audiences about plant-centered diets. He is a graduate of Columbia University, where he earned his master's degree in teaching writing. Much of *Vegan* was written while he was living in upstate New York. Mr. Marcus recently settled in the San Francisco area.

VEGAN.COM

Erik Marcus established Vegan.com as a way to convey frequently updated vegan news, resources, recipes, and information.

Visit Vegan.com's website at:
http://www.vegan.com

or send a blank or very short e-mail message to info@vegan.com. Letters and inquiries can also be mailed to:

Vegan.com
P.O. Box 1933
Cupertino, CA 95015-1933

Please enclose an SASE if a reply is desired.